BRIDGING PERSONAL AND BUSINESS PROSPERITY

FOUNDATIONS OF FINANCIAL EMPOWERMENT

BRIDGING PERSONAL AND BUSINESS PROSPERITY

M.L. RUSCSAK

Copyright © 2023 Trient Press

All rights reserved. No portion of this publication may be reproduced, distributed, or transmitted in any form or by any means, including photocopying, recording, or other electronic or mechanical methods, without the prior written permission of the publisher. This restriction excludes brief quotations utilized in critical reviews and certain other noncommercial usages as permitted by copyright law. For permission inquiries, direct correspondence to the publisher, marked "Attention: Permissions Coordinator," at the following address:

Trient Press
3375 S Rainbow Blvd
#81710, SMB 13135
Las Vegas, NV 89180

Criminal copyright infringement, including instances without financial gain, is subject to investigation by the FBI and incurs penalties of up to five years in federal imprisonment and a fine of $250,000.

Excepting the original narrative material authored by M.L. Ruscsak, all songs, song titles, and lyrics cited within Foundations of Financial Empowerment remain the exclusive property of their respective artists, songwriters, and copyright holders.

Ordering Information:
For quantity sales, Trient Press offers special discounts to corporations, associations, and other organizations. For detailed information, contact the publisher at the address provided above.
For orders by U.S. trade bookstores and wholesalers, please reach out to Trient Press at Tel: (775) 996-3844, or visit www.trientpress.com.

Printed in the United States of America
Publisher's Cataloging-in-Publication Data
Ruscsak, M.L.
Foundations of Financial Empowerment

Hardcover: 979-8-88990-175-4
Paperback: ISBN 979-8-88990-176-1
E-Book: 979-8-88990-177-8

Overview of financial literacy and its importance in personal and business contexts.
Chapter 1: Navigating Financial Health: Analysis, Assessment, and Application
Chapter 2: Strategic Financial Vision: Setting Goals and Crafting Success
Chapter 3: Mastering Financial Flow: The Art of Budgeting and Cash Management
Chapter 4: Liberating Finances: Pathways to Debt Freedom and Credit Vitality
Chapter 5: Investing in Your Future: Pathways to Wealth and Security
Chapter 6: Safeguarding Your Financial Journey: Risk Management and Emergency Preparedness

Navigating the Seas of Financial Literacy: Empowerment in Personal and Business Realms

In the grand tapestry of life, financial literacy stands as a beacon of knowledge, guiding individuals and businesses alike through the intricate labyrinth of economic decisions. It is not merely an asset but a necessity, akin to a compass for a sailor navigating uncharted waters. This overview explores the profound importance of financial literacy in both personal and business contexts, highlighting its role as a cornerstone of empowerment, stability, and growth.

The Essence of Financial Literacy

At its core, financial literacy encompasses a comprehensive understanding of financial principles and concepts, including budgeting, investing, saving, and the mechanics of loans and interest rates. It's the knowledge that allows one to make informed and effective decisions with all of their financial resources. Imagine setting sail on a voyage; financial literacy is your map and compass, essential for navigating through storms and reaching your desired destination.

Empowerment Through Personal Financial Literacy

In the realm of personal finance, literacy transforms uncertainty into confidence. It empowers individuals to:

- **Budget and Save Efficiently:** Understanding how to manage income and expenses effectively ensures that individuals can save for future goals, emergencies, and investments, securing their financial well-being.
- **Invest Wisely:** Knowledge of different investment vehicles and strategies enables individuals to build wealth over time, navigating the complexities of risk and return with a seasoned hand at the helm.
- **Manage Debt:** Insight into the nature of debt, including the implications of various types of loans and credit, arms individuals with the tools to avoid the pitfalls of debt traps, steering a course towards financial freedom.

- **Plan for the Future:** Financial literacy lays the foundation for robust retirement planning, ensuring that individuals can look forward to their later years with anticipation rather than apprehension.

The Business Horizon: Financial Literacy as a Pillar of Success

In the business world, financial literacy transcends individual benefit, becoming a pivotal factor in the organization's success and longevity. It empowers businesses to:

- **Make Informed Decisions:** Understanding financial statements, market trends, and economic indicators enables businesses to make strategic decisions, driving growth and innovation.
- **Manage Cash Flow:** Mastery over the nuances of cash flow management ensures that businesses can meet their obligations, invest in opportunities, and navigate the ebb and flow of their financial cycles with agility.
- **Access Capital:** Knowledge of financing options and the ability to present a compelling case to investors and lenders opens doors to capital, fueling expansion and development.
- **Mitigate Risks:** Financial literacy includes an understanding of risk management strategies, allowing businesses to identify potential threats and implement measures to safeguard their assets and ensure continuity.

The Ripple Effect of Financial Literacy

The benefits of financial literacy extend beyond the immediate financial health of individuals and businesses, contributing to a more stable and prosperous economy. Educated financial decisions lead to increased savings, investment, and consumption, which in turn, fuel economic growth and stability. On a societal level, financial literacy can reduce the gap between the financially informed and uninformed, fostering a more equitable economic landscape.

Charting the Course Forward

In conclusion, financial literacy is not merely a skill but a fundamental component of a prosperous life and successful business. It equips individuals and organizations with the knowledge to make prudent financial decisions, navigate challenges, and seize opportunities. As we continue to sail through the ever-evolving financial seas, let us embrace financial literacy as our guiding star, illuminating the path to financial empowerment, stability, and growth.

Chapter 1: Navigating Financial Health: Analysis, Assessment, and Application

Welcome to the first chapter of our journey together—a voyage into the heart of your financial landscape. As we stand at the threshold of this exploration, I invite you to consider this chapter not just as a collection of pages, but as a mirror reflecting the intricate details of your financial health. Whether you are embarking on this journey from a personal interest or with the aim to fortify your business finances, our goal remains unified: to navigate through the realms of analysis, assessment, and application with clarity, confidence, and a touch of creativity.

Our voyage is not just about numbers on a spreadsheet or abstract concepts in economic theory; it's about understanding the narrative behind those numbers, the stories they tell about our lives, businesses, and the decisions that shape them. As an advocate walking alongside you, I've navigated my own financial challenges and triumphs, and I bring these experiences into our discussions—not as a distant expert, but as a fellow traveler keenly aware of the terrain's complexities.

This chapter is designed to be your compass and map, guiding you through the foundational aspects of financial analysis and assessment. We will demystify the world of financial statements, ratios, and metrics, transforming them from intimidating jargon into tools of empowerment. You'll learn not only how to read these indicators but also how to interpret them, allowing you to make informed decisions that align with your financial goals and aspirations.

We'll share personal stories, not just as anecdotal evidence, but as lived experiences that illuminate the path from financial uncertainty to clarity and strength. These narratives are interwoven with actionable advice, step-by-step guides, and practical tips that you can apply immediately to your own situation. Whether you're evaluating your personal net worth, analyzing your business's cash flow, or planning for future investments, this chapter offers a hands-on approach to mastering these essential skills.

Moreover, we delve into the philosophical underpinnings of financial success, drawing on insights that have guided generations in overcoming psychological barriers to wealth. We'll explore the mindset shifts necessary for growth, emphasizing resilience, strategic planning, and the power of informed decision-making.

Understanding that financial education is not a one-size-fits-all endeavor, we present diverse examples and scenarios that reflect a broad spectrum of financial situations. Our discussions are enriched with interactive elements—exercises, reflection prompts, and action plans—that invite you to engage directly with the material, making your learning experience both dynamic and personal.

As we embark on this journey together, remember that navigating financial health is not solely about reaching a destination. It's about acquiring the knowledge, skills, and confidence to make the journey rewarding in itself. So, with a dash of humor to lighten our path and a commitment to clear, accessible explanations, let's set sail towards financial empowerment, guided by the principles of analysis, assessment, and application. Together, we will transform your financial landscape into one of abundance, stability, and enduring success.

Section 1: Introduction to Financial Analysis

In the grand tapestry of financial mastery, the skill of financial analysis stands as a beacon, guiding us through the fog of uncertainty and into the clarity of informed decision-making. It is the compass by which we navigate the vast seas of personal and business finance, enabling us to chart a course towards sustainability, growth, and prosperity.

Financial analysis, at its core, is the art and science of understanding the numbers that define our financial world. It goes beyond mere observation; it is about interpreting, predicting, and ultimately, making strategic decisions that align with our financial goals and aspirations. Whether we are managing a household budget, overseeing the finances of a burgeoning enterprise, or planning for future investments, the principles of financial analysis remain steadfast companions on our journey.

Why, you might ask, is financial analysis so critical? The answer lies in its power to transform abstract numbers into actionable intelligence. It equips us with the ability to assess the health of our finances, identify opportunities for growth, and foresee potential pitfalls before they become insurmountable obstacles. In the realm of personal finance, it empowers us to make decisions that enhance our financial well-being, from optimizing our spending habits to maximizing our savings and investment returns. For businesses, it serves as the foundation upon which strategic planning, budgeting, and financial management are built, ensuring that every decision is made with a clear understanding of its financial implications.

But financial analysis is not a monolith; it is a mosaic, composed of various techniques and tools that cater to the diverse needs of individuals and businesses alike. From the basic assessment of income and expenses to the complex evaluation of investment opportunities and market trends, the scope of financial analysis is as broad as it is deep. It encompasses everything from simple budgeting exercises to sophisticated financial modeling, each serving a unique purpose in our quest for financial clarity and success.

At its essence, financial analysis involves examining financial statements and related data to understand an entity's financial health, performance, and the underlying value. This analytical process is pivotal for making informed decisions, whether for personal finance management, investment evaluation, or guiding business strategies. It's a multifaceted discipline that encompasses various methods and tools, including ratio analysis, trend analysis, and cash flow analysis, each offering unique insights into financial health and potential future performance.

The Importance of Financial Analysis

1. Informed Decision Making: Financial analysis stands as the cornerstone of sound decision-making. By dissecting financial data, individuals and businesses can make decisions that are not based on gut feelings or speculation, but on concrete, quantitative analysis. This can range from deciding on investments, evaluating the profitability of a new project, to determining the feasibility of expanding a business.

2. Financial Health Assessment: For individuals, financial analysis provides a clear picture of one's financial situation, highlighting areas of strength and pinpointing vulnerabilities. It enables one to assess their net worth, understand their cash flow, and evaluate their saving and spending patterns. For businesses, it involves analyzing liquidity, solvency, and profitability, ensuring that the business can meet its short-term obligations, sustain operations, and grow in the long-term.

3. Risk Management: Through the identification of financial trends and potential red flags, financial analysis is instrumental in risk management. By understanding the financial stability and performance trends, both individuals and businesses can take preemptive actions to mitigate financial risks before they manifest into financial crises.

4. Strategic Planning: Financial analysis informs strategic planning by providing insights into market trends, competitive positioning, and financial forecasts. It enables businesses to allocate resources more efficiently, set realistic financial targets, and develop strategies to achieve long-term objectives.

5. Investment Decisions: At the heart of investment decisions lies financial analysis. For individual investors, it helps in assessing the viability and potential return on investments, ranging from stocks and bonds to real estate and startups. For businesses, it aids in evaluating the potential returns of investing in new ventures, technologies, or markets.

6. Enhancing Financial Communication: Financial analysis facilitates clearer communication between all stakeholders, including investors, creditors, and management. By presenting an objective, data-driven view of financial performance, it enhances transparency and builds trust.

The Application in Decision Making

Applying financial analysis in decision-making involves a systematic approach to gathering and interpreting financial data, then using this information to guide actions. This process starts with setting clear objectives, whether it's improving personal financial health, increasing a business's profitability, or making a successful investment. It then moves to collecting relevant financial data, analyzing this data using appropriate tools and techniques, and finally, interpreting the results to make informed decisions.

Financial analysis, therefore, is not just a technical skill; it's a critical thinking process that requires not only a grasp of numbers but also an understanding of the broader economic, social, and organizational context. It demands a balance between quantitative analysis and qualitative judgment, enabling decision-makers to navigate the complexities of the financial landscape with confidence and insight.

As we delve deeper into the nuances of financial analysis in the subsequent sections, remember that the ultimate goal is to empower you with the knowledge and tools to make informed, strategic decisions that lead to financial prosperity and stability.

Section 2: Understanding Financial Statements

Embarking on the exploration of financial statements is akin to unlocking a treasure chest of insights into one's financial health and the vitality of a business. These documents, rich in detail and depth, serve as the navigational stars guiding us through the financial universe. In this section, we delve into the core of financial literacy, illuminating the foundational knowledge of financial statements and underscoring their paramount significance in our journey towards informed financial decision-making.

Subsection 1: The Balance Sheet - A Snapshot of Financial Position
Objective: Introduce the balance sheet and explain its role in providing a comprehensive snapshot of an entity's financial position at a specific point in time.

Content: Explore the balance sheet's structure, including assets, liabilities, and shareholders' equity. Through personal anecdotes and simplified examples, we'll demystify how this statement reflects the net worth of an individual or the financial stability of a business. Engaging narratives will bring to life the balance sheet's ability to tell a story of financial resilience or vulnerability.

Subsection 2: The Income Statement - The Story of Profitability
Objective: Detail the purpose and structure of the income statement, emphasizing its importance in tracking revenue, expenses, and profitability over a period.

Content: Through relatable examples and case studies, we'll dissect the components of the income statement, from gross profit to net income. Personal stories will illustrate how understanding the income statement can lead to more informed spending, investing, and business strategy decisions, highlighting the direct impact of operational activities on financial health.

Subsection 3: The Cash Flow Statement - Understanding Liquidity
Objective: Explain the cash flow statement's critical role in revealing the liquidity and cash management of an individual or business.

Content: Dive into the dynamics of cash inflows and outflows, distinguishing between operating, investing, and financing activities. Interactive elements will invite readers to track their cash flows, revealing insights into how effectively cash resources are being managed. Real-life scenarios will underscore the significance of positive cash flow in sustaining operations and fostering growth.

Subsection 4: Interpreting Financial Statements - Beyond the Numbers
Objective: Equip readers with the skills to interpret and analyze financial statements, turning data into actionable intelligence.

Content: Introduce key financial ratios and metrics that unveil the stories behind the numbers. With a focus on practical application, this subsection will guide readers through exercises in ratio analysis, trend identification, and comparative assessment. Empowering readers with these analytical tools, we aim to transform the act of reviewing financial statements from a daunting task into an insightful, strategic exercise.

Subsection 5: The Integrated Financial Statement Framework
Objective: Illustrate how the balance sheet, income statement, and cash flow statement interconnect, providing a holistic view of financial health.

Content: Through engaging narratives, we'll explore the symbiotic relationship between these statements, demonstrating how changes in one can affect the others. This subsection aims to build a cohesive understanding, enabling readers to view the financial statements not as isolated documents but as interconnected pieces of a larger financial puzzle.

In navigating through this section, our journey transcends mere comprehension of financial documents. We embark on a quest to harness the power of financial statements as tools of empowerment, insight, and foresight. With each page turned, we move closer to mastering the art of financial analysis, equipped to make decisions that pave the way for financial prosperity and security. Through this exploration, we transform numbers on a page into narratives of aspiration, resilience, and success, charting a course toward achieving our most ambitious financial goals.

Subsection 1: The Balance Sheet - A Snapshot of Financial Position

Embarking on the exploration of the balance sheet, we venture into a realm where every figure tells a story, every line item has a backstory, and every total offers a glimpse into the financial soul of an individual or business. Considered by many as the cornerstone of financial analysis, the balance sheet does more than just list assets, liabilities, and shareholders' equity; it provides a comprehensive snapshot of financial position at a specific point in time, painting a picture of stability, resilience, or vulnerability.

The Structure of the Balance Sheet: An Overview

At its core, the balance sheet is elegantly simple, divided into two main sections: assets on one side, and liabilities and shareholders' equity on the other. Assets, from cash to real estate, represent what an entity owns. Liabilities, from loans to accounts payable, outline what it owes. The difference between these two—shareholders' equity—tells us the residual value that remains for the owners.

Assets: The Resources at Your Disposal

Imagine assets as the tools in your financial toolkit. Each tool, whether it's a hammer (cash in hand) or a saw (investments), has its purpose in building your financial future. Through personal stories, we'll explore how strategic acquisition and management of assets can fortify your financial edifice, making it resilient against the storms of economic uncertainty.

Liabilities: The Responsibilities You Bear

Just as assets are the wind in your sails, liabilities can be the anchor that either steadies or drags you down. Through engaging narratives, we'll delve into the stories of individuals and businesses alike, who navigated the treacherous waters of debt to find a harbor of financial stability. These stories will not only demystify liabilities but also highlight the strategic role they play in growth and expansion.

Shareholders' Equity: The Measure of Your Financial Worth

Shareholders' equity is the story of what remains when all obligations are met—a true reflection of net worth. It's a tale of endurance, of decisions made and risks taken. By sharing anecdotes of how equity can fluctuate with business decisions and economic changes, we'll provide insights into maintaining and increasing this crucial indicator of financial health.

Bringing the Balance Sheet to Life

To illustrate these concepts, let's consider the story of "Elena," a budding entrepreneur whose journey from startup to stability mirrors the evolution of a balance sheet. Elena's initial investments (assets) were minimal, funded by a small loan (liability) and her savings (equity). As her business grew, so did her assets—inventory, cash flow, investments. Her liabilities grew as well, but strategically, taking on debt to finance expansion at opportune moments. Over time, Elena's equity in the business expanded, reflecting her growing financial stability and success.

The Balance Sheet in Your Financial Narrative

Understanding the balance sheet is akin to understanding the heartbeats of your financial narrative. It's about recognizing the signs of health, the risks of over-leverage, and the potential for growth. As we dissect the balance sheet through simplified examples and interactive exercises, remember that each number, each ratio derived from this document, is a chapter in your ongoing story of financial resilience and aspiration.

Through this exploration, our aim is not just to acquaint you with the structure and significance of the balance sheet but to empower you with the knowledge to use it as a tool for financial insight and strategic planning. Whether assessing personal wealth or the financial stability of a business, the balance sheet stands as a beacon, guiding us towards informed decisions and a future of financial prosperity.

Subsection 2: The Income Statement - The Story of Profitability
Venturing deeper into the narrative of financial enlightenment, we now turn our focus to the income statement—a document that, much like the chapters of a compelling novel, unfolds the story of an entity's profitability over time. It's a tale of earnings and expenditures, of fiscal discipline and strategic foresight, narrated through the lens of revenue, expenses, and, ultimately, net income.

The Essence of the Income Statement

At its heart, the income statement serves as a financial scorecard, detailing the results of an entity's operational endeavors. It begins with revenue—the lifeblood of any financial entity, whether a multinational corporation or a solo entrepreneur's venture. From this starting point, we subtract the costs of doing business, including the direct costs of goods sold and the broader operational expenses, to arrive at the net income, the bottom line that tells us the outcome of all financial strategies and decisions.

Revenue: The Starting Line of Financial Success

Let's embark on this journey with a narrative close to my heart—the story of "Mia," a freelance graphic designer whose revenue streams from client projects represent the seeds of her financial growth. Mia's journey teaches us the importance of diversifying income sources and the impact of market demand on revenue generation. Through her story, we understand that revenue isn't merely about numbers; it's about the value created and delivered to customers.

Expenses: Navigating the Waters of Operational Costs

Expenses, the inevitable counterpart to revenue, encompass the costs incurred to generate earnings. Here, we delve into the tale of "The Cozy Café," a small business that transformed its expense management into a strategic tool for enhancing profitability. By closely monitoring their cost of goods sold and operational expenses, the café's owners learned to streamline operations without compromising on quality. Their story exemplifies how effective expense management can be a lever for financial health, turning potential losses into opportunities for sustainability and growth.

Net Income: The Culmination of Financial Endeavors

Net income, the climax of the income statement's story, represents the ultimate measure of profitability. It's the reward for financial acumen, operational efficiency, and strategic planning. To illustrate, consider the journey of "EcoTech," a startup specializing in green technologies. Despite initial challenges, their strategic decisions around product development and market positioning led to increased revenues and controlled expenses, culminating in a positive net income. EcoTech's story is a testament to the power of perseverance, innovation, and the strategic use of financial insights to drive profitability.

Bringing the Income Statement to Life

To truly grasp the essence of the income statement, we engage in practical exercises, breaking down its components through interactive examples and personal finance analogies. We'll explore how to analyze revenue trends, evaluate expense ratios, and interpret net income results, turning abstract figures into actionable insights.

Understanding the income statement is akin to mastering the art of financial storytelling, where each line item adds depth to the narrative of financial health and strategic decision-making. Through this exploration, we empower ourselves with the knowledge to craft our own stories of financial success, informed by the lessons of profitability and underpinned by the principles of revenue generation and expense management.

As we conclude this section, remember that the income statement is more than a financial document; it's a roadmap that guides us through the fiscal landscape, highlighting the milestones of success and the pitfalls of mismanagement. Armed with this understanding, we are better equipped to navigate the path to financial prosperity, turning the aspirations of today into the achievements of tomorrow.

Subsection 3: The Cash Flow Statement - Understanding Liquidity

In the journey of financial mastery, understanding the flow of cash within an entity is akin to navigating the life-giving rivers that sustain vibrant ecosystems. The cash flow statement, often overshadowed by its financial statement counterparts, plays a pivotal role in revealing the liquidity and cash management prowess of an individual or business. It is here, within the ebb and flow of cash inflows and outflows, that we uncover the essence of financial vitality and resilience.

The Essence of Cash Flows

The cash flow statement is the chronicle of an entity's financial liquidity over a period, categorized into three main activities: operating, investing, and financing. Each category offers a unique perspective on how cash is generated and utilized, providing a comprehensive view of financial health beyond mere profitability.

Operating Activities: The Heartbeat of Cash Flow

Operating activities represent the primary source of an entity's cash inflows, derived from its core business operations. To bring this concept to life, let's explore the story of "Luna's Boutique," a small retail business whose day-to-day sales activities are the lifeline of its cash flow. Through Luna's narrative, we witness how managing receivables, inventory, and payables can significantly impact cash flow, teaching us the importance of operational efficiency in maintaining liquidity.

Investing Activities: The Vision for Future Growth

Investing activities reflect an entity's expenditure on long-term assets and investments, crucial for future growth. Through the tale of "InnovateTech," a tech startup investing in research and development, we see the delicate balance between utilizing cash for expansion and ensuring sufficient liquidity for operational needs. InnovateTech's journey illustrates the strategic nature of investing activities, highlighting their role in shaping an entity's future.

Financing Activities: The Fuel for Expansion

Financing activities encompass transactions related to borrowing, repaying debt, and managing equity—essentially, how an entity finances its operations and growth. By delving into the story of "GreenEnergy," a company that leveraged loans and equity financing to fund its ambitious projects, we learn the complexities of managing cash flow in alignment with growth objectives and financial strategies.

Interactive Exploration of Cash Flow Management

To demystify the management of cash flows, we introduce interactive elements that engage readers in tracking and analyzing their cash inflows and outflows. By applying these concepts to personal finances or a business scenario, readers gain practical insights into the effectiveness of their cash management practices.

The Significance of Positive Cash Flow

Positive cash flow, the hallmark of financial stability, ensures that an entity can meet its obligations, invest in opportunities, and weather economic downturns. Through real-life scenarios and case studies, we underscore the critical importance of positive cash flow in sustaining operations and fostering growth.

Understanding the cash flow statement is not merely an academic exercise; it is a practical tool for navigating the financial currents of life. It empowers individuals and businesses alike to make informed decisions that enhance liquidity, ensure sustainability, and drive strategic growth. As we conclude this exploration, let us carry forward the insights gleaned from the dynamics of cash flow, applying them to cultivate a landscape of financial resilience and prosperity.

Subsection 4: Interpreting Financial Statements - Beyond the Numbers

As we venture further into our financial odyssey, we arrive at a crucial waypoint: the interpretation of financial statements. This is where the alchemy of turning data into actionable intelligence takes place. It's a transformative process, where numbers on a page morph into insights, strategies, and decisions. Our objective here is not just to look at financial statements but to see through them, to understand the stories they tell about past performances, present conditions, and future possibilities.

The Art of Ratio Analysis

Ratio analysis is akin to deciphering a secret code, where each ratio reveals a piece of the financial puzzle. We'll explore key financial ratios such as the debt-to-equity ratio, which speaks to a company's financial leverage; the current ratio, which measures liquidity; and the return on equity, which assesses profitability and efficiency. Through the story of "Zara's Zestful Zucchinis," a thriving organic farm, we'll see how these ratios can signal health, warn of danger, or uncover hidden opportunities.

Trend Identification: The Financial Compass

Understanding the direction in which an entity is moving financially is crucial for making informed decisions. We'll delve into trend identification, learning how to spot patterns in financial performance over time. By examining the ups and downs in the income statements and balance sheets of "TechTonic," an innovative electronics manufacturer, we'll demonstrate how identifying trends can guide strategic planning and operational adjustments.

Comparative Assessment: The Benchmark of Success

Comparative assessment involves measuring an entity's financial metrics against those of its peers or industry standards. This practice, akin to navigating by the stars, provides a benchmark by which to gauge relative performance. Through interactive exercises, we'll practice comparing the financial health of "Bella's Boutique" with its competitors, learning how to position a business advantageously within its market.

Empowering Readers with Analytical Tools

Equipping readers with the ability to analyze financial statements is about empowering them to take control of their financial destinies. This subsection will include practical exercises in ratio analysis, templates for trend identification, and guides for conducting comparative assessments. By engaging with these tools, readers will transform the act of reviewing financial statements from a daunting task into an insightful, strategic exercise.

Beyond the Numbers

Interpreting financial statements is about more than just understanding the numbers; it's about grasping the narrative they weave. As we conclude this section, remember that financial statements are a reflection of decisions made, strategies implemented, and challenges faced. They are a tool for reflection, a guide for the present, and a map for the future.

Armed with these analytical skills, we are better prepared to navigate the complex world of finance. We move forward, not just as passive observers of our financial journey but as informed participants, capable of shaping our path with wisdom, insight, and strategic foresight.

Subsection 5: The Integrated Financial Statement Framework

Embarking on the final leg of our journey through the landscape of financial statements, we reach a crucial understanding—the interconnectedness of the balance sheet, income statement, and cash flow statement. This trifecta of financial documentation forms a comprehensive framework that offers a panoramic view of an entity's financial health. Recognizing how these statements intertwine is akin to assembling a puzzle; each piece is critical, and when fitted together, they reveal the complete picture.

The Symbiosis of Financial Statements

Imagine a thriving ecosystem where every element is interdependent. Similarly, in the financial ecosystem, the balance sheet, income statement, and cash flow statement coexist in a state of dynamic interrelation. For instance, the income statement's net income feeds into the balance sheet's equity section, reflecting the entity's profitability over time. Meanwhile, the cash flow statement adjusts this income for non-cash items and changes in working capital, offering a clear view of actual cash generated or used during the period.

Narratives of Interconnection

To illuminate this concept, consider the story of "Cypress Solar," a renewable energy company. Cypress Solar's expansion into new markets increased its assets (balance sheet) through the purchase of new equipment, financed by a combination of debt (also on the balance sheet) and reinvested earnings (reflected in both the income statement as net income and the balance sheet as retained earnings). The cash flow statement captured the outflows for equipment purchases and inflows from financing, providing a lens through which to view the company's liquidity and operational efficiency.

Understanding Through Changes

Another avenue to explore the integrated financial statement framework is through changes—how an event or decision ripples across all three statements. For example, a decision to take on a new loan impacts the balance sheet (increase in liabilities), the income statement (interest expense affects net income), and the cash flow statement (cash inflow from financing activities). Through interactive scenarios, we'll engage readers in tracing such changes across the statements, enhancing their grasp of this interconnected framework.

Building a Cohesive Understanding

This subsection is designed to transcend the mere analysis of individual financial statements, guiding readers toward a holistic comprehension of financial health. By exploring how the statements are linked, we empower readers with a three-dimensional view of financial reality, enabling them to make more informed decisions based on a comprehensive analysis of financial performance and position.

The Integrated Framework in Practice

Engaging with the integrated financial statement framework through real-life narratives, case studies, and exercises, readers will learn to see beyond the surface of financial data. This perspective is not just about understanding the numbers; it's about appreciating the stories they tell and the strategies they suggest.

As we conclude this exploration, let us carry forward the insight that financial statements, much like chapters in a book, are most illuminating when read together. They provide a narrative arc that guides us through the past, illuminates the present, and helps us chart a course for the future. Armed with this integrated perspective, readers are equipped to navigate the complex world of finance with confidence, discernment, and strategic acumen.

As we transition from the intricate weave of financial statements to the next vital chapter in our financial narrative, we approach the realm of key financial ratios and metrics. This upcoming section represents a deep dive into the quantitative tools that distill complex financial information into digestible, actionable insights. Having laid the foundation with an understanding of how financial statements interconnect to provide a holistic view of financial health, we now turn our focus to the precision instruments that enable us to measure, compare, and interpret this health in a nuanced and meaningful way.

From Broad Strokes to Fine Details

Think of our journey thus far as having sketched the broad outlines of a landscape. We've traced the contours of hills (the balance sheet), charted the flow of rivers (the cash flow statement), and observed the changing seasons (the income statement). Now, with key financial ratios and metrics, we prepare to add depth, color, and detail to this landscape, bringing into focus the features that tell us not just about the beauty of the scene, but about the quality of the soil, the health of the ecosystem, and the patterns of the weather.

The Compass and Map of Financial Decision-Making

Key financial ratios and metrics serve as both compass and map, guiding us through the terrain of financial decision-making. They are the tools by which we navigate, allowing us to position ourselves and our endeavors in relation to our goals, challenges, and opportunities. Whether assessing liquidity through the current ratio, evaluating leverage with the debt-to-equity ratio, or measuring profitability via return on equity, these ratios offer a concise summary of financial health and operational effectiveness.

Empowering Through Precision

In the upcoming section, we will explore these tools in detail, empowering readers with the ability to not only calculate these ratios but also understand what they reveal about an entity's financial position and performance. Through practical examples, interactive exercises, and engaging narratives, we will demystify these metrics, transforming them from abstract concepts into concrete guides for action.

A Bridge to Strategic Insight

As we stand on the brink of this new chapter, let us embrace the power of financial ratios and metrics to provide strategic insight. These are the instruments that allow us to read between the lines of financial statements, to uncover the stories of efficiency, growth, and resilience that lie beneath the surface.

Join me as we continue our journey, moving from the broad understanding of financial health into the realm of precision analysis. Together, we will unlock the secrets held within key financial ratios and metrics, arming ourselves with the knowledge to make informed, strategic decisions that drive us toward our financial aspirations.

Section 3: Key Financial Ratios and Metrics

Objective: Educate readers on the essential financial ratios and metrics used in financial As we step into the realm of key financial ratios and metrics, we venture beyond the surface of financial statements to uncover the insights they hold. This section is dedicated to demystifying these vital tools, making them accessible and actionable for our readers. Financial ratios and metrics are the lenses through which we can view the financial health, efficiency, and potential of a business or personal finance with clarity and insight.

The Essence of Financial Ratios and Metrics

Financial ratios and metrics serve as the navigational stars in the vast sky of financial analysis, guiding us through decisions that shape our financial landscape. They offer a concise summary of complex financial data, providing benchmarks for performance, indicators of financial health, and signposts for future strategy.

Liquidity Ratios: The Lifeblood of Financial Health

Imagine liquidity as the lifeblood flowing through the veins of a business or personal finance, ensuring vitality and resilience. Liquidity ratios, such as the Current Ratio and Quick Ratio, measure the ability to meet short-term obligations with short-term assets. Through the journey of "Sara's Sustainable Startups," we explore how maintaining a healthy liquidity ratio enabled her venture to navigate the ebbs and flows of business cycles, illustrating the critical role of liquidity in sustaining operations.

Solvency Ratios: The Foundation of Financial Stability

Solvency ratios, including the Debt-to-Equity Ratio and Interest Coverage Ratio, delve into the long-term sustainability and debt management of an entity. The narrative of "Evergreen Enterprises" showcases how a strategic approach to leveraging and debt management, guided by solvency ratios, fortified its financial foundation against economic upheavals, offering lessons in building and maintaining financial stability.

Profitability Ratios: The Measure of Economic Success

Profitability ratios, such as the Net Profit Margin and Return on Assets, reflect the efficiency with which a business or individual converts effort into economic success. Through "Lily's Luxury Labels," a tale of transformation from a fledgling boutique to a thriving brand, we uncover how focusing on profitability ratios led to strategic decisions that maximized earnings and growth.

Efficiency Ratios: The Symphony of Operational Harmony

Efficiency ratios, including the Inventory Turnover Ratio and Receivables Turnover Ratio, assess how effectively resources are managed. "Orion's Optics" provides a compelling story of how optimizing operational efficiency, illuminated by these ratios, enhanced its market competitiveness and profitability.

Market Value Ratios: The Reflection of Investor Confidence
For businesses, market value ratios like the Price-Earnings Ratio and Market-to-Book Ratio offer insights into how the market perceives their value and potential. The ascent of "Techtronix" in the stock market, fueled by strategic innovations and investor confidence, demonstrates the power of market value ratios in attracting investment and driving growth.

Empowering Through Application
This section will not only elucidate these ratios and metrics but will also equip our readers with the tools to apply them through practical exercises, real-life scenarios, and interactive elements. By engaging directly with these analytical tools, readers transform theoretical knowledge into practical wisdom, capable of making informed decisions that navigate the path to financial prosperity.

As we journey through this section, let us embrace the power of financial ratios and metrics as our allies in the quest for financial success. They are the keys that unlock the stories behind the numbers, guiding us toward strategic decisions and enlightened financial management. With these tools in hand, we are empowered to write our own stories of financial achievement, marked by informed decisions, strategic growth, and sustainable success.

Key Financial Ratios and Metrics - Explanation and Application
In this pivotal section of our financial exploration, we decode the essence of liquidity ratios, profitability ratios, debt ratios, and efficiency ratios. Each of these metrics serves as a beacon, guiding us through the financial fog with clarity and precision. Let's dive into the mechanics and significance of these ratios, including their formulas and how to interpret them, transforming raw data into actionable insights.

Liquidity Ratios
Objective: Assess an entity's ability to meet short-term obligations with its short-term assets.

Current Ratio = Current Assets / Current Liabilities
Interpretation: A current ratio greater than 1 indicates a strong liquidity position, suggesting that the entity can cover its short-term obligations with its short-term assets. A ratio below 1 signals potential liquidity issues.

Quick Ratio = (Current Assets - Inventories) / Current Liabilities
Interpretation: Also known as the acid-test ratio, it measures the ability to meet short-term obligations without relying on the sale of inventories. Higher values indicate better liquidity and financial health.

Profitability Ratios
Objective: Evaluate how effectively a company or individual generates profit relative to sales, assets, and equity.

Net Profit Margin = Net Income / Revenue
Interpretation: Indicates how much of each dollar in revenue is converted into profit. Higher percentages signify greater efficiency in converting sales into actual profits.

Return on Assets (ROA) = Net Income / Total Assets
Interpretation: Measures how efficiently assets are used to generate profit. A higher ROA indicates efficient use of assets to produce earnings.

Debt Ratios
Objective: Measure the degree of an entity's leverage and its capacity to meet its debt obligations.

Debt-to-Equity Ratio = Total Liabilities / Shareholders' Equity
Interpretation: Indicates the proportion of equity and debt used to finance a company's assets. A higher ratio suggests more debt financing relative to equity.

Interest Coverage Ratio = Earnings Before Interest and Taxes (EBIT) / Interest Expenses
Interpretation: Assesses a company's ability to pay interest on its outstanding debt. Higher values suggest better capability to cover interest payments from operational earnings.

Efficiency Ratios
Objective: Assess how effectively a company or individual utilizes its assets and manages its operations.

Inventory Turnover Ratio = Cost of Goods Sold / Average Inventory
Interpretation: Indicates how many times a company's inventory is sold and replaced over a period. Higher turnover rates suggest efficient inventory management.

Receivables Turnover Ratio = Net Credit Sales / Average Accounts Receivable
Interpretation: Measures how quickly a company collects on its receivables. A higher ratio implies efficient collection processes and credit policies.

Empowering Financial Insights Through Ratios
Understanding and applying these ratios empower us to peel back the layers of financial statements, revealing the operational and financial nuances hidden within. They enable us to craft a narrative of financial health, sustainability, and efficiency, providing a comprehensive view that goes beyond mere numbers.

By integrating these ratios into our financial analysis toolkit, we transform abstract data into a cohesive story of fiscal strength and vulnerability. This story equips us with the insights needed to make informed decisions, whether we're steering a business towards growth, managing personal finances, or evaluating investment opportunities.

Let these ratios be your guide as you navigate the complex seas of financial analysis. Armed with these tools, you are well-equipped to interpret the financial landscapes you encounter, making decisions that are not just informed but inspired.

As we transition from the intricate world of financial ratios and metrics—a domain where numbers weave the tales of enterprises and economies—we embark on a journey closer to home: the assessment of personal financial health. This next section, Section 4: Personal Financial Health Assessment, marks a pivotal shift from the macro to the micro, from the broad strokes of business analysis to the fine details of individual financial scrutiny.

In the vast landscape of financial literacy, understanding the health of one's personal finances is akin to mastering the art of self-navigation in the wilderness of economic uncertainty. Here, the principles of financial analysis are not just tools for evaluating businesses but become integral to evaluating our financial well-being, setting goals, and charting a course towards financial independence and security.

Bridging the Divide

The journey thus far has equipped us with the analytical skills to dissect and interpret financial statements, to understand the stories told by ratios about profitability, liquidity, debt, and efficiency. Now, we turn these tools inward, applying them to our personal financial statements—our budgets, our savings, our debts, and our investments. The transition from analyzing a corporation's financial health to assessing personal financial health is not merely a change in scale but a change in perspective. The principles remain the same, but the application becomes deeply personal.

A Personal Touch

Section 4 is about more than numbers; it's about dreams, goals, challenges, and the strategies we employ to navigate them. It's about understanding where we stand financially, identifying where we want to be, and outlining the steps to get there. This section will introduce concepts such as net worth calculation, budgeting techniques, debt management strategies, and investment planning, all tailored to the individual.

Empowerment Through Understanding

Armed with the knowledge and skills from the previous sections, we are now poised to take a deep dive into our financial reality, to confront our financial fears, and to embrace our aspirations with confidence and clarity. This section aims to empower readers with the ability to conduct a thorough personal financial health assessment, transforming financial data into a personalized strategic plan for growth and stability.

From Insight to Action

As we segue into Section 4: Personal Financial Health Assessment, let us approach it with the understanding that personal finance is not just about managing money but about fostering a life of abundance, security, and freedom. The insights we gain from this assessment are not endpoints but beginnings—springboards from which we launch our most ambitious financial dreams into reality.

Join me on this journey of personal discovery, where each calculation, each assessment, and each plan we make is a step towards a future of financial empowerment and prosperity. Together, we will learn not just to navigate but to thrive in the ever-changing world of personal finance.

Section 4: Personal Financial Health Assessment

In this vital section, we pivot our focus towards the personal, embarking on a journey of self-discovery in the realm of financial health. This exploration is about more than numbers on a spreadsheet; it's about understanding your financial narrative, where you currently stand, and where you aspire to be. Let's dive into the essential practices of net worth and cash flow analysis, presenting them as tools not just for assessment but for empowerment.

Subsection 1: Calculating Your Net Worth

Objective: Equip readers with the knowledge and skills to calculate their net worth, providing a clear snapshot of their financial position.

Net Worth = Total Assets - Total Liabilities

Assets: Begin with a comprehensive inventory of your assets. These are what you own: savings accounts, investments, real estate, and personal property. We'll share stories of individuals who discovered hidden assets they hadn't considered, highlighting the importance of thoroughness in this process.

Liabilities: List all your debts and obligations. These include mortgages, loans, credit card debts, and any other liabilities. Through relatable anecdotes, we'll explore common pitfalls in underestimating liabilities and strategies to address them.

Interpretation: Your net worth is the distilled essence of your financial reality. It's a baseline for tracking financial progress over time. We'll guide you through creating a personalized net worth statement, turning abstract concepts into a tangible, actionable plan.

Subsection 2: Mastering Cash Flow Analysis

Objective: Teach readers how to conduct a cash flow analysis, understanding how money moves in and out of their personal finances.

Cash Flow = Income - Expenses

Income: Catalogue your sources of income, not just your salary but any side hustles, investments, or passive income streams. Inspirational stories from individuals who diversified their income sources will motivate readers to explore new opportunities.

Expenses: Examine your spending habits, categorizing your expenses from necessities to discretionary spending. We'll offer practical tips and exercises for tracking and categorizing expenses, including how to identify areas for adjustment.

Interpretation: Cash flow analysis reveals the liquidity of your personal finances, highlighting opportunities to enhance savings and invest in your future. Engaging narratives will demonstrate how positive cash flow changes have transformed financial destinies.

Empowering Actionable Change

This section is designed not just to inform but to transform. It's structured around interactive exercises, reflective prompts, and actionable plans that encourage readers to engage directly with their financial data. By calculating net worth and conducting cash flow analysis, readers embark on a path of financial enlightenment, equipped with the knowledge to make informed decisions that align with their financial goals and aspirations.

Bridging Theory and Practice

Through the personal stories shared, the practical advice given, and the philosophical insights offered, this section bridges the gap between theoretical financial concepts and real-world application. It's about empowering readers to take control of their financial narrative, turning challenges into opportunities for growth and uncertainty into clarity.

As we navigate through this section, remember that assessing personal financial health is a continuous journey, not a one-time event. It's a process of regular reflection, adjustment, and action. Armed with these tools and insights, you are well on your way to achieving financial health, independence, and prosperity. Let's embark on this journey together, transforming financial dreams into achievable realities.

Calculating Net Worth: Steps to Determine Personal Net Worth

Embarking on the journey to calculate your net worth is akin to mapping the contours of your financial landscape. It provides a clear picture of where you stand and lays the groundwork for future financial planning. Here's how to approach this crucial assessment:

List Your Assets

Begin with Liquid Assets: These are assets that can be quickly converted into cash, such as checking and savings accounts, cash on hand, and money market instruments.

Include Invested Assets: This category covers stocks, bonds, mutual funds, retirement accounts, and other investments.

Consider Personal Assets: Add the value of your home, vehicles, jewelry, and other personal property. Be realistic in your appraisal, using market value where applicable.

Inspirational Insight: Reflect on the story of Emma, who realized her extensive collection of vintage guitars was a significant personal asset, adjusting her financial planning to reflect this value.

Identify Your Liabilities

Short-term Liabilities: These include credit card balances, personal loans, and other debts due within a year.

Long-term Liabilities: List mortgages, student loans, auto loans, and any other long-term obligations.

Empowering Example: Consider the case of Alex, who tackled his liabilities by listing them in order of interest rate, focusing on paying off high-interest debt first to improve his net worth more efficiently.

Calculate Your Net Worth

Subtract Total Liabilities from Total Assets: The result is your net worth.

Interpretation and Action: A positive net worth indicates that your assets exceed your liabilities, a sign of financial health. A negative net worth suggests the need for strategic financial adjustments.

Analyzing Cash Flow: How to Create and Analyze a Personal Cash Flow Statement

Understanding your cash flow involves tracking the movement of money in and out of your personal finances. This analysis is pivotal for managing your financial life with precision and foresight.

Track Your Income

Regular Income: This includes wages, salaries, bonuses, and any consistent income streams.

Irregular Income: Factor in freelance earnings, dividends, and interest payments. The tale of Lucas, who supplemented his regular income with freelance photography, underscores the value of diverse income sources.

Categorize Your Expenses

Fixed Expenses: These are regular, predictable costs such as rent or mortgage, insurance premiums, and loan payments.

Variable Expenses: Costs that fluctuate, like groceries, utility bills, and leisure spending. Tracking variable expenses reveals potential areas for savings, as Maria discovered by analyzing her spending on dining out.

Calculate Net Cash Flow

Subtract Total Expenses from Total Income: The result is your net cash flow.

Positive vs. Negative Cash Flow: A positive cash flow means you're living within your means, with surplus funds for savings and investments. A negative cash flow indicates spending exceeds income, necessitating adjustments.

Review and Adjust

Regular Review: Monthly analysis helps identify trends, adjust for unexpected expenses, and realign with financial goals.

Strategic Adjustments: Use insights from your cash flow analysis to make informed decisions—boosting savings, reducing unnecessary expenses, or exploring additional income opportunities.

By meticulously calculating net worth and analyzing cash flow, you equip yourself with a comprehensive understanding of your financial health. These processes, illuminated by real-life examples and actionable advice, are not just exercises in financial management but steps towards financial empowerment and independence. Through regular assessment and adjustment, you can navigate your financial journey with confidence, ensuring your actions today lay the groundwork for a prosperous tomorrow.

As we transition from the personal to the professional, our journey through financial literacy takes us to the next crucial phase: Business Financial Health Assessment. Having navigated the terrain of personal finance, where we've learned to calculate net worth and analyze cash flows, we're now ready to apply these principles on a larger scale. This new section extends the framework of financial analysis into the realm of business, where the stakes are higher, and the complexities magnified, yet the core principles of sound financial management remain universal.

Bridging Personal Insight to Business Acumen

The leap from personal financial health to assessing the financial health of a business is significant, yet it is built on the same foundational principles we've explored. The skills honed in personal finance—meticulous analysis, strategic planning, and disciplined execution—serve as the bedrock for understanding business finance. The difference lies in scale and scope, where individual strategies are amplified to meet the demands of organizational growth, sustainability, and profitability.

Expanding Our Financial Toolkit

In Section 5, we delve into the intricacies of business finance, exploring how to assess a company's financial health through a broader array of tools and metrics. We'll examine balance sheets, income statements, and cash flow statements from a business perspective, interpreting these documents to extract meaningful insights about operational efficiency, financial stability, and growth potential.

From Theory to Application

This section is designed not only to educate but to empower entrepreneurs, business owners, and financial enthusiasts to make informed decisions that drive business success. Through engaging narratives, we'll explore real-world scenarios that highlight common challenges and strategic triumphs in business financial management. These stories will serve as a bridge, connecting theoretical knowledge with practical application.

Navigating Business Finance with Confidence

Our journey through Business Financial Health Assessment will equip you with the knowledge to:

Conduct thorough financial analyses of businesses,
Understand key financial ratios and metrics in a business context,
Identify strengths, weaknesses, and opportunities in business financial statements,
Develop strategies for financial improvement and growth.

As we embark on this exploration, let's approach it with the same curiosity and commitment to growth that guided us through personal finance. The transition from personal to business financial health assessment is not just a step up in complexity; it's an expansion of our financial literacy, empowering us to navigate the broader financial landscape with confidence and insight.

Join me as we continue our journey, applying our sharpened financial skills to the world of business, where each analysis and strategic decision can lead to profound impacts on operational success and long-term sustainability. Together, we will unlock the secrets to business financial health, setting the stage for informed decision-making and strategic growth.

Section 5: Business Financial Health Assessment

Welcome to a transformative journey into the heart of business finance. This section is your gateway to mastering the art of assessing a business's financial health. Whether you're an entrepreneur, a business leader, or a financial enthusiast, the insights and tools we share here are designed to empower you with the knowledge necessary to make informed decisions that foster growth and ensure sustainability. Let's demystify the complex process of financial assessment together, turning it into a powerful catalyst for strategic decision-making.

Understanding Business Financial Statements

Discovering the Financial Narrative: Dive into the core of business financial statements—the balance sheet, income statement, and cash flow statement. These documents are interconnected chapters of your business's financial story, revealing its well-being and operational efficiency. Through an interactive guide, you'll learn to read and interpret these statements, gaining insights into your company's liquidity, profitability, and cash management.

From Theory to Practice: Real-life case studies from a variety of sectors will bring the dry numbers to life. By examining how different businesses analyze their financial statements, you'll learn to spot common pitfalls and emulate strategies that lead to financial success.

Key Financial Ratios for Businesses

Mastering the Metrics: Financial ratios are the compass that guides businesses through the economic landscape. We'll introduce you to essential ratios that assess liquidity, profitability, debt, and efficiency. Through practical exercises and real-business examples, you'll learn how these ratios can be calculated and interpreted to inform strategic decisions.

Strategic Insights: Gain philosophical insights and actionable advice on leveraging financial ratios for your business's benefit. Whether it's making operational improvements or crafting investment strategies, these ratios will become invaluable tools in your strategic toolkit.

Cash Flow Analysis for Business

Ensuring Operational Stability: A thorough analysis of your business's cash flow statement reveals the dynamics of cash inflows and outflows. This knowledge is crucial for maintaining operational stability and identifying growth opportunities. Through stories of real businesses that navigated cash flow challenges successfully, you'll learn effective cash management strategies.

Hands-on Tools: We provide templates and tools to help you conduct your cash flow analysis, encouraging you to apply these concepts directly to your business scenario.

Conducting a Comprehensive Business Health Assessment
A Holistic View: This subsection synthesizes insights from financial statements, ratio analysis, and cash flow analysis into a comprehensive evaluation of your business's financial health. By adopting a holistic approach, you'll consider not just the numbers, but also the broader context—your business model, market conditions, and competitive landscape.

Creating Action Plans: Equipped with a thorough assessment, we guide you in developing action plans that address weaknesses, leverage strengths, and capitalize on growth opportunities.

Empowering Financial Leadership
As we conclude this section, remember that assessing the financial health of a business is not just about learning; it's about doing. This journey equips you with the confidence and skills to take charge of your business's financial destiny, guiding it toward sustainability and success with strategic foresight and informed decision-making.

By the end of this section, you will not only have a deep understanding of how to assess a business's financial health but also the practical ability to apply these insights in real-world scenarios. This knowledge is a stepping stone to becoming a more empowered leader, ready to navigate the complexities of the business world with assurance and agility.

Empowering Your Financial Journey in Business
As we wrap up Section 5: Business Financial Health Assessment, we reflect on the journey we've embarked upon together. This exploration has not merely been about acquiring the technical skills to analyze financial statements or compute ratios; it's been about nurturing the mindset of a strategic leader who uses financial insights to guide business decisions. Here, we consolidate our learning and look ahead to how you can apply these insights to foster the growth and resilience of your business.

Integrating Financial Insights into Strategic Planning
Bridging Analysis with Action: The transition from understanding to action is critical. The insights gleaned from financial statements and ratios are not endpoints but the beginning of a strategic dialogue within your organization. Use these insights to initiate discussions about operational efficiency, cost management, investment opportunities, and potential areas for expansion.

Scenario Planning: Armed with financial data, engage in scenario planning. Consider various future scenarios, including market expansions, product launches, or economic downturns, and assess how these could impact your financial health. This exercise not only prepares you for potential challenges but also uncovers opportunities for strategic innovation.

Building a Culture of Financial Literacy
Fostering Team Engagement: Financial health is not the sole responsibility of the finance team. Encourage a culture of financial literacy across your organization by sharing key insights and involving team members in financial planning and analysis. This inclusive approach demystifies finance and aligns the team towards common financial goals.

Continuous Learning: The landscape of business finance is ever-evolving. Commit to ongoing education for yourself and your team. Workshops, seminars, and courses on financial management can provide fresh perspectives and update your team on best practices and emerging trends.

Leveraging Technology for Financial Management
Adopting Financial Tools: Leverage technology to streamline financial analysis and planning. From accounting software to advanced analytics platforms, the right tools can automate routine tasks, provide real-time financial data, and enable sophisticated scenario analysis.

Data-Driven Decisions: In the age of big data, harnessing financial and operational data can provide a competitive edge. Use this data to identify patterns, predict trends, and make informed strategic decisions that drive business growth.

Looking Ahead: Strategic Growth and Financial Sustainability
Strategic Review and Adaptation: Make financial health assessment an integral part of your strategic review process. Regularly revisit your financial analysis to adapt to changes in the business environment, ensuring that your strategies remain aligned with your financial goals.

Growth Mindset: View every financial challenge as an opportunity for growth. Whether it's optimizing cash flow, managing debt, or expanding your market presence, approach each situation with a mindset geared towards innovation and improvement.

Conclusion: Your Path to Financial Empowerment
As this section concludes, your journey to financial empowerment is just beginning. The tools and insights you've gained are your compass and map in the complex world of business finance. With them, you are better equipped to navigate your business towards financial health, operational excellence, and strategic growth.

Remember, the true measure of financial literacy is not just in understanding but in application. It's in the decisions you make every day, the strategies you implement, and the vision you have for your business's future. Armed with knowledge, insight, and a proactive approach to financial management, you are poised to lead your business into a future marked by success and sustainability.

As we pivot from the foundational principles and strategic applications of business financial health assessment, we now transition towards a vivid illustration of these concepts in action. Section 6: Case Studies, serves as a bridge connecting theoretical knowledge with practical implementation. This section is meticulously designed to showcase real-world applications, challenges, and triumphs in the financial journey of businesses from diverse industries and scales.

Bringing Theory to Life

In this next phase, we delve into a curated collection of case studies that breathe life into the financial strategies, analyses, and principles we've explored. Each case study is a narrative, rich with lessons learned, strategic insights, and actionable takeaways. These stories are not just recountings of financial decisions made; they are roadmaps laid by those who navigated the complex terrain of business finance, offering guidance and inspiration for your journey.

Learning from Successes and Failures
Diverse Perspectives: The case studies span a range of scenarios—from startups grappling with cash flow challenges to established corporations strategizing for global expansion. This diversity offers a panoramic view of the financial landscape, illustrating how the principles of financial health assessment are universally applicable yet uniquely executed.

Strategic Decision-Making: Through these narratives, we will dissect the decision-making processes, exploring how financial data informed strategic moves, the impact of external economic factors, and the role of leadership in steering financial outcomes.

Interactive Engagement
Analytical Exercises: Accompanying each case study are interactive exercises that invite you to apply your analytical skills, challenging you to identify what you would have done differently, how you might apply similar strategies in your context, or how certain decisions align with the financial principles discussed in previous sections.

Discussion Prompts: Engage with thought-provoking questions that spur deeper reflection on each case, encouraging you to draw parallels to your own business scenarios and consider how you might leverage similar insights.

Synthesizing Knowledge into Action
Actionable Insights: Each case study concludes with key takeaways, distilling the essence of the narrative into practical insights you can apply to your business. These lessons bridge the gap between theory and practice, empowering you with strategies tested by the fires of real-world application.

Empowerment Through Example: As we journey through these case studies, the aim is to empower you with not just knowledge, but the confidence to apply this knowledge. The real-world examples serve as a testament to the power of informed financial decision-making, demonstrating how understanding and application of financial principles can drive businesses to thrive.

Conclusion: A Foundation for Your Future Success
Section 6 is more than just a collection of stories; it's a source of inspiration, a toolkit for problem-solving, and a guide for strategic thinking. As we transition into these case studies, let us do so with the intent to learn, adapt, and envision how we might write our own success stories. This section stands as a testament to the transformative power of financial literacy and strategic planning, offering a beacon for your path towards financial empowerment and business success.

Section 6: Case Studies

Welcome to Section 6, where the theoretical meets the tangible in the vibrant world of finance. This section is a curated gallery of real-life scenarios, each case study meticulously chosen to illuminate the path from financial analysis to actionable insight. Here, we apply the principles, strategies, and tools we've discussed, breathing life into them through the experiences of individuals and businesses alike. Our objective is clear: to transform theoretical knowledge into a prism through which real-life financial scenarios are not only understood but mastered.

Personal Finance in Action
Case Study: Navigating Financial Milestones with Emily
Background

Emily, a 32-year-old software engineer, found herself at a crossroads common to many professionals in her age group. With a stable job and a growing desire to lay down roots, she aspired to purchase her first home. Additionally, Emily harbored ambitions of early retirement, hoping to travel and dedicate time to her passions. However, achieving these goals required more than just a steady income; it demanded strategic financial planning and a deep dive into personal cash flow analysis.

The Challenge

Despite her technical background, Emily initially felt overwhelmed by the intricacies of personal finance. She faced several challenges:

Saving for a Home Down Payment: With housing prices steadily rising, amassing a sufficient down payment for her dream home seemed daunting.

Retirement Planning: Emily's goal of early retirement necessitated aggressive savings and investment strategies but finding the right balance without compromising her current lifestyle was puzzling.

Debt Management: Student loans and minor credit card debt loomed over her financial landscape, requiring careful management and strategic repayment.

Strategy and Implementation

Cash Flow Analysis: Emily began her financial overhaul by conducting a meticulous cash flow analysis. She tracked her income versus her expenses, categorizing her spending to identify areas where she could cut back without significantly impacting her quality of life.

Reducing Expenses: Emily discovered she was spending a considerable amount on dining out and subscription services. By cooking more at home and streamlining her subscriptions, she was able to allocate more funds toward her down payment and retirement savings.

Debt Snowball Method: For her debts, Emily employed the debt snowball method, prioritizing the repayment of smaller debts first to build momentum before tackling her larger student loans.

Automated Savings: To ensure consistency in her savings, Emily automated transfers to her down payment and retirement accounts immediately after receiving her paycheck, treating these contributions as non-negotiable expenses.

Investment in Knowledge: Recognizing the importance of informed investment decisions, Emily dedicated time to educating herself on various investment vehicles. She diversified her retirement savings across stocks, bonds, and real estate investment trusts (REITs), based on her risk tolerance and retirement timeline.

Regular Financial Health Assessments: Emily committed to regular reviews of her financial plan, adjusting her budget, savings rate, and investments as her income grew and her financial knowledge deepened.

Outcomes

Two years into her strategic financial plan, Emily achieved her goal of purchasing her first home. Her disciplined savings strategy, coupled with a favorable market, allowed her to make a 20% down payment, avoiding private mortgage insurance (PMI) and securing a favorable mortgage rate.

Furthermore, Emily's retirement accounts showed robust growth, thanks to her diversified investment strategy and consistent contributions. Her debt was also significantly reduced, with her credit card debt cleared and her student loans on track to be paid off within five years.

Lessons Learned

Emily's journey underscores the power of proactive financial planning and the tangible benefits of personal financial health assessment. Key takeaways include:

The Importance of Cash Flow Analysis: Understanding how money moves in and out of your personal finances is crucial for setting and achieving financial goals.

The Value of Financial Education: Investing time in learning about personal finance and investment strategies can significantly impact your financial well-being.

Flexibility and Regular Assessment: Regularly reviewing and adjusting your financial plan is essential as your income, expenses, and life circumstances evolve.

Emily's story is a testament to how leveraging personal finance knowledge to navigate life's financial milestones can lead to tangible achievements and set the foundation for a secure financial future.

Case Study: Overcoming Debt - Marco's Path to Financial Empowerment

Background

Marco, a 28-year-old marketing specialist, found himself entangled in a web of debt, a mix of student loans, credit card balances, and an auto loan. While Marco's job provided a decent income, his monthly debt payments were a constant source of stress, limiting his ability to save for the future or enjoy life's simple pleasures. Determined to change his financial trajectory, Marco embarked on a journey to eliminate his debt and reclaim his financial freedom.

The Challenge

Marco's financial challenges were multi-faceted:

High-Interest Debt: Credit card balances with high-interest rates were rapidly accruing, exacerbating his financial strain.

Lack of Savings: The majority of Marco's income was allocated towards debt payments, leaving little for emergencies or future goals.

Feeling Overwhelmed: The sheer volume of debt and complexity of managing multiple payments left Marco feeling defeated, unsure where to begin.

Strategy and Implementation

Debt Analysis and Prioritization: Marco started by listing all his debts, noting the balance, interest rate, and minimum payment for each. Recognizing the impact of high interest on his financial health, he decided to tackle the debts with the highest interest rates first.

Debt Avalanche Method: Marco adopted the debt avalanche method, allocating extra payments towards the debt with the highest interest rate while maintaining minimum payments on the others. This strategy not only reduced the amount paid in interest over time but also accelerated the debt repayment process.

Budget Overhaul: To free up more money for debt repayment, Marco overhauled his budget, identifying non-essential expenses he could reduce or eliminate. He cut back on dining out, renegotiated his phone plan, and canceled unused subscriptions.

Emergency Fund: Despite his focus on debt repayment, Marco understood the importance of having an emergency fund. He committed a small portion of his budget to build a modest emergency fund, which provided a financial cushion and reduced the need to rely on credit cards for unexpected expenses.

Financial Ratio Analysis: To gauge his progress and maintain motivation, Marco utilized financial ratios, such as the debt-to-income ratio, tracking improvements over time. This analytical approach allowed him to see the tangible results of his efforts, reinforcing his commitment to his financial plan.

Outcomes

After two years of disciplined effort, Marco's strategy bore fruit:

Debt Reduction: Marco successfully paid off all credit card debt and the auto loan, significantly reducing his total debt burden.

Improved Financial Ratios: Marco's debt-to-income ratio improved markedly, reflecting his enhanced financial health and resilience.

Increased Savings: With the elimination of several high-interest debts, Marco was able to redirect funds towards savings, building a solid financial foundation for the future.

Lessons Learned

Marco's journey from debt-laden stress to financial empowerment offers valuable lessons:

Strategic Debt Repayment Works: The debt avalanche method, combined with budget adjustments, proved effective in tackling high-interest debt.

Emergency Savings are Crucial: Even modest emergency savings can prevent the cycle of debt by providing a buffer against unforeseen expenses.

The Power of Financial Analysis: Regularly tracking financial ratios can provide motivation and insight, turning abstract numbers into milestones of progress.

Marco's narrative is more than a story of overcoming debt; it's a blueprint for financial resilience, demonstrating that with strategy, discipline, and a bit of financial education, regaining control over one's finances is within reach.

Case Study: Startup Growth and Sustainability - The BloomTech Story

Background

BloomTech, a burgeoning tech startup, embarked on a mission to revolutionize the way businesses utilize artificial intelligence for market analysis. Founded by a trio of tech enthusiasts, the startup quickly gained traction, attracting attention from investors and clients alike. However, with rapid growth came the daunting challenges of scalability, financial management, and securing additional funding to fuel expansion.

The Challenge

BloomTech faced several critical financial challenges as it scaled:

Securing Funding: To sustain growth and invest in technology development, BloomTech needed to secure additional funding from investors who demanded clear evidence of financial health and potential for return on investment.

Managing Rapid Growth: BloomTech's rapid client acquisition and product development placed significant strain on its financial resources, necessitating meticulous cash flow management.

Scalability Concerns: The startup needed to strategically manage its operational costs and investment in growth to ensure long-term sustainability without compromising product quality or market position.

Strategy and Implementation

Leveraging Financial Ratios: The founders of BloomTech recognized the importance of using key financial ratios not only as internal health indicators but also as tools to communicate the company's value proposition to potential investors.

Gross Margin Ratio: By optimizing their production processes and cost management, BloomTech improved its gross margin ratio, demonstrating to investors the company's ability to generate profit relative to its sales.

Current Ratio: BloomTech diligently managed its current assets and liabilities to maintain a healthy current ratio, assuring investors of its liquidity and short-term financial stability.

Burn Rate Analysis: Understanding the criticality of cash flow management, BloomTech conducted regular burn rate analyses to ensure they had sufficient runway to achieve their next milestones before requiring further capital.

Strategic Funding Rounds: With solid financial ratios and a clear growth trajectory, BloomTech strategically approached funding rounds. They prepared detailed financial projections and used their improved financial ratios as a testament to their business model's viability and scalability.

Operational Efficiency: To address scalability challenges, BloomTech implemented automation and streamlined operations to manage costs without sacrificing innovation or market responsiveness.

Outcomes

BloomTech's strategic focus on financial health and transparent communication with investors paid off:

Successful Funding: The startup secured significant investment in subsequent funding rounds, providing the capital necessary for expansion and technology development.

Sustainable Growth: With a keen eye on financial ratios and operational efficiency, BloomTech managed to scale its operations sustainably, maintaining a strong market position and continuing innovation.

Increased Investor Confidence: The clear demonstration of financial acumen and strategic planning significantly increased investor confidence, opening doors for future partnerships and funding opportunities.

Lessons Learned

BloomTech's journey offers valuable insights into the financial strategies behind startup sustainability and growth:

The Power of Financial Ratios: Key financial ratios are indispensable tools for assessing a startup's health and communicating its value to investors.

Strategic Financial Planning: Proactive and strategic financial planning is crucial for managing rapid growth and ensuring scalability.

Investor Relations: Transparency and financial literacy are key to building trust and confidence with investors, crucial for securing funding and support for future growth.

BloomTech's story demystifies the complex landscape of startup finance, illustrating how strategic use of financial ratios and mindful growth management can pave the way for sustainable success in the competitive tech industry.

Case Study: Turning Challenges into Opportunities - The Gourmet Galore Journey
Background

Gourmet Galore, a cherished family-owned restaurant nestled in the heart of a bustling city, has been serving up culinary delights for over a decade. Known for its innovative dishes and warm, inviting atmosphere, the restaurant had built a loyal customer base. However, when an unexpected economic downturn hit, the once-thriving establishment faced a sharp decline in patronage, putting its financial stability at risk.

The Challenge

The economic downturn posed several significant challenges for Gourmet Galore:

Decreased Revenue: With fewer customers dining out, the restaurant saw a dramatic drop in daily sales, directly impacting its revenue.

High Operational Costs: Fixed costs such as rent, utilities, and salaries remained unchanged, exacerbating the financial strain.

Cash Flow Management: Managing cash flow became a critical concern, with the need to cover operational expenses and maintain quality without compromising the business's financial health.

Strategy and Implementation

In-depth Cash Flow Analysis: The family decided to take a proactive approach by conducting a thorough analysis of the restaurant's cash flow statement. This analysis helped identify key areas where adjustments could be made to navigate the downturn effectively.

Cost Optimization: Gourmet Galore revisited its operational expenses, identifying opportunities for cost reduction without affecting customer experience. This included negotiating with suppliers for better rates, reducing waste, and optimizing staff schedules to align with customer traffic patterns.

Revenue Diversification: Understanding the need to adapt, the restaurant diversified its revenue streams. It introduced catering services, developed a line of packaged gourmet products, and enhanced its takeout and delivery options to cater to customers preferring to dine at home.

Community Engagement: To strengthen its connection with the community and drive patronage, Gourmet Galore launched themed dining events and participated in local food festivals. These efforts not only increased revenue but also reinforced the restaurant's presence in the community during challenging times.

Financial Planning and Monitoring: With a revised strategy in place, Gourmet Galore implemented a system for regular financial monitoring, allowing for agile responses to any fluctuations in cash flow and ensuring that the restaurant remained on a stable financial footing.

Outcomes
Gourmet Galore's strategic response to the economic downturn yielded remarkable results:

Financial Stability: Through diligent cost management and the introduction of new revenue streams, the restaurant stabilized its finances, maintaining a positive cash flow despite the challenging economic climate.
Brand Loyalty: The efforts to engage with the community and adapt to changing customer preferences deepened customer loyalty and attracted new patrons, setting the stage for sustained growth.
Resilience and Growth: The experience of navigating through the downturn not only demonstrated the restaurant's resilience but also positioned it for future growth. Gourmet Galore emerged stronger, with a more diversified business model and a reinforced bond with its community.

Lessons Learned
Gourmet Galore's journey through economic adversity underscores several key lessons for businesses facing similar challenges:

The Importance of Adaptability: Flexibility and the willingness to adapt business strategies are crucial for navigating economic downturns.
Proactive Financial Management: Regular analysis of cash flow and financial health enables businesses to make informed decisions and take timely action.
Engagement and Innovation: Maintaining customer engagement and exploring innovative revenue streams can transform potential vulnerabilities into strengths.
Gourmet Galore's story is a testament to the power of effective cash management, adaptability, and community engagement in turning business challenges into opportunities for growth and resilience.

Interactive Learning and Application: From Case Studies to Real-World Strategies
In the journey through our case studies—Emily's meticulous financial planning, Marco's debt liberation saga, BloomTech's strategic growth, and Gourmet Galore's resilience in adversity—we've traversed diverse financial landscapes. Now, we turn these narratives into interactive learning experiences, encouraging you to engage directly with each scenario. This hands-on approach is designed not only to enhance your understanding but to equip you with practical tools for financial analysis and strategic planning.

Engage with Each Scenario
Analytical Exercises: For each case study, we present analytical exercises that challenge you to dive into the financial details. You'll calculate net worth adjustments like Emily, prioritize debt repayment strategies alongside Marco, assess key financial ratios to guide BloomTech, and analyze cash flow adjustments to aid Gourmet Galore. These exercises aim to sharpen your financial acumen, offering a practical framework for applying theoretical knowledge.

Scenario Simulation: Imagine yourself in the shoes of each protagonist. How would you navigate the financial challenges presented? What decisions would you make differently, and why? These simulations encourage you to apply the financial concepts and tools discussed, personalizing the learning experience.

Discussion and Reflection

Reflective Questions: Accompanying each case study are reflective questions that prompt deeper thought. How could the strategies employed by Emily or Marco be adapted to your personal financial situation? What lessons from BloomTech and Gourmet Galore can be applied to your business or entrepreneurial endeavors?

Community Engagement: We encourage sharing insights and reflections within a learning community. This collaborative discussion can unveil diverse perspectives and innovative strategies, enriching the learning experience.

Empowering Insights for Action
From Insight to Strategy: The culmination of each case study is a set of actionable insights. These are practical takeaways that you can implement in your financial journey or within your business operations. Whether it's adopting a disciplined savings plan, employing strategic debt repayment, leveraging financial ratios for business growth, or diversifying revenue streams for resilience, these insights serve as a bridge from theory to action.

Strategic Planning Template: To facilitate the application of these insights, we provide templates for strategic planning. These tools help you to outline your action plans, set measurable goals, and track progress, turning the lessons learned into concrete steps toward financial empowerment.

Inspiration for Your Financial Journey
As you engage with the case studies and their interactive components, let the stories of Emily, Marco, BloomTech, and Gourmet Galore inspire you. Their journeys illuminate the path to financial resilience, strategic growth, and personal empowerment. The challenges they faced, the strategies they implemented, and the successes they achieved demonstrate the transformative power of applying financial knowledge with strategic foresight.

Conclusion: A Path Forward
These case studies, with their interactive exercises and reflective questions, are more than educational content; they are a call to action. They invite you to embrace financial challenges with courage, to apply strategic insights with intention, and to navigate your financial journey with confidence. Let these stories and the lessons they impart guide you toward financial empowerment, illuminating your path to success in personal finance and business endeavors alike.

As we conclude Section 6, with its rich tapestry of narratives that span from the personal triumphs over financial hurdles to the strategic victories within the business arena, we recognize the profound impact of financial literacy when applied to the challenges and opportunities of the real world. These stories transcend mere anecdotes; they serve as potent lessons in financial empowerment, strategic decision-making, and the relentless pursuit of both financial independence and business excellence.

With the wisdom gleaned from these case studies, we stand at the threshold of a new chapter in our financial education journey—Section 7: Practical Application. This upcoming section is designed to transition us from the realm of theory and narrative insight into the tangible world of action. It's here that the abstract principles of financial analysis, the strategies for sustainable growth, and the resilience needed to overcome obstacles become tools in your hands, ready to be wielded in the crafting of your financial future.

Transitioning to Action

As we step into Section 7, we carry forward the inspiration and insights from the stories of Emily, Marco, BloomTech, and Gourmet Galore. Their journeys underscore a fundamental truth: while each financial path is unique, the core principles guiding those journeys hold universal relevance. It's these principles, coupled with the strategies and resilience illustrated through their experiences, that we aim to transform into actionable steps in the next section.

From Insight to Implementation

Section 7: Practical Application is where insight meets implementation. It's dedicated to empowering you with the skills, tools, and confidence to apply what you've learned directly to your financial life and business endeavors. Whether it's crafting a budget that reflects your financial goals, devising a debt repayment plan, strategizing for business growth, or navigating the complexities of investment decisions, this section is about putting knowledge into practice.

Hands-on Learning

Prepare to engage with practical exercises, step-by-step guides, and interactive tools designed to facilitate the application of financial principles in your personal and professional life. This hands-on approach will not only deepen your understanding but also enhance your ability to make informed, strategic financial decisions.

Building Your Financial Future

As we transition into Section 7, let the case studies from Section 6 serve as both a guide and a source of inspiration. Remember, the journey toward financial empowerment is a continuous process of learning, applying, and adapting. With the foundations laid in the preceding sections and the actionable strategies outlined in what follows, you are well-equipped to navigate the path toward achieving your financial goals and realizing your vision of success.

Let's move forward with purpose, applying the lessons learned to forge a path of financial empowerment and success. Welcome to Section 7: Practical Application, the next step in your journey towards mastering the art and science of financial decision-making.

Section 7: Practical Application

Welcome to Section 7, where the journey we've embarked upon transitions from the landscape of theory into the tangible realm of practice. This section is crafted with a singular purpose: to empower you, the reader, to apply the wealth of knowledge and insights you've gathered to your own financial narrative. Whether navigating the complexities of personal finance or steering a business toward sustainable growth, the focus now shifts to practical application, turning learning into action.

Making Theory Tangible

Personal Finance in Practice: Armed with the insights from Emily's and Marco's stories, you're now equipped to tackle your financial milestones and challenges. From crafting a detailed budget that mirrors your financial aspirations to devising a strategic plan for debt reduction, this section offers step-by-step guides and checklists designed to translate theory into practical, actionable steps.

Budgeting Workshop: Engage in an interactive budgeting exercise, using templates inspired by real-life scenarios to create a budget that's not just a spreadsheet but a reflection of your financial goals and lifestyle.

Debt Reduction Simulator: Apply Marco's principles to your own situation with a debt reduction simulator that helps you visualize the impact of different repayment strategies on your finances over time.

Business Finance - Strategy Implementation: Drawing from BloomTech's and Gourmet Galore's experiences, this segment empowers business owners and entrepreneurs to apply strategic financial analysis and planning to their enterprises.

Financial Ratio Dashboard: Utilize a customizable dashboard to calculate and monitor key financial ratios for your business, turning raw data into strategic insights.

Cash Flow Management Exercise: Participate in a cash flow management workshop, employing tools and techniques to optimize your business's cash flow, ensuring operational stability and funding future growth.

Bridging Insight with Implementation

Action Plans for Financial Empowerment: Each module in this section concludes with the creation of a personalized action plan. These plans are your roadmap to financial empowerment, detailing specific steps, timelines, and milestones based on the strategies discussed.

Personal Finance Action Plan: From saving for a down payment to planning for retirement, outline the steps you'll take to achieve your financial goals, inspired by Emily's proactive planning.

Business Financial Strategy Plan: Drawing on BloomTech's growth strategies and Gourmet Galore's adaptability, craft a plan that addresses your business's unique financial health and growth aspirations.

Engaging with Your Financial Future

Interactive Challenges and Reflections: Throughout this section, you'll encounter interactive challenges designed to test your application of the principles covered. Reflection prompts will encourage you to consider how these strategies fit into your personal or business financial context, fostering a deeper connection between knowledge and practice.

Community Sharing and Feedback: Engage with a community of learners to share insights, successes, and challenges. This collaborative approach enriches the learning experience, offering diverse perspectives and mutual support as you apply these concepts to your life or business.

Conclusion: Empowerment Through Application

Section 7 is more than just the next step in your financial education—it's a commitment to action. It represents the bridge between understanding financial concepts and living them, between aspiring for financial independence and actively pursuing it. As you utilize the tools, exercises, and strategies provided, remember that each action you take is a building block in the foundation of your financial future.

Let the practical application of the knowledge gained be your guide to navigating financial decisions with confidence and precision. This section is your invitation to take control of your financial narrative, transforming aspirations into achievements through informed, strategic action. Welcome to the path of empowered financial decision-making.

In this section, we provide a suite of templates and tools designed to facilitate both personal and business financial assessments. These resources are crafted to help you apply the concepts discussed, transforming theory into practical action. Additionally, exercises based on hypothetical scenarios will allow you to practice financial analysis, reinforcing your understanding and application of financial principles.

Personal Finance Worksheets

Net Worth Calculator:

- **Description**: A spreadsheet designed to help you calculate your current net worth by listing all assets and liabilities.
- **Components**: Asset categories (cash, investments, personal property), liability categories (loans, credit card debt), and a formula to automatically calculate net worth.

Monthly Budget Planner:

- **Description**: A detailed template for planning monthly income and expenses, allowing for tracking against actual spending.
- **Components**: Income sources, fixed and variable expenses categories, savings goals, and an automatic calculation of surplus or deficit.

Debt Repayment Planner:

- **Description**: A tool to outline strategies for debt repayment, including the snowball and avalanche methods.
- **Components**: List of debts (amount, interest rate, minimum payment), repayment strategy selector, and a schedule generator to visualize the repayment timeline.

Business Finance Tools

Financial Ratios Dashboard:

- **Description**: An interactive dashboard for calculating and monitoring key financial ratios relevant to your business.
- **Components**: Ratios for liquidity, profitability, debt, and efficiency, with benchmarking capabilities against industry standards.

Cash Flow Forecast Template:

- **Description:** A spreadsheet to project future cash flows based on current income and expense trends, aiding in financial planning.
- **Components:** Monthly cash inflow and outflow sections, a section for adjustments based on anticipated changes, and a cumulative cash flow calculation.

Break-Even Analysis Tool:

- **Description:** A calculator to determine the break-even point for products or services, crucial for pricing and sales strategy.
- **Components:** Fixed costs, variable costs per unit, price per unit, and a formula to calculate the break-even quantity.

Exercises for Financial Analysis Practice

Personal Finance Scenario:

- **Scenario:** Imagine you're planning to buy a home in 3 years. You currently have $15,000 in savings, $2,000 in credit card debt, and you save an additional $500 per month. Using the provided Monthly Budget Planner, calculate how much you can realistically save in 3 years and decide if you need to adjust your plan.

Business Finance Exercise:

- **Scenario:** "TechInnovate," a startup, has revenue of $500,000, COGS of $200,000, operating expenses of $150,000, and an interest expense of $10,000. Utilize the Financial Ratios Dashboard to calculate TechInnovate's gross margin ratio, net profit margin, and interest coverage ratio. Discuss what these ratios indicate about TechInnovate's financial health.

Debt Management Exercise:

- **Scenario:** You have three credit cards with balances and interest rates as follows: Card 1 - $5,000 at 20%, Card 2 - $3,000 at 15%, Card 3 - $2,000 at 10%. Using the Debt Repayment Planner, outline a repayment plan using both the avalanche and snowball methods. Determine which method allows you to pay off the debt faster and with less interest paid.

These worksheets, tools, and exercises are designed to enhance your financial literacy by providing hands-on experience with real-world applications. By engaging with these resources, you'll deepen your understanding of financial principles and sharpen your skills in financial analysis and planning.

Section 8: Conclusion and Next Steps

As we draw this chapter to a close, we stand at a pivotal juncture in our financial education journey. Together, we've traversed the landscapes of personal and business finance, delved into practical applications, and engaged with real-world scenarios that bring the principles of financial literacy to life. This journey has been about more than acquiring knowledge; it's been a process of empowerment, designed to equip you with the tools necessary for informed financial decision-making.

Reflecting on Our Journey

We began by exploring the foundations of financial health, from calculating net worth to mastering cash flow analysis. We ventured into the realm of debt management and investment strategies, learning from the triumphs and challenges of individuals like Emily and Marco. Transitioning to the business world, we drew insights from BloomTech and Gourmet Galore, embracing the complexities of business finance and the strategies that drive growth and sustainability. Through interactive exercises and engaging narratives, we've endeavored to transform theory into actionable wisdom.

Key Takeaways

- **Financial Literacy is Empowering:** Understanding the principles of finance is the first step toward financial independence and success.
- **Actionable Insights are Transformative:** The real value of financial knowledge lies in its application. By utilizing the worksheets, tools, and exercises provided, you can translate insights into action.
- **Regular Assessment is Crucial:** Just as a navigator regularly checks their course, conducting regular financial assessments ensures you remain aligned with your financial goals.

Moving Forward with Confidence

As you move forward, I encourage you to embrace regular financial assessments, both personal and business, as a cornerstone of your financial strategy. Let the insights you've gained serve as a foundation for informed decision-making. Here are a few steps to guide you on this path:

Schedule Regular Financial Reviews: Mark your calendar for regular financial health check-ups. Use these opportunities to update your financial plans, recalibrate your goals, and make necessary adjustments.

Stay Informed and Curious: The world of finance is ever-evolving. Commit to lifelong learning by staying informed about financial trends, new investment opportunities, and emerging financial tools and technologies.

Build a Supportive Network: Surround yourself with a community of like-minded individuals. Whether it's joining financial forums, participating in workshops, or engaging with a financial advisor, a supportive network can provide valuable insights and encouragement.

Embrace Challenges as Opportunities: Remember, every financial challenge is an opportunity for growth. Use the strategies and insights from this chapter to navigate challenges with confidence and strategic foresight.

Your Next Steps

- **Implement Your Action Plans:** Begin by implementing the action plans you've developed. Whether it's tackling debt, optimizing your business's financial health, or planning for retirement, take those first steps with confidence.
- **Reflect and Adapt:** Financial planning is dynamic. Reflect on your progress, celebrate your successes, and be prepared to adapt your strategies as circumstances change.
- **Share Your Journey:** Your financial journey can inspire and empower others. Consider sharing your experiences, challenges, and triumphs with your community.

In Closing

Our exploration of financial literacy does not end here; it's a continuous journey of growth, learning, and adaptation. Armed with the knowledge and tools from this chapter, you are well-equipped to chart a course toward financial empowerment and success. Remember, the principles of financial analysis, strategic planning, and resilience in the face of adversity are your allies on this journey. May the insights and strategies you've gleaned serve as stepping stones to greater financial independence and prosperity.

Chapter 2: Strategic Financial Vision: Setting Goals and Crafting Success

Welcome to Chapter 2: "Strategic Financial Vision: Setting Goals and Crafting Success." In this chapter, we embark on a vital journey towards understanding the profound impact of setting financial goals, not as mere wishes for the future, but as the bedrock upon which personal and business financial success is built. This exploration is about illuminating the path from where you are now to where you aspire to be, guided by a strategic financial vision that serves as the compass for your decision-making and action planning.

The Essence of a Strategic Financial Vision

Imagine standing at the threshold of a vast landscape, your future stretching out in all directions. A strategic financial vision is like having a map and compass in hand, offering clarity and direction amidst the expanse of possibilities. It's about envisioning a future shaped by financial independence, security, and success, then charting a course to make that vision a reality.

The Power of Goal Setting

Goal setting is not just a practice; it's an art. It's the process of translating your financial vision into tangible targets, each acting as a milestone on your journey towards financial empowerment. Whether it's saving for a down payment on a home, becoming debt-free, or ensuring your business thrives in competitive markets, each goal is a step towards realizing your broader financial aspirations.

The Journey Ahead

In this chapter, we will navigate the process of defining your strategic financial vision and setting achievable goals. From personal savings targets to business growth objectives, we'll delve into practical strategies and tools designed to bring your financial dreams within reach. Along the way, we'll share inspiring stories of individuals and entrepreneurs who have transformed their financial landscapes through disciplined planning and strategic action.

Crafting Your Financial Roadmap

Personal Financial Goals: We start by examining how to conduct a thorough personal financial assessment, laying the groundwork for setting SMART (Specific, Measurable, Achievable, Relevant, Time-bound) financial goals. You'll learn how to balance the demands of today with the dreams of tomorrow, ensuring your financial planning reflects both your immediate needs and long-term aspirations.

Business Financial Objectives: For the entrepreneurs and business leaders, we delve into establishing clear financial objectives that not only aim for profitability but also sustainability and growth. We'll explore how to use financial analysis to set solid foundations for your business, identify growth opportunities, and navigate challenges.

Bringing Your Vision to Life

Through interactive exercises, reflective prompts, and step-by-step guides, this chapter is designed to be your hands-on workshop for financial success. You'll be equipped to:

- **Translate Vision into Action:** Learn how to turn your financial vision into actionable goals, breaking down the journey into manageable steps.
- **Navigate Financial Challenges:** Gain insights on overcoming the hurdles that may arise on your path, armed with strategies for resilience and adaptation.
- **Celebrate Progress:** Discover the importance of recognizing and celebrating each milestone achieved, reinforcing your commitment to your financial journey.

Conclusion

As we conclude this chapter, remember that setting a strategic financial vision is not a one-time event but an ongoing process of growth and refinement. Your financial goals, both personal and business, are the beacons guiding you towards a future of success and fulfillment. With the tools and strategies shared in this chapter, you are well-prepared to set your sights on the horizon, chart your course, and embark on the journey towards turning your financial aspirations into reality. Let this chapter be the catalyst that propels you from dreaming to doing, from planning to achieving, as you craft your story of financial success.

Section 1: Understanding Financial Vision and Goals

Welcome to the foundational step of your journey toward financial mastery—cultivating a Strategic Financial Vision and setting purposeful Goals. This section is not just about setting targets; it's about understanding the essence of what you aim to achieve financially, both personally and in your business endeavors. It's about bridging the gap between where you are today and where you want to be tomorrow, next year, or a decade from now. Let's embark on this enlightening path together, exploring the significance of a well-defined financial vision and the art of goal setting.

The Essence of a Strategic Financial Vision

A strategic financial vision serves as your guiding star, illuminating the path through the often complex world of personal and business finance. It is a vivid, compelling picture of your future financial state, crafted with intention and clarity. Whether it's achieving financial freedom, building a thriving business, or creating a legacy, your financial vision is a reflection of your deepest aspirations and values.

Personal Insight: Consider the story of Maya, who visualized owning a home where her family could create lasting memories. This vision guided her financial decisions, motivating her to save diligently, even when it meant making sacrifices in the short term.

Setting Financial Goals: The SMART Way

Your financial vision becomes attainable when broken down into specific, measurable, achievable, relevant, and time-bound (SMART) goals. This approach transforms lofty visions into tangible targets, providing a clear roadmap for your financial journey.

Short-Term Goals: These are your immediate focus—saving for an emergency fund or paying off credit card debt within a year. They are the stepping stones that provide momentum and confidence.

Medium-Term Goals: Medium-term goals, such as saving for a down payment on a home or launching a new product line in your business, often require a few years to accomplish. They bridge the gap between immediate actions and long-term aspirations.

Long-Term Goals: These are the pillars of your financial vision, such as achieving financial independence, funding your retirement, or expanding your business internationally. Long-term goals demand patience, discipline, and sustained effort.

The Psychology Behind Goal Setting

Understanding the psychological aspects of goal setting—motivation, discipline, and visualization—can significantly enhance your ability to achieve your financial objectives. The process of setting and pursuing goals activates our intrinsic motivation, pushing us to overcome obstacles and maintain focus on the end goal.

Motivational Example: Alex, an entrepreneur, visualized his startup becoming a market leader. This vision fueled his motivation, driving him to work tirelessly, even when faced with setbacks.

Discipline in Practice: Discipline is the bridge between goals and accomplishment. It's about making consistent choices that align with your financial objectives, even when they're not the easiest or most immediate path to pleasure.

Power of Visualization: Visualization is a potent tool in achieving financial goals. By vividly imagining the achievement of your goals, you reinforce your commitment and enhance your motivation to pursue them.

Conclusion

As we conclude this section, remember that your strategic financial vision and the goals you set are deeply personal. They should reflect not only your financial aspirations but also the values and dreams that give your life meaning. Armed with a clear vision and SMART goals, you're now ready to embark on the journey of turning your financial dreams into reality, equipped with the motivation, discipline, and visualization techniques needed to navigate the path ahead.

In the next sections, we will dive deeper into how to apply these concepts to set actionable personal and business financial goals, and develop strategies to achieve them, ensuring that your financial vision becomes an integral part of your journey toward success.

Section 2: Setting Personal Financial Goals

Embarking on the journey of setting personal financial goals begins with a critical first step: conducting a thorough personal financial assessment. This process is akin to drawing a map of your current financial landscape—it lays bare where you stand today and helps chart a course to where you want to be tomorrow. Let's navigate this process together, transforming the abstract into actionable, and turning dreams into achievable goals.

Conducting a Personal Financial Assessment

Step 1: Gather Your Financial Data

Overview: Start by collecting information on all your assets (what you own) and liabilities (what you owe). This includes bank account balances, investment accounts, property values, outstanding debts, and monthly expenses.

Personal Insight: Imagine you're like Sarah, who once felt overwhelmed by her finances. She began by simply listing her assets and debts, which clarified her financial situation and alleviated her stress.

Step 2: Analyze Your Cash Flow

Overview: Understanding your cash flow involves examining your income sources and spending habits. This step is crucial for identifying potential savings and understanding how much money can be allocated toward achieving your goals.

Actionable Advice: Create a monthly cash flow statement. Track your income and expenses over a month. This exercise can reveal surprising insights into your spending patterns, just as it did for Michael, who discovered how minor adjustments could lead to significant savings.

Step 3: Identify Your Financial Goals

Overview: With a clear understanding of your financial situation, it's time to identify your goals. These should be a mix of short-term (saving for an emergency fund), medium-term (down payment for a house), and long-term goals (retirement planning).

Engaging Narrative: Take inspiration from Lisa, who set a goal to pay off her student loans within five years. By prioritizing this goal, she not only freed herself from debt but also built a strong foundation for her financial future.

Step 4: Prioritize Your Goals

Overview: Not all financial goals are created equal. Some will be essential (emergency savings), while others may be desirable (vacation fund). Prioritizing your goals helps focus your financial resources on what matters most to you.

Philosophical Insight: Remember, the art of prioritization is also the art of sacrifice. It's about choosing which dreams to chase now and which to save for later, much like Alex did when he decided to prioritize saving for a home over buying a new car.

Step 5: Set SMART Goals

Overview: Transform your priorities into SMART (Specific, Measurable, Achievable, Relevant, Time-bound) goals. This framework ensures your financial goals are clear and attainable.

- **Example:** If your goal is to save for a home, a SMART goal might be, "Save $20,000 for a down payment in three years by setting aside $555 each month."

Step 6: Create an Action Plan

- **Overview:** With your SMART goals in hand, the final step is to create an action plan. This includes setting up automatic savings, adjusting your budget to cut unnecessary expenses, and finding ways to increase your income if necessary.
- **Interactive Element:** Utilize the provided template to build your personalized action plan. Reflect on how each action aligns with your goals, ensuring you're on the path to success.

Conclusion

Setting personal financial goals is not merely a task but a transformative process that empowers you to take control of your financial destiny. By conducting a detailed financial assessment and applying the principles of SMART goal setting, you lay the groundwork for a future characterized by financial security and success.

Remember, the journey to achieving your financial goals is as personal as your dreams. Inspired by the stories of Sarah, Michael, Lisa, and Alex, let their experiences guide you, their strategies empower you, and their successes inspire you. Armed with a clear financial vision and actionable goals, you're now ready to turn the page and begin crafting your success story.

Personal financial goals vary widely depending on individual circumstances, aspirations, and life stages. However, some goals are nearly universal in their importance for securing financial stability and growth. Here are detailed examples of common personal financial goals, along with strategies for achieving them:

1. Building an Emergency Fund

Goal: Create a safety net of funds to cover unexpected expenses, such as medical emergencies, car repairs, or sudden job loss.

- **Strategy:** Start by setting a target to save three to six months' worth of living expenses. Begin small, saving a portion of your income each month, and gradually increase the amount as your financial situation improves. Consider opening a high-yield savings account specifically for this fund to maximize your savings growth.

2. Debt Reduction

Goal: Minimize or eliminate outstanding debts, including credit card balances, student loans, and personal loans, to reduce financial stress and increase net worth.

Strategy: Assess all your debts to prioritize them based on interest rates (consider the debt avalanche method) or balances (consider the debt snowball method). Allocate extra payments toward the prioritized debt while maintaining minimum payments on others. Revisit your budget to find additional funds for debt repayment and consider consolidating or refinancing high-interest debts to lower rates.

3. Retirement Savings

Goal: Ensure financial security in retirement by accumulating sufficient funds to cover living expenses, healthcare, and leisure activities.

Strategy: Take advantage of employer-sponsored retirement plans like 401(k)s, particularly if they offer matching contributions. Additionally, open an Individual Retirement Account (IRA) to further your savings. Determine your desired retirement lifestyle to estimate the necessary savings, and invest early to benefit from compound interest. Regularly review and adjust your contributions based on career advancements, salary increases, and any changes in retirement goals.

4. Investment Strategies

Goal: Grow wealth over time through informed investment in stocks, bonds, mutual funds, real estate, or other vehicles.

Strategy: Define your investment goals based on your risk tolerance, time horizon, and financial objectives. Diversify your portfolio to spread risk across different asset classes. Consider low-cost index funds for a balanced approach or specific stocks and sectors if you have more knowledge and interest. Stay informed about market trends and adjust your strategy as needed, but avoid reactionary decisions based on short-term market volatility. For many, consulting with a financial advisor can provide personalized advice and strategy planning.

Implementing Your Goals

For each of these goals, the key to success lies in careful planning, regular review, and adaptation to changing financial circumstances. Setting SMART (Specific, Measurable, Achievable, Relevant, Time-bound) goals can transform these broad objectives into actionable plans. For instance, instead of vaguely aiming to "save more for retirement," a SMART goal would be "to increase my 401(k) contributions by 2% each year until I reach a 15% contribution rate."

By focusing on these foundational financial goals, you create a robust framework for personal financial health that can support more specific or ambitious goals over time. Remember, the journey to financial well-being is marathon, not a sprint, and every step taken towards these goals is a step towards greater financial freedom and security.

Crafting SMART (Specific, Measurable, Achievable, Relevant, Time-bound) financial goals.

Tools and techniques for tracking progress towards personal financial goals.

Crafting SMART (Specific, Measurable, Achievable, Relevant, Time-bound) financial goals is a strategic approach to setting targets that are not only clear and actionable but also aligned with your personal values and long-term vision. Let's explore how to apply the SMART framework to financial goal-setting, followed by an overview of tools and techniques for tracking your progress.

Crafting SMART Financial Goals

Specific

Your financial goals should be clear and specific enough to focus your efforts and feel real. Instead of saying, "I want to save money," specify what you're saving for, such as 'I want to save $10,000 for a down payment on a house."

Measurable

A goal should be measurable so that you have tangible evidence of your progress. Determine how you will measure your goal, like tracking the amount saved each month towards your $10,000 down payment.

Achievable

Ensure your goal is realistic and attainable to avoid setting yourself up for failure. If saving $10,000 in a year requires saving more than you earn, adjust your goal to fit your financial capabilities.

Relevant

Your goals should be relevant to your life and align with your broader financial plans and aspirations. Saving for a home should fit into your long-term plan of homeownership and financial stability.

Time-bound

Every goal needs a deadline to provide a sense of urgency and motivation. Decide on a feasible timeline for your goal, such as 'I will save $10,000 for a down payment in two years.'

Tools and Techniques for Tracking Progress

Budgeting Apps

Many budgeting apps are available that can help you track your savings and expenses against your goals. Look for apps that allow you to categorize transactions and set specific savings goals, offering insights into your spending patterns and progress.

Spreadsheets

Customizable and versatile, spreadsheets can be powerful tools for tracking your financial goals. Use them to create a detailed budget, track expenses, and monitor savings towards specific goals over time. You can find templates online or create one tailored to your needs.

Financial Planning Software

For more comprehensive financial planning, consider using financial planning software. These tools often offer more in-depth features for tracking investments, retirement planning, and other financial goals, providing a holistic view of your financial health.

Automated Alerts and Reminders

Setting up automated alerts for bill payments, savings deposits, and goal milestones can help keep you on track. Many banking apps and financial tools offer customization options for these reminders.

Regular Reviews

Schedule regular financial check-ins with yourself (monthly or quarterly) to review your progress towards your goals. Use this time to adjust your strategies if needed, celebrate successes, and recommit to your plans.

Implementing Your SMART Goals

With your SMART goals defined, utilize these tools and techniques to embark on your journey towards achieving them. Remember, the path to financial success is often iterative. Regularly revisiting your goals and the progress made towards them not only keeps you aligned with your financial vision but also empowers you to make informed decisions and adjustments as your financial landscape evolves.

Embrace these strategies with a spirit of resilience and adaptability, and watch as your financial goals transform from aspirations into achievements, marking your journey towards financial empowerment and success.

As we transition from the personal sphere of financial goal-setting in Section 2, where we navigated the intricacies of crafting SMART personal financial goals and the tools to track their progress, we now pivot to the broader, yet equally critical, arena of business finance. In Section 3: Establishing Business Financial Objectives, we extend the principles of strategic planning and disciplined execution into the realm of business operations. This shift marks a progression from the individual to the collective, from personal aspirations to shared business ambitions.

The journey thus far has equipped you with a robust framework for setting and achieving personal financial goals. The discipline, clarity, and strategic foresight you've harnessed on a personal level lay the groundwork for success in the business context. However, the landscape here expands; the stakes are higher, and the dynamics more complex. Businesses must navigate a myriad of financial considerations—cash flow management, profitability, growth funding, and more—all underpinned by the overarching need for sustainability and strategic growth.

In Section 3, we delve into how to translate the vision of a thriving business into concrete financial objectives. Just as personal goals are anchored in a broader financial vision, business financial objectives stem from the company's mission and strategic direction. These objectives are not just numbers on a balance sheet; they are milestones on the path to realizing your business's potential. From establishing a solid foundation for cash flow management to setting ambitious yet attainable targets for revenue growth and profitability, this section is designed to guide entrepreneurs and business leaders through the process of defining, measuring, and achieving their financial objectives.

We'll explore how to apply the SMART criteria in a business setting, ensuring that financial objectives are not only clear and achievable but also aligned with the broader goals of the business. Moreover, we'll introduce tools and methodologies tailored to the unique needs of businesses, facilitating effective tracking, management, and adjustment of financial strategies in response to changing market dynamics and internal growth milestones.

As we embark on this next phase of our financial journey, remember that the principles of discipline, strategic planning, and continuous learning apply as much to business finance as they do to personal finance. The transition from personal financial goals to business financial objectives represents a natural progression in your journey towards comprehensive financial mastery. Let the insights and strategies you've gleaned thus far inspire and inform your approach to establishing and achieving the financial objectives that will drive your business forward. Welcome to Section 3: Establishing Business Financial Objectives.

Section 3: Establishing Business Financial Objectives

In the dynamic world of business, the clarity of your financial objectives can be the beacon that guides your enterprise through turbulent markets and towards sustainable growth. As we pivot from the realm of personal finance to the broader landscape of business operations, it's time to focus on establishing solid financial objectives that will serve as the foundation of your company's success. This section is dedicated to empowering entrepreneurs, business leaders, and visionaries with the knowledge and tools necessary to conduct thorough financial analyses, set meaningful objectives, and navigate the path to financial prosperity.

Conducting a Financial Analysis for Your Business

The first step towards setting actionable financial goals is conducting a comprehensive financial analysis of your business. This process involves a deep dive into your company's financial statements—balance sheets, income statements, and cash flow statements—to assess its current health and identify areas for improvement.

Actionable Advice: Begin by reviewing your revenue streams, cost of goods sold (COGS), operating expenses, and net profit margins over the past few years. This historical analysis will help you understand trends, pinpoint inefficiencies, and forecast future performance.

Interactive Element: Utilize our financial analysis template to systematically review your financial data. This tool will guide you through calculating key ratios and metrics that reveal the financial strengths and weaknesses of your business.

Setting Business Financial Objectives

With a clear understanding of your business's financial health, you can now set precise financial objectives. These goals should be tailored to your company's unique situation, market position, and long-term vision.

1. Cash Flow Management

Efficient cash flow management is crucial for the survival and growth of any business. Your objective should focus on maintaining a positive cash flow, ensuring that your business can meet its obligations and invest in growth opportunities.

Example: Implement a monthly cash flow forecasting system to predict incoming cash and outgoing expenses. This foresight allows for proactive adjustments, ensuring liquidity and financial stability.

2. Profit Maximization

While profitability is a fundamental goal for any business, setting specific targets for profit maximization requires strategic planning and operational efficiency.

- **Personal Anecdote:** Consider the story of "EcoWear," a startup that set a goal to increase its net profit margin by 5% within two years. Through cost reduction strategies and pricing optimizations, they exceeded their target, demonstrating the power of focused financial objectives.

3. Capital Structure Optimization

Optimizing your capital structure involves finding the right balance between debt and equity to finance your business operations and expansion. The goal is to minimize the cost of capital while maximizing financial flexibility.

- **Philosophical Insight:** The journey to optimizing your capital structure is akin to walking a tightrope. It requires a careful balance between leveraging debt for growth and maintaining enough equity to ensure stability and investor confidence.

Tools and Techniques for Achieving Financial Objectives

Achieving your business financial objectives requires diligent monitoring, strategic decision-making, and continuous adaptation.

Tracking and Monitoring: Adopt financial dashboards and KPIs to monitor progress towards your objectives regularly. These tools provide real-time insights, enabling swift adjustments to strategy as needed.

Strategic Decision-Making: Use your financial analysis and objectives as the basis for strategic decisions, from investment opportunities to cost-cutting measures. Let data drive your decision-making process.

Adaptation and Flexibility: The business landscape is ever-changing. Be prepared to revisit and adjust your financial objectives as market conditions, competitive environments, and your business needs evolve.

Conclusion

As we wrap up this section, remember that establishing solid business financial objectives is not a one-time exercise but a critical ongoing process. It's about setting a course for your business that aligns with your vision, understanding the financial implications of your decisions, and adapting to the ever-changing business environment. Armed with a strategic financial vision, actionable objectives, and the right tools for tracking and analysis, you are now poised to lead your business toward a future marked by financial success and growth.

Utilizing Financial Projections and Forecasts

The ability to look ahead with accuracy is a key facet of successful business management, particularly when it comes to financial planning. Financial projections and forecasts are indispensable tools that allow business leaders to set realistic and achievable financial targets. These forward-looking statements are based on historical data, current market analysis, and assumptions about future market trends.

Creating Financial Projections:

- Start with a comprehensive review of your past financial performance, including revenue, expenses, and cash flow patterns.
- Analyze market trends, competitor actions, and potential economic shifts to inform your projections.
- Develop detailed revenue forecasts by product line or service offering, considering factors like market penetration, pricing strategies, and sales channels.
- Project your expenses, factoring in both fixed costs (like rent and salaries) and variable costs that may fluctuate with business volume.
- Incorporate planned business initiatives, such as expansions or new product launches, assessing their financial impact on revenue, costs, and cash flow.

Setting Achievable Targets:

- Use your financial projections to establish specific, measurable financial targets for the short and medium term. These might include revenue growth rates, profit margins, or cash reserve levels.
- Ensure these targets are aligned with your broader business goals and strategic vision, providing a clear direction for your team.

Scenario Planning:

- Prepare for uncertainty by creating multiple forecast scenarios (e.g., best case, worst case, most likely case). This approach allows you to anticipate potential challenges and opportunities, making your business more resilient.

Implementing Key Performance Indicators (KPIs)

Key Performance Indicators (KPIs) are vital metrics that provide insights into the financial and operational health of your business. They enable ongoing monitoring and fine-tuning of your financial objectives, ensuring your business remains on track towards achieving its goals.

Selecting the Right KPIs:

- Choose KPIs that are directly related to your critical business objectives. For a startup focused on growth, relevant KPIs might include customer acquisition cost, lifetime value of a customer, and monthly recurring revenue.
- Ensure your KPIs are measurable and provide actionable insights. Each KPI should have a clear calculation method and benchmark for success.

Implementing KPI Monitoring:

- Develop a dashboard or use business intelligence software to track your KPIs in real-time. This visibility allows for prompt decision-making and adjustments.
- Schedule regular review meetings to assess KPI performance against targets. Use these discussions to celebrate wins, identify areas for improvement, and adjust strategies as needed.

Adjusting Business Financial Objectives:

- Use the insights gained from your KPI analysis to refine your financial projections and targets. For example, if customer acquisition costs are rising, you may need to revise your sales and marketing strategies.
- Be prepared to pivot your business model or financial strategies based on what your KPIs reveal about market dynamics and internal performance.

Conclusion

The strategic use of financial projections, forecasts, and KPIs transforms the art of setting business financial targets from a guessing game into a precise science. By looking ahead with informed projections, setting achievable targets, and implementing rigorous KPI monitoring, you empower your business to navigate the complexities of the market with confidence. This proactive approach not only ensures your financial objectives are grounded in reality but also equips you with the agility to adapt and thrive in an ever-changing business landscape.

As we transition from the foundational work of establishing business financial objectives, utilizing projections, forecasts, and implementing KPIs for ongoing monitoring, we pivot towards the actionable realm in Section 4: Strategies for Achieving Financial Goals. This next chapter is designed to bridge the gap between setting ambitious financial targets and the practical steps required to turn these aspirations into tangible achievements.

In the journey so far, we've equipped ourselves with the tools and insights necessary for laying down clear, measurable, and achievable objectives. We've also embraced the discipline of monitoring progress through KPIs, ensuring our strategies are data-driven and aligned with our overarching business goals. Now, it's time to delve deeper into the specific strategies, methodologies, and practices that can propel a business from the planning stage to the realization of its financial ambitions.

Section 4 is about action. It's where planning meets execution. Here, we'll explore a variety of strategies that successful businesses employ to navigate growth, manage resources efficiently, and overcome the myriad challenges that emerge on the path to financial success. From optimizing cash flow and managing debt effectively to leveraging growth opportunities and scaling operations, this section provides a comprehensive guide to actionable steps businesses can take to achieve their financial goals.

Expect to uncover:

- **Cash Flow Optimization Techniques:** Practical steps for ensuring your business maximizes its operational liquidity without compromising on investment opportunities for growth.
- **Debt Management Strategies:** Insightful approaches to managing and leveraging debt in a way that supports your business objectives while maintaining financial health.
- **Growth Financing Options:** Exploration of various financing avenues, including equity financing, debt financing, and alternative funding sources, each with its nuances and strategic implications.
- **Efficiency and Cost Reduction Tactics:** Methods for streamlining operations, reducing wasteful expenditure, and enhancing overall business efficiency to boost your bottom line.
- **Revenue Maximization Strategies:** Innovative ways to increase your business's revenue streams, improve product offerings, and enhance market penetration.

Each strategy will be dissected to provide a clear understanding of its implementation, challenges, and the measurable impact it can have on your business's financial performance. Moreover, this section will not shy away from the realities of navigating the complexities of business growth, offering wisdom on adapting strategies in response to both internal developments and external market changes.

As we move forward, remember that the journey to achieving your business's financial goals is iterative and dynamic. It requires persistence, flexibility, and a willingness to learn from both successes and setbacks. Section 4: Strategies for Achieving Financial Goals is your roadmap to action, designed to empower you with the knowledge and tools to drive your business towards its financial vision with confidence and clarity. Let's embark on this next phase of our journey with a commitment to strategic action and an eye towards the successful realization of our financial aspirations.

Section 4: Strategies for Achieving Financial Goals

Embarking on the path to financial success requires more than just setting goals; it demands a comprehensive action plan that breaks down those goals into actionable steps. In this section, we'll guide you through developing a robust plan to achieve your financial goals, whether personal or business-related. Moreover, we'll tackle the inevitable challenges you'll face along this journey, offering strategies to overcome obstacles, maintain motivation, and adapt your plans as necessary.

Developing an Action Plan

Step-by-Step Approach:

Clarify Your Goals: Begin with a clear understanding of your financial goals. Whether it's achieving a debt-free life, expanding your business, or securing a comfortable retirement, specificity is key.

Break It Down: Divide each goal into smaller, manageable tasks. For instance, if your goal is to save for a down payment, determine the amount you need to save monthly and identify ways to adjust your budget accordingly.

Assign Deadlines: Set realistic deadlines for each task. Deadlines create urgency and help prioritize actions, keeping you on track towards your larger goal.

Identify Resources: Determine what resources you'll need to accomplish each step. This could include financial tools, advice from a financial advisor, or educational materials to improve your financial literacy.

Monitor Progress: Regularly review your plan to track progress, celebrate achievements, and adjust your strategies as needed.

Actionable Advice:

Automate Savings: For personal savings goals, automation can be a game-changer. Setting up automatic transfers to a savings account can help ensure consistency in your savings effort.

Leverage Technology: Utilize financial management software to monitor business cash flows, track expenses, and manage invoices efficiently.

Overcoming Common Obstacles

Addressing Setbacks:

Financial journeys are rarely smooth. Unexpected expenses, economic downturns, or business challenges can derail your plans. When setbacks occur:

Stay Calm and Assess: Take a step back and assess the situation. Understand the impact on your goals and consider your options.

Adjust Your Plan: Be flexible and willing to adjust your plans. Sometimes, extending a deadline or revising a goal is necessary to align with new realities.

Maintaining Motivation:

Staying motivated, especially with long-term goals, can be challenging. To keep your motivation high:

Celebrate Small Wins: Recognize and celebrate milestones, no matter how small. These victories build momentum and reinforce your commitment to your goals.

Visualize Success: Regularly visualize achieving your goals. This mental exercise can reinforce your determination and help maintain focus.

Adjusting Strategies:

As you progress towards your goals, you may find that some strategies are more effective than others. Being adaptable is crucial:

Seek Feedback: Don't hesitate to seek advice from mentors, advisors, or financial professionals. Fresh perspectives can provide valuable insights.

Learn from Experience: Embrace both successes and failures as learning opportunities. Each experience provides valuable lessons that can refine your approach.

Conclusion

Creating a detailed action plan and being prepared to navigate the hurdles along the way are essential components of financial success. Remember, the path to achieving your financial goals is not linear. It requires persistence, flexibility, and a proactive mindset. Armed with a clear strategy, the ability to overcome obstacles, and the willingness to adapt, you are well on your way to realizing your financial aspirations. Let this section serve as your guide and inspiration as you take concrete steps towards financial empowerment and success.

The role of financial education and professional advice in achieving financial goals.

As we delve further into the strategies for achieving financial goals, it becomes imperative to recognize the pivotal role of financial education and professional advice. These elements are not just supplementary; they are fundamental to navigating the complex terrain of financial planning and decision-making. This segment explores how a commitment to ongoing learning and seeking expert guidance can significantly enhance your ability to meet and exceed your financial objectives.

The Role of Financial Education

Empowerment Through Knowledge:

Financial education equips you with the knowledge to make informed decisions about your money. Understanding concepts such as budgeting, investing, debt management, and financial planning empowers you to take control of your financial destiny.

- **Actionable Advice:** Dedicate time each week to learning about financial topics relevant to your goals. This could involve reading books, attending workshops, or enrolling in online courses. Websites and podcasts offer a wealth of information that can broaden your understanding and keep you updated on financial trends and strategies.

Informed Decision-Making:

The more you know, the better you can navigate financial challenges and opportunities. Education enables you to evaluate the pros and cons of different financial decisions, from investment choices to debt repayment strategies, with a critical eye.

Interactive Element: Engage with financial simulations or calculators available online to understand the implications of different financial decisions, such as the impact of additional mortgage payments on interest over time or the potential returns from various investment portfolios.

Seeking Professional Advice

Accessing Expertise:

Financial advisors, accountants, and tax professionals can provide personalized advice tailored to your unique financial situation and goals. Their expertise can be invaluable in areas where specialized knowledge is required.

Personal Anecdote: Consider the story of James, who, despite his best efforts to manage his growing business's finances, sought the advice of a financial advisor. The advisor identified tax-saving opportunities James had overlooked, significantly improving the business's financial health.

Strategic Planning and Accountability:

A financial professional can help you develop a comprehensive financial plan that aligns with your goals, risk tolerance, and life stage. They can also serve as an accountability partner, helping you stay on track towards your objectives.

Engaging Narrative: Emily and her partner, aiming to retire early, worked with a financial planner to map out a detailed investment strategy. Their advisor's insights and regular check-ins provided the discipline and motivation needed to adhere to their aggressive savings plan.

The Synergy of Education and Professional Advice

Combining personal financial education with professional advice creates a powerful synergy. While education empowers you with foundational knowledge and confidence, professional advice offers depth, personalization, and strategic oversight. Together, they form a comprehensive approach to achieving your financial goals, ensuring you're not just following a path but charting it with insight and expertise.

Conclusion

The journey toward financial goals is enriched by the knowledge gained through education and the strategic guidance provided by financial professionals. As you continue to navigate your financial path, remember that these resources are not merely optional; they are integral to crafting a future marked by financial success and security. Embrace the pursuit of financial education as a lifelong endeavor and consider professional advice as a valuable investment in your financial well-being. Together, they will serve as your compass and map in the journey to achieving your financial dreams.

Continuing from our exploration of the roles of financial education and professional advice in achieving financial goals, let's delve into the real-world impact these elements can have through a series of case studies. These success stories of individuals and businesses illuminate the path to achieving strategic financial visions, showcasing the transformative power of informed decision-making, strategic planning, and professional guidance.

Case Study 1: Personal Financial Transformation

The Individual: Sofia, a marketing professional in her early thirties, faced a common predicament: living paycheck to paycheck despite a decent salary. Saddled with student loan debt and credit card debt, her dream of owning a home seemed distant.

The Strategy: Sofia embarked on a journey of financial education, dedicating time each week to learn about personal finance management. She utilized online courses, financial podcasts, and books to build her knowledge base. Armed with this information, Sofia sought the advice of a financial planner who helped her prioritize her debts using the avalanche method, set realistic savings goals, and create a budget that allowed for savings growth.

The Outcome: Within three years, Sofia not only paid off her high-interest debts but also saved enough for a down payment on her first home. Her commitment to financial education and willingness to seek professional advice were key to transforming her financial situation.

Case Study 2: Startup Success Story

The Business: "EcoTech," a startup focused on sustainable technology solutions, struggled to secure funding and manage cash flow efficiently in its early stages. The founders had a strong vision but lacked the financial acumen to bring their ideas to fruition.

The Strategy: Recognizing their limitations, the EcoTech team decided to invest in both their financial education and professional consultancy. They attended workshops on startup finance and engaged a seasoned financial advisor specializing in startups. The advisor helped them refine their business model, develop a solid financial plan, and prepare pitches that eventually won them significant funding.

The Outcome: EcoTech not only secured the necessary funding but also implemented robust financial management practices that propelled their growth. Today, they are a leading player in the sustainable technology market, with a clear path toward long-term profitability and success.

Case Study 3: Overcoming Business Adversity

The Business: "Bella's Boutique," a small family-owned retail business, faced the brink of closure when a major economic downturn hit. With sales plummeting and debts rising, the future looked bleak.

The Strategy: The owners of Bella's Boutique took a proactive approach to turn their business around. They sought the advice of a business financial advisor, who helped them renegotiate their debts, identify cost-cutting measures, and pivot their business model to include an online storefront. Concurrently, they educated themselves on digital marketing and e-commerce to adapt to the changing retail landscape.

The Outcome: The strategic pivot to online sales, combined with improved financial management, allowed Bella's Boutique to not only survive the downturn but thrive. Their online store attracted a wider customer base, and the boutique became profitable again within a year.

Conclusion

These case studies underscore the profound impact that a commitment to financial education, coupled with the strategic use of professional advice, can have on achieving financial goals. Whether navigating personal financial challenges or steering a business towards its strategic vision, the combination of knowledge, strategic planning, and expert guidance can unlock pathways to success previously thought unreachable.

As we reflect on these stories, let them serve as both inspiration and a blueprint. They remind us that with the right approach, achieving our financial visions, no matter how ambitious, is within our grasp.

As we transition from the inspiring tales of individuals and businesses who transformed their financial destinies through education, strategy, and professional guidance, we embark on the next crucial chapter in our financial journey—Section 5: Integrating Technology and Tools in Financial Planning. This section heralds a shift towards the practical, exploring how modern technology and innovative tools can be harnessed to streamline financial planning, enhance decision-making, and ultimately, achieve your financial goals with greater efficiency and precision.

The case studies we delved into illuminated the path to financial success through informed decisions and strategic partnerships. Now, we extend that foundation by embracing the digital revolution that has transformed the landscape of financial management. In today's digital age, a plethora of tools and technologies are at our fingertips, offering unprecedented opportunities to optimize our financial planning processes, from personal budgeting to comprehensive business financial management.

In Section 5, we will explore:

Financial Management Software: Discover how software solutions can offer detailed insights into your financial health, automate tedious tasks, and facilitate more informed financial decisions.

Budgeting Apps: Learn about the array of apps designed to help you manage your personal finances, track spending, and save towards your goals, all from the convenience of your smartphone.

Investment Platforms: Delve into the world of online investment platforms that democratize access to the stock market, allowing for portfolio diversification and real-time monitoring of investments.

Analytical Tools: Uncover how advanced analytical tools can parse vast amounts of financial data to provide predictive insights, helping businesses anticipate market trends and adjust strategies accordingly.

Blockchain and Cryptocurrency: Explore the emerging technologies of blockchain and cryptocurrency and their implications for personal and business finance, from enhancing transaction security to offering new investment opportunities.

Technology has the power to transform the abstract into the actionable, making our financial goals more attainable than ever before. However, integrating these tools into our financial planning requires a thoughtful approach, balancing the benefits of automation and digital insights with the need for personal oversight and customization.

As we move forward into Section 5, keep in mind that technology is not just about convenience; it's about empowerment. It's about leveraging digital advancements to craft a financial strategy that is not only effective but also aligned with our values and aspirations. Let us embrace the digital age, using technology as a catalyst to propel us towards our financial visions with confidence and clarity.

Section 5: Integrating Technology and Tools in Financial Planning

In the dynamic landscape of today's financial world, the integration of technology and tools in financial planning represents a leap towards efficiency, accessibility, and strategic depth. This section is dedicated to unveiling the myriad of financial technology tools available for both personal and business finance management. These digital solutions not only streamline financial operations but also enhance decision-making processes, allowing individuals and businesses alike to navigate their financial journeys with greater precision and insight.

Financial Management Software

For Personal Use: Imagine a world where every aspect of your personal finances, from budgeting to investment tracking, can be managed with a few clicks. Financial management software such as Quicken or Mint offers a comprehensive view of your financial health, integrating bank accounts, investments, and upcoming bills into one dashboard. The convenience and clarity provided by these tools demystify financial planning, making it accessible to everyone.

Actionable Advice: Schedule a weekly finance review using your chosen software. Use this time to check on your spending patterns, evaluate your budget, and adjust your savings goals as needed.

For Business Use: On the business front, platforms like QuickBooks and Xero transform how companies manage their finances. From invoicing to expense tracking and financial reporting, these tools offer real-time insights into a business's financial performance, enabling timely decisions that can drive growth and efficiency.

Engaging Narrative: Consider "LunaTech," a small tech startup that streamlined its cash flow management using Xero. This not only saved countless hours on financial administration but also provided the founders with clear insights into their financial health, aiding in strategic decision-making.

Budgeting Apps

Personal Budgeting Made Simple: Budgeting apps such as YNAB (You Need A Budget) or PocketGuard simplify the process of tracking income and expenses, offering features like goal setting and spending alerts. By providing a real-time overview of your finances, these apps empower you to make informed spending decisions and stick to your financial goals.

Personal Anecdote: Sarah discovered she was spending an unsustainable amount on dining out. By using YNAB, she was able to set a stricter dining out budget, redirecting those funds towards her emergency savings goal.

Investment Platforms

Democratizing Investing: The advent of online investment platforms like Robinhood and E*TRADE has democratized access to the stock market, allowing individuals to trade stocks, bonds, and other securities with ease. These platforms often offer educational resources, making investing more approachable for beginners.

Philosophical Insight: The essence of investing lies not just in the potential financial return but in the growth of one's financial literacy and confidence. Embrace these tools as both a means to wealth and a learning opportunity.

Analytical Tools

Data-Driven Decision Making: For businesses, analytical tools embedded within financial software can parse through vast amounts of data, offering predictive insights and identifying trends. This capability allows for data-driven decision-making, crucial in today's fast-paced business environment.

- **Interactive Element:** Utilize the analytical features within your business financial software to conduct a quarterly review. Assess key metrics and trends that could inform your strategy moving forward.

Blockchain and Cryptocurrency

Exploring New Frontiers: Blockchain technology and cryptocurrencies represent the frontier of financial technology, offering new ways to think about currency, transactions, and investments. While navigating this space requires caution, it also presents unique opportunities for diversification and innovation.

- **Empathy and Understanding:** While the volatility of cryptocurrencies can be daunting, educating yourself on blockchain technology's potential and risks can provide a balanced perspective on these digital assets.

Conclusion

As we wrap up this section, remember that the journey through financial technology is one of empowerment and opportunity. Whether managing personal finances or steering a business, the right tools can illuminate your path, making your financial goals not just aspirations but achievable realities. Embrace these technologies with an open mind and a strategic approach, and let them propel you towards financial success.

How to leverage apps, software, and online resources for budgeting, investment, and financial tracking.

Building upon our exploration of the wide array of financial technology tools available for both personal and business finance management, let's delve deeper into practical ways to leverage apps, software, and online resources to enhance budgeting, investment, and financial tracking endeavors. These digital tools not only simplify financial management but also empower users with actionable insights, fostering a proactive approach to achieving financial goals.

Leveraging Budgeting Apps

Maximizing the Potential of Budgeting Apps:

Customization is Key: Select a budgeting app that allows you to customize categories according to your spending habits and financial goals. Tailoring the app to reflect your unique financial landscape can provide a clearer picture of where your money is going and where you can cut back.

Set Realistic Budgeting Goals: Utilize the app's goal-setting features to establish realistic and achievable budgeting targets. Remember, the objective is to create a sustainable budget that balances your current needs with your future financial aspirations.

Review Regularly: Make it a habit to review your budget regularly within the app. Many apps offer weekly or monthly summaries of your spending against your budget, which can help identify patterns and make necessary adjustments promptly.

Utilizing Investment Platforms

Smart Investing Through Online Platforms:

Start with Education: Many investment platforms offer tutorials, webinars, and articles that can help demystify the investment process. Take advantage of these resources to build your knowledge base before making investment decisions.

Diversify Your Portfolio: Use online investment platforms to diversify your portfolio across different asset classes. These platforms often provide tools to analyze your current portfolio's diversity and suggest ways to balance your investments.

Monitor Investments Efficiently: Set up alerts for your investments to stay informed about significant market movements. This feature can help you make timely decisions based on the performance of your portfolio.

Harnessing Financial Tracking Software

Enhancing Financial Oversight with Tracking Software:

Automate Expense Tracking: Choose software that offers the ability to link your bank accounts and credit cards for automatic transaction categorization. This feature can save time and provide an up-to-date view of your finances.

Utilize Dashboards for a Holistic View: Financial tracking software often includes dashboards that offer a holistic view of your financial health, including net worth, cash flow, and upcoming bills. Regularly consulting these dashboards can help you stay on top of your financial situation and adjust your plans as needed.

Set and Track Financial Goals: Use the software's goal-tracking features to set specific financial goals and monitor your progress towards achieving them. This functionality can be particularly motivating, providing visual progress indicators and reminders.

Exploring Online Financial Resources

Expanding Knowledge and Skills:

Financial Blogs and Websites: There's a wealth of knowledge available on financial blogs and websites. Whether you're looking for investment advice, tips on saving money, or strategies for debt repayment, there's likely a resource that matches your needs.

Online Financial Calculators: Utilize online calculators for everything from planning your retirement savings to calculating mortgage payments. These tools can provide quick answers to complex financial questions and aid in decision-making.

Joining Online Communities: Participate in online forums and communities related to personal finance and investing. These platforms can offer support, advice, and shared experiences from individuals who are navigating similar financial journeys.

Conclusion

As we conclude this section, it's clear that the integration of technology into financial planning offers unparalleled opportunities for enhancing our understanding, efficiency, and effectiveness in managing our finances. By thoughtfully selecting and utilizing budgeting apps, investment platforms, financial tracking software, and leveraging online resources, you can take control of your financial future. These tools not only simplify the complex world of finance but also empower you to make informed decisions, track your progress towards your goals, and adjust your strategies in real-time. Embrace these digital solutions as key allies on your journey to financial success.

The importance of cybersecurity and data privacy in using financial technology.

As we navigate the digital landscape of financial planning, leveraging apps, software, and online resources to optimize our financial management, the importance of cybersecurity and data privacy cannot be overstated. In this era where financial transactions and personal data are increasingly managed online, protecting this information from cyber threats and ensuring privacy becomes paramount. Let's delve into why cybersecurity and data privacy are critical in the use of financial technology and how you can safeguard your financial digital footprint.

The Significance of Cybersecurity and Data Privacy

Guarding Against Cyber Threats:

In the realm of financial technology, your personal and financial data represent a valuable target for cybercriminals. From identity theft to unauthorized access to your financial accounts, the risks are significant. Cybersecurity measures are essential to protect against such threats, ensuring that your financial aspirations are not derailed by malicious actors.

     Actionable Advice: Regularly update your financial apps and software to the latest versions. These updates often include security patches that protect against newly discovered vulnerabilities.

Maintaining Privacy and Control:

Data privacy is about maintaining control over your personal information. In the financial sector, this means having a say in how your financial data is collected, used, and shared. Ensuring data privacy means that sensitive information, like your spending habits or investment choices, remains confidential, used only in ways that benefit you and are in line with your expectations.

     Engaging Narrative: Imagine the peace of mind that comes from knowing your investment platform uses end-to-end encryption for your transactions, ensuring that your investment decisions remain your own, shielded from prying eyes.

Strategies for Enhancing Cybersecurity and Data Privacy

Utilize Strong Authentication Methods:

Adopting strong authentication methods, such as two-factor authentication (2FA), adds an extra layer of security to your financial accounts. This can significantly reduce the risk of unauthorized access, even if your password is compromised.

     Interactive Element: Activate 2FA on all financial platforms that offer it. Consider using a secure password manager to generate and store complex passwords for each of your accounts.

Be Vigilant About Phishing Attempts:

Phishing scams, designed to trick you into revealing personal information or financial details, are increasingly sophisticated. Being able to recognize these attempts is crucial for protecting your data.

- **Empathy and Understanding:** Sarah, after attending a webinar on cybersecurity, recognized a phishing email masquerading as a message from her bank. Her newfound awareness prevented a potential breach of her financial data.

Secure Your Internet Connection:

Using public Wi-Fi to access financial accounts or conduct transactions can expose your data to interception. Ensure that your internet connection is secure and consider using a virtual private network (VPN) when accessing financial information on public networks.

- **Philosophical Insight:** The convenience of technology comes with the responsibility to protect our digital selves. Just as we would lock our doors in the physical world, securing our online financial activities is a fundamental practice in our digital lives.

Conclusion

Incorporating technology into our financial planning offers immense benefits in terms of convenience, efficiency, and insights. However, the flip side is the increased responsibility to safeguard our financial data against cyber threats and ensure its privacy. By adopting robust cybersecurity measures and being vigilant about data privacy, we can enjoy the advantages of financial technology with confidence and security. Let this awareness of cybersecurity and data privacy be a cornerstone of your financial technology use, ensuring that your journey towards financial success is both fruitful and secure.

As we conclude our exploration of integrating technology and tools into financial planning, and underscore the critical importance of cybersecurity and data privacy, we stand at the precipice of a vital phase in our financial journey. The path we have traversed has equipped us with the knowledge and tools necessary to navigate the complexities of modern financial management. Now, it's time to turn our attention to the crucial practice of reflection and adaptation in Section 6: Revisiting and Revising Your Financial Vision.

The dynamic nature of life, coupled with the ever-evolving financial landscape, necessitates periodic reassessment of our financial strategies and goals. Just as the technology we use to manage our finances continues to evolve, so too must our financial visions adapt to reflect changes in our personal lives, the economy, and our understanding of what we value most.

In Section 6, we will delve into:

The Importance of Regular Financial Reviews: Discover how periodic reviews of your financial plan can highlight achievements, uncover new opportunities, and identify areas requiring adjustment. This process ensures your financial strategies remain aligned with your evolving goals and life circumstances.

Adapting to Life's Changes: Life is replete with changes—career transitions, family dynamics, and personal aspirations all evolve. We'll explore how to adjust your financial vision and goals to remain relevant and supportive of your current and future needs.

Leveraging New Financial Knowledge and Tools: As you grow in your financial journey, new insights, tools, and strategies become available. Integrating these resources can enhance your approach to financial management, making your path to success more efficient and aligned with best practices.

Case Studies on Financial Adaptation: Be inspired by stories of individuals and businesses that have successfully navigated significant shifts in their financial landscapes. These narratives will demonstrate the power of resilience, flexibility, and strategic revision in achieving financial well-being.

The journey through the financial landscape is not a straight line but a series of adjustments and course corrections. It's about taking stock of where you are, envisioning where you want to be, and mapping out the most effective route to get there, even as the destination evolves.

As we prepare to embark on Section 6, remember that revisiting and revising your financial vision is not just about responding to change—it's about embracing it. It's an opportunity to refine your goals, rediscover your aspirations, and renew your commitment to financial success with a fresh perspective. Let's move forward with the understanding that our financial visions are living entities, shaped by our experiences, enriched by our learning, and refined by our growth. Welcome to the journey of continuous evolution in pursuit of financial excellence.

Section 6: Revisiting and Revising Your Financial Vision

In the ever-evolving journey of personal and professional growth, the practice of regularly revisiting and revising your financial vision stands as a pivotal cornerstone. It's an acknowledgment that as we navigate through life's various stages, our priorities, circumstances, and aspirations inevitably shift. This section is dedicated to empowering you with strategies for ensuring your financial goals remain aligned with your evolving vision, thereby maximizing your potential for success and fulfillment.

The Imperative of Financial Reflection

Embrace Change as a Constant:

Change is the only constant in life, and this holds particularly true in the realm of financial planning. The goals you set yesterday may not serve the reality of today or the dreams of tomorrow. Regular reviews of your financial plan allow you to pivot and adapt, ensuring your strategies are always in service of your current and future aspirations.

- **Actionable Advice:** Schedule bi-annual financial reviews. Use these checkpoints to assess progress towards your goals, adjust for any life changes, and recalibrate your financial plan as necessary.

Adapting to Life's Milestones

**Life's milestones—marriage, the birth of a child, career changes, or retirement—demand a reassessment of your financial goals. Each of these events can significantly impact your financial priorities and strategies.

- **Personal Anecdote:** Consider Maria, who, upon the arrival of her first child, realized her financial goals needed a major overhaul. Her priority shifted towards securing her family's future, leading her to adjust her savings strategy and explore education funds.

The Role of New Financial Knowledge

Stay Informed and Agile:

As you grow in your financial journey, new insights, products, and changes in the economic landscape will emerge. Staying informed and integrating new knowledge into your financial plan can uncover opportunities to optimize your approach and achieve your goals more efficiently.

- **Engaging Narrative:** Alex, once a novice investor, dedicated time to learning about diversified investment portfolios. This new knowledge empowered him to adjust his investment strategy, significantly enhancing his financial growth and reducing risk.

Leveraging Technology for Dynamic Planning

Technology as a Catalyst for Adaptation:

Modern financial tools and apps not only simplify the management of your finances but also facilitate the regular review and adjustment of your financial plan. These digital solutions can provide alerts, generate reports, and offer insights that inform timely revisions to your strategy.

Interactive Element: Utilize financial apps that offer customizable dashboards and goal-tracking features. These tools can visually map your progress and highlight when adjustments are needed, keeping your financial vision in sharp focus.

Celebrating Progress and Setting New Horizons

Recognize Achievements and Aspire for More:

Revisiting your financial vision isn't just about making adjustments; it's also an opportunity to celebrate the milestones you've achieved. Acknowledging your successes reinforces your motivation and sets the stage for aspiring to new heights.

Philosophical Insight: The journey of financial planning is akin to navigating a river—it requires both steering to avoid obstacles and recognizing when to let the current of new opportunities carry you forward to new explorations and achievements.

Conclusion

The process of revisiting and revising your financial vision is integral to a holistic financial strategy. It ensures that your financial goals evolve in tandem with your life's journey, reflecting your current priorities, dreams, and the wisdom you've gathered along the way. By regularly reviewing your financial plan, adapting to new circumstances, integrating fresh knowledge, and leveraging technology, you can navigate the path to financial success with confidence and agility. Let this practice of continuous reflection and adaptation be your guiding principle, enabling you to realize a financial vision that truly resonates with the life you aspire to live.

Strategies for adapting financial plans in response to life changes, economic shifts, and business growth.

Building upon the crucial practice of revisiting and revising your financial vision, let's explore specific strategies for adapting your financial plans in response to life changes, economic shifts, and business growth. These strategies are designed to equip you with the agility and foresight needed to maintain alignment between your evolving circumstances and your financial objectives, ensuring resilience and progress towards your goals.

Adapting to Life Changes

Anticipate and Plan for Major Life Events:

- **Proactive Planning:** Begin by anticipating potential life changes, such as starting a family, buying a home, or planning for retirement. Adjust your financial plan to include savings goals and insurance coverage that align with these future needs.
- **Emergency Fund:** Ensure you have an emergency fund that can cover unexpected life events, such as job loss or medical emergencies. This fund acts as a financial buffer, protecting your long-term plans from short-term upheavals.

Responding to Economic Shifts

Stay Informed and Flexible:

- **Market Awareness:** Keep abreast of economic trends and market conditions. Understanding the broader economic environment can help you anticipate changes that may impact your investments, savings, or earning potential.
- **Diversification:** In times of economic uncertainty, diversification becomes even more critical. Spread your investments across different asset classes to mitigate risk and protect your portfolio from volatility.

Fueling Business Growth

Scale Strategically:

- **Reinvest Profits:** As your business grows, reinvesting profits back into the business can fuel further growth. Be strategic about where you allocate these funds, whether it's expanding your product line, investing in marketing, or enhancing operational efficiency.
- **Flexible Financing:** Explore different financing options to support expansion efforts, such as loans, equity financing, or crowdfunding. Choose the option that aligns with your business's financial health and growth trajectory.

Practical Steps for Financial Adaptation

Review and Revise Regularly:

- **Scheduled Reviews:** Establish a routine, such as quarterly or bi-annual reviews, to assess your financial plan. Use these reviews to adjust your budget, savings targets, and investment strategies based on your current financial situation and future outlook.

Leverage Financial Advising:

Professional Guidance: Consider working with a financial advisor who can provide personalized advice tailored to your unique circumstances. An advisor can offer valuable insights for adjusting your financial plan in response to life changes, economic shifts, and business growth.

Embrace Technological Tools:

Digital Resources: Utilize financial planning software and apps that offer predictive analytics, budget tracking, and scenario planning. These tools can help you visualize different financial outcomes based on varying conditions and make informed adjustments to your plan.

Cultivate Financial Resilience:

Build Flexibility: Incorporate flexibility into your financial plan by identifying areas where adjustments can be made quickly if needed. This might involve having a portion of your investment portfolio in more liquid assets or setting aside a contingency fund for your business.

Conclusion

Adapting your financial plan in response to life changes, economic shifts, and business growth is an ongoing process that requires vigilance, flexibility, and strategic thinking. By anticipating potential changes, staying informed about the economic landscape, leveraging professional advice, and utilizing technology, you can ensure that your financial plan remains robust and responsive to the ever-changing tapestry of life. Embrace these strategies as fundamental practices in your journey toward financial success, viewing each adaptation as a step closer to achieving your evolving financial vision.

Building flexibility into financial planning to accommodate unforeseen circumstances.

Building flexibility into financial planning is a crucial strategy for navigating the unpredictable nature of life and the economy. This approach ensures that your financial plan can withstand and adapt to unforeseen circumstances, whether they arise from personal life changes, economic downturns, or unexpected opportunities. Here, we delve into practical measures for embedding flexibility into your financial strategy, enabling you to maintain progress toward your goals even when the unexpected occurs.

Establishing a Flexible Financial Foundation

Emergency Funds: A Must-Have Safety Net

Prioritize Savings: An emergency fund is your first line of defense against unforeseen financial shocks. Aim to save at least three to six months' worth of living expenses. This fund provides the financial breathing room needed to navigate sudden changes without derailing your long-term plans.

Adaptable Investment Strategies

- **Dynamic Asset Allocation:** Adopt an investment strategy that allows for adjustments based on market conditions and your personal situation. Consider a mix of assets that can be easily realigned in response to changing economic landscapes, ensuring your portfolio remains balanced and aligned with your risk tolerance.

Fluid Budgeting Practices

Adjustable Budget Categories

- **Flexibility Within Categories:** Design your budget with flexibility in mind. Allocate funds to different categories in a way that allows for adjustments. For example, if unexpected expenses arise in one category, you can temporarily reduce spending in another to compensate.

Contingency Planning

- **Plan for the Unknown:** Incorporate contingency plans into your financial strategy. Identify potential financial risks and develop actionable plans to address them should they materialize. This could involve setting aside additional funds for specific risks or having alternative income sources.

Leveraging Technology for Adaptability

Financial Planning Software and Apps

- **Real-Time Adjustments:** Utilize financial planning apps that allow for easy adjustments to your budget and savings goals. Many modern apps provide scenario analysis tools, enabling you to test how different financial decisions could impact your overall plan.

Insurance as a Flexibility Tool

Comprehensive Coverage

- **Protect Your Assets and Income:** Ensure you have adequate insurance coverage for major life assets and your income. This includes health insurance, life insurance, disability insurance, and property insurance. Proper coverage can mitigate the financial impact of unexpected events, preserving your financial plan's integrity.

Continuous Learning and Adjustment

Embrace a Growth Mindset

Lifelong Financial Education: Commit to continuous learning about financial planning and management. Staying informed about financial strategies, products, and economic conditions empowers you to make timely adjustments to your plan.

Regular Financial Check-Ins

Scheduled Reviews: Conduct regular financial reviews to assess your progress and adapt your plan as needed. These check-ins provide opportunities to realign your financial strategies with your current circumstances and future aspirations.

Conclusion

Incorporating flexibility into your financial planning is not just a strategy; it's a mindset that acknowledges the fluidity of life and the economy. By preparing for unforeseen circumstances through emergency funds, adaptable investment strategies, flexible budgeting, comprehensive insurance, and the strategic use of technology, you can create a financial plan that endures and evolves. This approach ensures that you are not just reacting to changes but proactively managing your financial journey, ready to adjust and capitalize on opportunities as they arise. Embrace flexibility as a core principle of your financial planning, and you'll navigate life's uncertainties with confidence and resilience.

As we navigate the intricacies of building flexibility into our financial planning to accommodate the unforeseeable twists and turns of life, we are reminded that the foundation of enduring financial resilience and adaptability lies not just in the strategies we employ, but equally in the mindset we cultivate. This realization seamlessly bridges us to our next crucial exploration in Section 7: Cultivating a Mindset for Financial Success. Here, we delve deeper into the psychological and emotional underpinnings that empower us to thrive in our financial journey, transcending mere tactical adjustments to embody a holistic approach to achieving and sustaining financial well-being.

This section invites us to examine the core attitudes, beliefs, and perspectives that constitute a mindset geared toward financial success. It's about embracing a proactive stance towards our financial health, where adaptability, continuous learning, and resilience become ingrained in our approach to financial planning and decision-making.

In Section 7, we will explore:

The Psychology of Financial Decision-Making: Understanding the cognitive biases and emotional factors that influence our financial choices and how to navigate them with awareness and intention.

Resilience and Adaptability: Strategies for developing emotional resilience and adaptability in the face of financial challenges, ensuring that setbacks are viewed as opportunities for growth and learning rather than insurmountable obstacles.

Growth and Abundance Mindset: Shifting from a scarcity mindset, which focuses on limitations and fears, to a growth and abundance mindset, which opens up possibilities, fosters optimism, and encourages taking calculated risks for financial growth.

The Power of Goals and Visualization: Harnessing the power of setting clear, compelling financial goals, and using visualization techniques to maintain focus, motivation, and alignment with your financial vision.

Building Financial Confidence: Cultivating confidence in your financial decision-making by accumulating knowledge, gaining experience, and celebrating achievements along the way.

As we prepare to embark on this transformative exploration in Section 7, it's essential to recognize that the journey to financial success is as much about shaping our external strategies as it is about nurturing our internal world. The strategies we've discussed for adapting financial plans are vital, but their effectiveness is magnified when applied with a mindset attuned to success, resilience, and growth.

Let us step forward into Cultivating a Mindset for Financial Success with the understanding that our financial destinies are not just shaped by the plans we make but by the mindset with which we approach them. Armed with a robust financial strategy and a mindset geared towards success, we are well-equipped to navigate the complexities of our financial journey, transforming challenges into stepping stones towards our ultimate vision of financial well-being.

Section 7: Cultivating a Mindset for Financial Success

In the journey toward financial success, the strategies we implement and the numbers we crunch are just one part of the equation. Equally crucial is the mindset with which we approach our financial endeavors. Cultivating a mindset geared towards success involves more than just wishful thinking; it requires deliberate psychological strategies to maintain focus, foster resilience, and embrace adaptability. In this section, we delve into the transformative power of a positive mindset, the unyielding strength of resilience, and the dynamic flexibility of adaptability in achieving financial goals.

Embracing a Positive Mindset

Focusing on Opportunities, Not Obstacles:

Optimism in Action: A positive mindset starts with focusing on opportunities rather than dwelling on obstacles. This approach doesn't ignore challenges but chooses to view them as stepping stones towards greater achievements.

Actionable Advice: Start each day by jotting down three financial aspirations or positive affirmations related to your financial goals. This daily practice primes your mind to recognize opportunities and approach financial decisions with optimism.

Building Resilience

Overcoming Setbacks with Strength:

The Power of Perseverance: Financial journeys are marred with setbacks and challenges. Resilience is about bouncing back stronger, learning from these experiences, and refusing to let them define your financial future.

Personal Anecdote: Consider the story of Emma, who faced a significant financial loss in her investment portfolio. Instead of succumbing to despair, she sought to educate herself further on investment strategies, gradually rebuilding her portfolio with more diversification and risk awareness.

Cultivating Adaptability

Navigating Change with Agility:

Flexibility as a Virtue: In a world where economic conditions and personal circumstances are constantly changing, adaptability is key. Being able to adjust your financial plans in response to life's shifts ensures you remain on course towards your goals.

Engaging Narrative: Tom's career took an unexpected turn, forcing him to rethink his financial strategy. By adopting a flexible approach, he shifted his investment focus and revised his budget, ultimately finding a more fulfilling career path and maintaining his financial stability.

Integrating Psychological Strategies into Financial Planning

Creating a Mindful Financial Routine:

Mindfulness and Financial Decisions: Integrating mindfulness into your financial routine can enhance decision-making clarity and reduce impulsive behaviors. Before making significant financial decisions, take a moment to reflect on how this aligns with your long-term goals and values.

Seeking Growth Through Learning:

- **Lifelong Financial Education:** Cultivating a mindset for financial success also means committing to continuous learning. The financial world is ever-evolving, and staying informed helps you navigate it with confidence.

Leveraging Community and Support:

- **Strength in Numbers:** Surround yourself with a community that supports your financial aspirations. Whether it's online forums, financial literacy groups, or a circle of like-minded friends, sharing experiences and advice can bolster your journey.

Conclusion

Cultivating a mindset for financial success is a dynamic process that involves more than just positive thinking. It requires actionable strategies that foster optimism, resilience, and adaptability. By integrating these psychological strategies into your financial planning, you transform not only your approach to managing money but also your overall journey towards financial well-being. Remember, the path to financial success is as much about shaping your mindset as it is about implementing effective financial strategies. Let this holistic approach guide you towards achieving your financial goals with a balanced, informed, and positive outlook.

The role of community and support networks in achieving financial success.

The journey toward financial success, while deeply personal, is significantly enriched and often accelerated by the presence of a supportive community and robust support networks. The role of community in achieving financial success cannot be overstated; it provides a unique blend of motivation, insight, shared experiences, and accountability that can transform the financial planning process from a solitary endeavor into a collaborative journey. In this exploration, we delve into how community and support networks contribute to financial success, offering practical advice on leveraging these resources to enhance your financial journey.

The Power of Community in Financial Planning

Sharing Knowledge and Experiences:

- **Collective Wisdom:** Communities, whether formed around personal finance blogs, forums, or local finance clubs, serve as reservoirs of collective wisdom. Members share their successes and setbacks, offering invaluable lessons and strategies that can inform your financial decisions.

- **Actionable Advice:** Actively participate in finance-related forums or social media groups. Ask questions, share your experiences, and take advantage of the diverse perspectives and advice offered by the community.

Accountability and Encouragement:

Staying on Track: A support network provides not just advice but also accountability. Sharing your goals with a trusted group creates a sense of commitment and can motivate you to stay on track, even when challenges arise.

Engaging Narrative: Maya found that joining a monthly investment club meeting motivated her to stick to her savings goals. The encouragement and accountability provided by the group played a crucial role in her achieving her financial objectives.

Building and Leveraging Support Networks

Seeking Mentors and Advisors:

Guidance from Those Who've Been There: Mentors who have navigated their own financial journeys successfully can offer personalized advice and guidance. Their experience can help you avoid common pitfalls and make more informed decisions.

Personal Anecdote: Alex credits much of his investment success to the mentorship he received from a seasoned investor he met through a mutual connection. This relationship provided him with insights and confidence that were instrumental in shaping his investment strategy.

Utilizing Professional Networks:

Access to Expertise: Professional networks, often formed through industry associations or professional events, can connect you with experts in financial planning, investment, and wealth management. These connections can be invaluable in providing specialized advice and opening doors to new opportunities.

Fostering Peer Support:

Shared Journeys: Building relationships with peers who are at similar stages in their financial journeys allows for the sharing of challenges and strategies in a relatable context. These peer networks can become a source of inspiration, motivation, and mutual support.

Interactive Element: Consider starting a finance-focused book club or a monthly budgeting workshop with friends or colleagues. These gatherings can be an enjoyable way to learn and discuss financial concepts, keeping each other motivated towards personal financial goals.

The Impact of Community on Financial Resilience

Enhancing Financial Resilience:

The support and knowledge gained from community and networks not only aid in achieving financial success but also in building financial resilience. During times of economic uncertainty or personal financial strain, the collective wisdom and encouragement of a community can provide both practical solutions and emotional support.

Conclusion

The role of community and support networks in achieving financial success is profound. By engaging with communities, seeking out mentors, leveraging professional networks, and fostering peer support, you can enrich your financial journey with collective wisdom, accountability, and encouragement. Remember, the path to financial success is often paved with the support and insights of those who walk alongside us. Embrace the power of community and support networks as integral components of your strategy for achieving financial well-being.

Continuous learning and growth as fundamental principles of financial success.

Embarking on the path to financial success is akin to setting sail on a vast and ever-changing ocean. The waters of financial management and investment are deep and wide, with currents that shift with the winds of economic change, technological advancement, and personal evolution. At the heart of navigating these waters successfully are the fundamental principles of continuous learning and growth. These principles are not just accessories to the journey; they are the very sails and rudder that guide us toward our financial destinations.

The Essence of Continuous Learning

Embracing the Journey of Financial Education: Continuous learning in finance means acknowledging that there is always something new on the horizon—new strategies to explore, new laws to understand, and new technologies to adopt. This journey is lifelong and dynamic, reflecting the ever-evolving nature of the financial landscape.

- **Actionable Advice:** Dedicate time each week to financial education. Whether it's reading articles, attending webinars, or participating in workshops, each learning opportunity broadens your horizon and deepens your understanding.

Growth Through Experience

Learning from Successes and Setbacks: Growth in financial success is as much about learning from setbacks as it is about building on successes. Each investment that doesn't pan out as hoped, and every financial goal met, offers invaluable lessons that shape smarter, more resilient financial strategies.

- **Personal Anecdote:** Reflect on the journey of Clara, who ventured into the world of stock market investing with enthusiasm. Her initial losses were disheartening, but instead of retreating, she used these experiences to deepen her understanding of market trends and risk management. Today, Clara's portfolio reflects not just financial growth but the profound personal growth that came from navigating those early challenges.

The Role of Adaptability

Staying Agile in a Changing World: Adaptability in financial planning means being ready to adjust your sails as the winds change. It's about having the flexibility to revise your financial plan in response to life changes, market shifts, and new goals. This agility is crucial for long-term financial success and security.

Engaging Narrative: Consider the story of Marco, whose career took an unexpected turn. By adapting his financial plan to his new circumstances, including a shift towards more aggressive savings and a foray into freelance work, Marco turned a potential financial setback into a launching pad for entrepreneurial success.

Cultivating a Supportive Community

Learning and Growing Together: The journey towards financial success is enriched by the company we keep. A community of like-minded individuals offers a space for sharing knowledge, experiences, and encouragement. This collective journey fosters a deeper understanding and a broader perspective on financial management.

Interactive Element: Join a financial literacy group or start a small investment club with friends or colleagues. These groups provide a platform for discussion, learning, and mutual support, making the journey towards financial success a shared adventure.

Conclusion

Continuous learning and growth are the compass and map that guide us through the complex terrain of personal finance and investment. They remind us that financial success is not a destination but a journey—one marked by constant exploration, adaptation, and evolution. By embracing these principles, we not only enhance our financial well-being but also embark on a path of lifelong learning and personal development. Let us move forward with the understanding that every step taken in the pursuit of knowledge and growth brings us closer to our financial aspirations and beyond.

Conclusion

As we draw this exploration to a close, it's essential to reflect on the journey we've embarked upon together—a journey towards setting a strategic financial vision and meticulously crafting a path to success. Through the chapters, we've traversed the landscapes of financial analysis and assessment, strategic planning, budgeting, investment strategies, and the indispensable role of continuous learning and adaptability. Each segment has contributed to a comprehensive framework designed to empower you with the knowledge, strategies, and mindset necessary for financial success.

Key Takeaways

Strategic Financial Vision: Establishing a clear and strategic financial vision is the foundation upon which all successful financial plans are built. It involves understanding your current financial landscape, identifying your long-term goals, and crafting a strategic plan that aligns with your aspirations.

Adapting to Change: Flexibility and adaptability are crucial in navigating the ever-evolving financial and economic landscapes. The ability to adjust your financial plans in response to personal life changes, economic shifts, and new opportunities is key to maintaining resilience and progressing towards your goals.

The Power of Community and Continuous Learning: Engaging with a community of like-minded individuals and committing to continuous education are fundamental to achieving and sustaining financial success. They provide a support network, foster accountability, and ensure you remain informed and adaptable.

Encouragement to Take the First Steps

Taking the first step towards defining and pursuing your personal and business financial goals can be daunting, yet it is the most critical action you will take on your journey to financial empowerment. Begin by articulating your financial vision, however broad or specific it may be. Then, set actionable, measurable goals that serve as milestones on the path to realizing this vision. Remember, the journey of a thousand miles begins with a single step. Let that step be taken today, with confidence and a commitment to your financial well-being.

Final Thoughts on the Journey of Financial Empowerment

The pursuit of financial independence is more than just a series of financial transactions and investment decisions; it's a journey of empowerment, growth, and self-discovery. It requires discipline, resilience, and a willingness to learn and adapt. However, the rewards of this journey extend far beyond monetary gains. Financial independence brings with it freedom—the freedom to make choices that align with your values, the freedom to pursue your passions, and the freedom to create a legacy that lasts.

As you embark on or continue your journey towards financial empowerment, remember that the path is not always linear. There will be successes and setbacks, times of clarity and periods of uncertainty. Yet, with each step forward, you gain more than just financial wealth; you build a wealth of knowledge, experience, and confidence that will guide you through all facets of life.

In closing, let this exploration serve as a beacon, illuminating the path to financial success. Embrace the journey with an open heart and mind, ready to seize the opportunities that lie ahead. Financial empowerment is within your reach, and the time to start is now. Let your journey be guided by strategic planning, informed by continuous learning, and enriched by the community and connections you build along the way. Here's to your success, in finance and beyond.

Exercises and Action Plans
Practical exercises for setting personal and business financial goals.
Embarking on the journey of financial empowerment involves not just understanding the theoretical aspects of personal and business finance but also engaging in practical exercises that bring these concepts to life. These exercises are designed to help you set clear, achievable financial goals, laying the groundwork for a strategic plan that aligns with your personal aspirations and business objectives. Let's dive into some practical exercises to get you started on setting your financial goals.

Exercise 1: Vision Board for Financial Goals

Objective: Create a visual representation of your financial goals to serve as a constant reminder and source of motivation.

Materials Needed:

- Poster board or digital collage app
- Magazines, printouts, or digital images
- Markers, pens, or digital text tool

Steps:

- **Reflect:** Spend some time thinking about what financial success looks like for you personally and, if applicable, for your business. Consider short-term goals (1 year), medium-term goals (1-5 years), and long-term goals (5+ years).
- **Visualize:** Find images and words that represent your financial goals. This could include pictures of a dream home for personal goals or a successful storefront for business aspirations.
- **Create:** Arrange and attach your images and words on the poster board or digital collage, grouping them into short-term, medium-term, and long-term goals.
- **Display:** Place your vision board somewhere you will see it daily to keep your financial goals top of mind.

Exercise 2: Goal-Setting Worksheet

Objective: Clearly define your financial goals with specific details and actionable steps.

Materials Needed:

- Worksheet template (create your own or find a template online)
- Pen and paper or digital document

Steps:

- **List Your Goals:** Write down your financial goals, separating them into personal and business categories if necessary.
- **Make Them SMART:** For each goal, apply the SMART criteria—Specific, Measurable, Achievable, Relevant, Time-bound. This might involve setting a specific savings target, defining how you'll measure progress, ensuring the goal is realistic, aligning it with your broader financial vision, and setting a deadline.
- **Action Steps:** Break down each goal into smaller, actionable steps. For example, if your goal is to save for a down payment, one step could be to set up an automatic transfer to a savings account each payday.
- **Review Regularly:** Set a schedule for reviewing your goals and progress. Adjust your action steps as needed to stay on track.

Exercise 3: Financial Roadmap Creation

Objective: Develop a detailed plan that maps out how you will achieve your financial goals over time.

Materials Needed:

- Large sheet of paper or digital planning tool
- Markers or digital text tool

Steps:

- **Timeline:** Draw a timeline on your paper or digital tool, marking out the next 1, 5, and 10 years.
- **Plot Goals:** Place your short-term, medium-term, and long-term goals along the timeline at their expected completion points.
- **Identify Milestones:** For each goal, identify key milestones that will indicate progress. Write these along the timeline.
- **Resources and Actions:** Next to each goal, note the resources (e.g., financial tools, education) you'll need and the primary actions you'll take to achieve the goal.

Exercise 4: Budget Breakdown for Goals

Objective: Create a budget that supports achieving your financial goals by allocating resources effectively.

Materials Needed:

    Budget template (digital or paper)
    Recent financial statements

Steps:

    Current Expenses: List your current monthly income and expenses. Identify any areas where you can reduce spending.

    Allocation: Decide how much of your monthly budget can be allocated towards your financial goals. This might involve setting aside a certain percentage of your income for savings, investment, or debt repayment.

    Adjustments: Look for opportunities to adjust your budget to better support your goals, such as cutting unnecessary expenses or finding additional income sources.

    Monitor: Commit to monthly budget reviews to ensure your spending aligns with your goals and adjust as needed.

These practical exercises are designed to transform the abstract concept of financial goal-setting into tangible, actionable plans. By dedicating time to these exercises, you're taking concrete steps towards defining and achieving both your personal and business financial goals, laying a solid foundation for financial success.

Templates for creating actionable financial plans.

Creating an actionable financial plan requires a structured approach to define your goals, assess your current financial situation, and map out the steps you need to take to achieve your objectives. Below are templates designed to guide you through this process, making it easier to visualize and track your progress toward financial success. These templates can be adapted for personal use, business planning, or a combination of both.

Template 1: Financial Goals Worksheet

Objective: Define and prioritize your financial goals.

Time Frame	Goal	Amount Needed	Priority	Action Steps	Deadline
Short-term	Example: Build an	$5,000	High	Set up automatic savings of	12

Time Frame	Goal	Amount Needed	Priority	Action Steps	Deadline
(within 1 year)	emergency fund			$416/month	months
Medium-term (1-5 years)	Example: Down payment for a house	$20,000	Medium	Research home prices, save $333/month, increase income	5 years
Long-term (5+ years)	Example: Retirement savings	$500,000	High	Max out IRA contributions, invest in a diversified portfolio	30 years

Instructions: Fill in each column, detailing your financial goals across different time frames, how much money you'll need to achieve each goal, their priority level, the specific action steps you'll take, and the deadline for achieving each goal.

Template 2: Monthly Budget Planner

Objective: Track your income and expenses to manage your cash flow effectively.

Category	Estimated Amount	Actual Amount	Difference
Income			
Salary/Wages	$	$	$
Additional Income	$	$	$
Total Income	$	$	$
Expenses			
Housing (rent/mortgage)	$	$	$
Utilities	$	$	$
Groceries	$	$	$
Transportation	$	$	$
Savings/Investments	$	$	$
Entertainment	$	$	$
Total Expenses	$	$	$
End of Month Balance	$	$	$

Instructions: Use this template to plan your monthly budget. Compare your estimated amounts with the actual amounts spent or earned to identify areas for improvement.

Template 3: Debt Repayment Plan

Objective: Organize your debts and create a strategy for paying them off.

Creditor	Total Amount Owed	Interest Rate	Monthly Payment	Payoff Goal Date
Credit Card 1	$2,000	19%	$60	Dec 2023
Student Loan	$10,000	5%	$150	Jun 2028
Auto Loan	$5,000	3%	$150	May 2025

Instructions: List all your debts, including the total amount owed, the interest rate for each, your current monthly payment, and your goal date for paying off each debt. Adjust payments as necessary to focus on high-interest debts first (avalanche method) or smallest debts for quick wins (snowball method).

Template 4: Investment Tracking Sheet

Objective: Monitor your investments and their performance.

Investment	Type	Purchase Date	Amount Invested	Current Value	Return on Investment (ROI)
XYZ Mutual Fund	Mutual Fund	Jan 2020	$5,000	$5,500	10%
ABC Corp Stock	Stocks	Mar 2021	$2,000	$2,200	10%

Instructions: Keep track of your investments, including the type of investment, when you purchased it, how much you invested, its current value, and the return on investment. This template can help you assess the performance of your portfolio and make informed decisions.

These templates are starting points for creating actionable financial plans. Customize them according to your specific financial situation and goals. Regular review and updates to these documents will help you stay on track and adjust your strategies as needed.

Reflection prompts to personalize the strategies discussed in the chapter.

Reflecting on the strategies discussed throughout the chapter is a crucial step in personalizing your financial plan and ensuring it aligns with your unique circumstances, goals, and values. The following reflection prompts are designed to facilitate deeper thought, helping you internalize the concepts covered and tailor the strategies to your personal and business financial journey.

Reflection Prompt 1: Defining Your Financial Vision

What does financial success look like to me personally, and if applicable, for my business?

- How do my current financial actions align with this vision, and where do I see discrepancies?
- What are the most significant changes I need to make to align my financial habits with my vision for success?

Reflection Prompt 2: Adapting to Change

- Reflect on a past financial challenge or unexpected change. How did I respond, and what did I learn from that experience?
- Considering potential future changes (e.g., career changes, economic fluctuations), how can I prepare my finances to be more resilient?
- What strategies can I implement to ensure my financial plan remains flexible and adaptable to changes in my personal life or business?

Reflection Prompt 3: Continuous Learning and Growth

- What areas of personal finance or business finance do I feel least confident about, and what resources can help me improve my understanding?
- How can I incorporate continuous learning into my routine to stay informed about financial strategies, market trends, and economic changes?
- Reflect on a financial decision that didn't turn out as expected. What did I learn, and how can I use this knowledge to inform future decisions?

Reflection Prompt 4: Leveraging Community and Support Networks

- What role have community and support networks played in my financial journey so far, and how can I engage more effectively with these resources?
- Are there specific financial goals or challenges where seeking mentorship or joining a community could provide additional insight and support?
- How can I contribute to my financial community or support network to help others and strengthen my understanding and accountability?

Reflection Prompt 5: Cultivating a Mindset for Financial Success

- What mental or emotional barriers have hindered my financial progress, and how can I overcome them?
- In what ways can I cultivate a more positive, growth-oriented mindset towards my finances?
- How does my current mindset influence my financial decisions, and what shifts are necessary to foster a mindset that supports my financial vision and goals?

These reflection prompts are designed to be revisited periodically as your financial situation and goals evolve. Writing down your responses can be particularly effective, providing a tangible record of your thoughts and plans that you can refer back to and adjust over time. Engaging with these prompts can deepen your understanding of the financial strategies discussed, ensuring that your financial plan is not only tailored to your unique situation but also imbued with personal insight and intention.

Chapter 3: Mastering Financial Flow: The Art of Budgeting and Cash Management

In the realm of personal and business finances, the mastery of budgeting and cash management stands as a cornerstone of success. This chapter is not merely a discourse on the mechanics of budgeting or a bland treatise on cash flow analysis. Instead, it's a journey into the very heart of how we can harness our financial resources to build a future that resonates with our deepest aspirations.

As someone who has navigated the treacherous waters of financial uncertainty and emerged with insights, I can affirm that mastering these skills is not just about keeping your bank account in the black. It's about crafting a life and a business that are both sustainable and fulfilling.

Let me share a personal anecdote. Early in my career, I grappled with the unpredictable ebbs and flows of income and expenses. It was a period marked by sleepless nights and constant anxiety about the future. The turning point came when I realized that budgeting and cash management were not just about numbers; they were about setting priorities, making conscious decisions, and ultimately, about taking control of my life. This epiphany was transformative.

In this chapter, we will delve into the practicalities of budgeting and managing cash flow, but we will do so through a lens that is both empowering and empathetic. We'll explore how to create budgets that are not just feasible, but that also align with your personal values and business goals. You'll learn not just how to manage your expenses, but how to make your money work for you in the most efficient way possible.

We'll also address the unique challenges and opportunities that women face in the financial arena. It's a perspective that's often overlooked, yet critically important. The stories of successful women in finance and entrepreneurship will not only provide inspiration but will also offer practical insights that you can apply to your own journey.

So, as we embark on this chapter, remember that this is more than just learning about numbers. It's about equipping yourself with the tools and knowledge to build a future of financial stability and independence. Let's turn the page and begin this empowering journey together.

Overview: The Importance of Budgeting and Cash Management

At the heart of financial stability and growth lies the art of budgeting and cash management. This is true for both individuals and businesses. In this section, we set the stage for understanding why these skills are not just necessary, but crucial for maintaining and enhancing financial health.

Budgeting, at its core, is about understanding and directing where your money goes. It involves planning your spending and savings based on your income and financial goals. For individuals, this could mean planning for major life events, securing a comfortable retirement, or simply ensuring that monthly expenses never outstrip income. For businesses, effective budgeting is key to sustaining operations, fueling growth, and maximizing profitability.

Cash management, on the other hand, involves the active handling of cash inflows and outflows. It is about ensuring that you have enough liquidity to meet your needs at any given time. For an individual, this could mean having enough money for everyday expenses and emergency funds. For a business, it means maintaining sufficient working capital to operate smoothly and having the ability to invest in opportunities as they arise.

The mastery of these disciplines offers numerous benefits. It leads to better financial decision-making, as you are more aware of your financial situation and can plan accordingly. It reduces financial stress, as you gain control over your finances. Moreover, it allows for the accumulation of wealth over time, whether through savings, investments, or the profitable growth of a business.

However, budgeting and cash management are not without their challenges. They require discipline, foresight, and a willingness to make sometimes difficult choices. But the rewards are significant. By mastering these skills, you unlock the potential for financial freedom and security, allowing you to pursue your personal and professional aspirations with confidence.

In the subsequent sections of this chapter, we will delve into the strategies, tools, and mindsets that can help you effectively manage your budget and cash flow. Whether you're an individual looking to improve your personal finances or a business owner seeking to optimize your company's financial health, this chapter aims to provide you with the knowledge and inspiration you need to succeed.

Objective: Equipping Readers with the Tools for Effective Financial Flow Management

The primary objective of this chapter is to empower you, the reader, with the knowledge and tools required for effective management of your financial flow. This encompasses a comprehensive understanding of budgeting and cash management, both crucial elements in achieving and maintaining financial health and independence.

To achieve this, the chapter will focus on several key areas:

Fundamentals of Budgeting: You will be introduced to the basic principles of budgeting. This includes understanding your income sources, categorizing expenses, and setting financial goals. We will explore various budgeting techniques and tools that cater to different financial situations and preferences.

Advanced Cash Management Strategies: Moving beyond the basics, we will delve into advanced strategies for managing cash flow. This will cover topics such as optimizing cash reserves, managing debt efficiently, and planning for both short-term liquidity and long-term investments.

Personalizing Your Financial Plan: Recognizing that financial situations are unique, the chapter will guide you in tailoring these principles to fit your personal or business financial context. This includes adapting budgeting strategies to your specific income and expense patterns and aligning cash management tactics with your financial goals.

Tools and Resources: Practical tools, apps, and resources will be discussed to help you implement these strategies effectively. This will include software recommendations, templates for budgeting, and resources for further learning.

Overcoming Challenges: We will address common challenges and pitfalls in budgeting and cash management, offering solutions and tips to overcome them. This includes maintaining discipline in spending, adjusting to changing financial circumstances, and dealing with unexpected expenses or income fluctuations.

Case Studies and Examples: To illustrate these concepts, the chapter will include real-life case studies and hypothetical scenarios. These will demonstrate how individuals and businesses have successfully navigated their financial journeys through effective budgeting and cash management.

By the end of this chapter, you will not only understand the importance of budgeting and cash management but also possess the practical know-how to implement these strategies in your own financial life. This knowledge will serve as a foundation for financial empowerment, enabling you to make informed decisions and take control of your financial destiny.

Segue into Section 1: Understanding Financial Flow

Having established the overarching objective of mastering budgeting and cash management, let us now transition to the first crucial step in this journey: Understanding Financial Flow.

Imagine your financial life as a dynamic river. The flow of this river, with its currents and tributaries, represents your financial transactions - income, expenses, savings, and investments. Just as a river's health is gauged by its flow's quality and consistency, the health of your financial life can be similarly assessed by the effectiveness of your financial flow.

In this section, we shall embark on a thorough exploration of what constitutes financial flow. This will not only entail a comprehensive understanding of your income streams and expenditure patterns but also an examination of the nuances that influence this flow – from fluctuating income to variable expenses.

We will dissect the anatomy of financial flow, segmenting it into its core components:

Income Analysis: This involves a detailed examination of your income sources. For individuals, this might mean salaries, dividends, or rental income. For businesses, it might encompass sales revenue, returns on investments, or other income streams. Understanding your income is the first step in mastering your financial flow.

Expense Categorization: Here, we delve into the nature of your expenses. From fixed obligations such as rent or loan payments to variable expenses like entertainment or travel. We will learn to categorize and prioritize these expenses, understanding their impact on your overall financial health.

The Interplay Between Income and Expenses: This is where we analyze how your income and expenses interact. We will explore how to balance these elements to avoid financial shortfalls and how to plan for surplus periods.

Identifying Financial Leakages: Often, unnoticed or uncontrolled expenses can disrupt your financial flow. We will learn to identify and plug these leakages to ensure a healthier financial state.

Adapting to Financial Variabilities: Life is unpredictable, and so is financial flow. We will discuss strategies to adapt to changes in your financial landscape, be it an unexpected expense or a sudden change in income.

By gaining a deep understanding of your financial flow, you lay the groundwork for effective budgeting and cash management. This section is designed not just to provide theoretical knowledge but to equip you with practical insights that you can apply to your own financial situation. As we proceed, remember that understanding your financial flow is akin to learning the language of your finances – a fundamental step towards achieving financial fluency and independence.

Section 1: Understanding Financial Flow

Concept of Financial Flow: Explaining the Dynamics of Income, Expenses, Savings, and Investments

Income: The Foundation of Your Financial Edifice

Let us begin by examining the bedrock of financial flow: income. For many, this is synonymous with a paycheck, but it can encompass a broader spectrum, including investments, side hustles, and passive income sources. Like a river fed by various streams, your total income may come from multiple sources.

I recall a time when I had to diversify my income streams to navigate through a challenging economic climate. This experience taught me the importance of not solely relying on a single source. It's not just about the quantity of your income, but its quality and stability.

Expenses: The Necessary Outflows

Expenses, the counterpart to income, are often viewed with a tinge of negativity. However, they are an essential part of the financial ecosystem. The key lies in understanding and managing them effectively. Think of expenses as the riverbanks that guide the flow of your financial river – necessary and defining.

I learned early in my career the impact of unchecked spending. It was a humbling experience that underscored the importance of budgeting and prioritizing expenses. This is where the art of distinguishing 'needs' from 'wants' becomes crucial.

Savings: The Reserve Pool

Savings represent the reservoir that you build over time. It's not just about setting aside a portion of your income; it's about creating a buffer for unforeseen circumstances and opportunities. As I navigated my financial journey, I realized that robust savings provided not just security, but also peace of mind.

Investments: The Growth Engine

Investments are where your money works for you. They can be intimidating, yet they are essential for long-term financial growth. I remember my first investment - a mix of apprehension and excitement. The key is to start small, understand your risk tolerance, and grow your portfolio over time.

The Interconnectedness of These Elements

The beauty of financial flow lies in the interconnectedness of these elements. Your income fuels your expenses and savings, and your savings enable investments, which in turn can increase your income. It's a cyclical process, each component feeding into and supporting the others.

To master your financial flow, you need to understand and manage each of these elements effectively. This chapter is designed to guide you through this process, offering practical advice, personal anecdotes, and exercises to help you build a strong, healthy financial flow. Remember, mastering your finances is not just about numbers; it's about making informed choices that align with your goals and values. Let's embark on this journey together, transforming our financial understanding into empowerment and success.

Cash Flow Analysis: Deciphering the Currents of Your Finances

The Essence of Cash Flow Analysis

Cash flow analysis is akin to a financial health checkup. It involves a meticulous examination of the money flowing in and out of your personal or business accounts. By understanding your cash flow, you become adept at navigating your financial journey, much like a skilled captain steering through the ebullient waves of the ocean.

Step-by-Step Guide to Analyzing Cash Flow

Gathering Financial Data: Start by collecting all relevant financial information. This includes bank statements, bills, pay stubs, and any records of other income sources. The goal is to have a comprehensive view of your financial landscape.

Categorizing Transactions: Divide your transactions into categories such as income, fixed expenses (like rent or mortgage), variable expenses (such as groceries and entertainment), savings, and investments. This classification provides clarity and helps identify patterns.

Identifying Income Patterns: Look for consistency in your income. Are there fluctuations, and if so, what causes them? Understanding your income patterns is crucial for effective budgeting and planning.

Assessing Expenses: Scrutinize your expenses. Which are necessary, and which can be trimmed? Are there any surprises or irregularities? Reflect on how your spending aligns with your financial goals.

Comparing Income and Expenses: This is the crux of cash flow analysis. Are you living within your means, or is your spending outpacing your income? This comparison will reveal much about your financial health.

Identifying Opportunities for Improvement: Look for ways to enhance your cash flow. Can you increase your income through side projects or investments? Are there expenses you can reduce without significantly impacting your quality of life?

Planning for the Future: Use your analysis to forecast future cash flows. This will help you plan for big expenses, investment opportunities, and potential financial challenges.

Personal Experience and Empathy in Cash Flow Analysis

I remember the first time I conducted a thorough cash flow analysis for myself. It was an eye-opening experience. I discovered expenses that were unnecessarily high and identified investment opportunities I was missing. This process helped me align my financial habits with my long-term aspirations.

The Importance of Regular Review

Cash flow analysis is not a one-time activity. Regular reviews – monthly or quarterly – are essential. They help you stay on track and adapt to changes in your financial situation. Think of it as a periodic course correction on your financial journey.

Empowering Readers Through Cash Flow Analysis

As you embark on your cash flow analysis, remember that knowledge is power. This process is not just about numbers; it's about gaining control over your financial destiny. With each analysis, you will grow more confident and capable in your financial decision-making, bringing you closer to your goals of financial freedom and security.

Transition to Effective Budgeting

Having navigated the intricate details of cash flow analysis, we now stand on the threshold of a pivotal aspect of financial management – budgeting. Just as understanding your cash flow is akin to reading a map of your financial landscape, effective budgeting is about charting a course towards your financial goals. It involves not only discipline and foresight but also a keen understanding of your own financial narrative.

Section 2: Principles of Effective Budgeting

In this section, we delve into the art and science of budgeting. Budgeting is not merely about constraining expenses or limiting pleasures; it is a strategic tool for empowering your financial journey. It's about making informed decisions that align your financial resources with your life's goals and aspirations.

The Philosophy Behind Budgeting

Much like a gardener carefully plans the layout of a garden, ensuring each plant has the space and resources to flourish, effective budgeting requires thoughtful allocation of your financial resources. It's a balance between the present needs and future aspirations, between the joy of spending and the security of saving.

Embracing Budgeting as a Lifestyle

Budgeting should not be viewed as a restrictive practice but rather as a lifestyle choice that enables freedom and independence. By taking control of your finances through budgeting, you are essentially choosing to live life on your own terms, free from the stresses of financial uncertainty.

In the upcoming segments, we will explore the foundational principles of budgeting, practical tips for creating and sticking to a budget, and how to make budgeting a seamless part of your daily life. This journey into budgeting is not just about numbers; it's a transformative process that empowers you to realize your dreams and secure your financial future.

Section 2: Principles of Effective Budgeting

Budgeting Basics: Types of Budgets and Their Purposes

In the realm of budgeting, one size does not fit all. Different types of budgets serve various purposes and cater to distinct financial situations and goals. Understanding these varieties is crucial in selecting a budgeting method that aligns with your personal and business financial objectives.

1. The Zero-Based Budget

The zero-based budget operates on a simple yet powerful principle: Income minus Outgoing equals Zero. Every dollar of your income is assigned a specific purpose, be it expenses, savings, or investments, leaving no money unaccounted for. This meticulous approach to budgeting is particularly effective for those who seek total control over their finances.

2. The Envelope System

A method as old as money itself, the envelope system involves dividing cash into envelopes designated for different spending categories. Once an envelope is empty, spending in that category ceases until the next budget cycle. This tangible approach to budgeting is exceptionally effective for visual learners and those who prefer a hands-on method to manage their finances.

3. The 50/30/20 Rule

Popularized for its simplicity, this budgeting technique suggests allocating 50% of your income to needs, 30% to wants, and 20% to savings or debt repayment. It's an excellent starting point for beginners and those seeking a balanced approach to budget management.

4. The Automated Budget

In the age of digital banking and online transactions, the automated budget takes advantage of technology to manage your finances. By setting up automatic transfers to savings, investments, and bill payments, this method ensures that key financial activities occur without the need for constant oversight.

5. The Flexible Budget

Ideal for those with fluctuating income or irregular expenses, the flexible budget adapts to changes in financial circumstances. It allows for adjustments in spending and saving allocations, providing a dynamic approach to financial planning that can accommodate the unpredictability of life.

6. The Project-Based Budget

Particularly relevant for entrepreneurs and businesses, a project-based budget focuses on the financial planning for specific projects or ventures. It involves allocating funds to various components of a project and is crucial for evaluating its financial feasibility and tracking its progress.

Understanding these budgeting methods empowers you to select a strategy that resonates with your financial temperament and goals. Remember, the best budget is the one that you can adhere to consistently and that supports your journey towards financial well-being.

Setting Realistic Budgets: A Guide to Achievable and Sustainable Financial Planning

The cornerstone of effective financial management lies in setting realistic budgets. A budget that is both achievable and sustainable serves as a roadmap, guiding you towards financial stability and growth. However, the challenge often lies in balancing ambition with practicality.

1. Assess Your Financial Situation

Begin by conducting a thorough analysis of your current financial state. This includes an examination of your income, expenses, debts, and savings. Understanding where you stand financially provides a solid foundation for setting realistic budgetary goals.

2. Identify Financial Priorities and Goals

Establish clear financial priorities. Are you aiming to pay off debt, save for a significant purchase, or invest in your business's growth? Setting specific, measurable, attainable, relevant, and time-bound (SMART) goals can guide your budgeting process, ensuring that your financial plan aligns with your objectives.

3. Create Customized Categories

While standard budget categories are a good starting point, customize your budget to reflect your unique financial situation. Differentiating between fixed expenses (like rent or mortgage payments) and variable expenses (such as dining out or entertainment) can provide greater clarity and control over your spending.

4. Be Realistic with Spending Limits

One of the most common pitfalls in budgeting is setting overly restrictive spending limits. While it's essential to control spending, setting unrealistic limits can lead to frustration and budget abandonment. Allocate sufficient funds for both necessities and occasional indulgences to maintain a balanced and realistic budget.

5. Plan for Unexpected Expenses

An often-overlooked aspect of budgeting is the allocation for unexpected expenses. Life is unpredictable, and having a buffer can prevent financial derailment in the face of unforeseen costs. This could involve setting aside a specific percentage of your income into an emergency fund.

6. Monitor and Adjust Your Budget Regularly

A budget is not set in stone. Regular monitoring and adjustment of your budget are necessary to accommodate changes in income, expenses, and financial goals. This ongoing process ensures that your budget remains relevant and effective in achieving your financial objectives.

7. Use Tools and Resources

Leverage budgeting tools and resources to streamline the process. From spreadsheets to budgeting apps, these tools can simplify tracking and managing your finances, making it easier to stick to your budget and achieve your financial goals.

In conclusion, setting a realistic budget requires a balanced approach that considers your financial situation, priorities, and lifestyle. By following these guidelines, you can create a budget that not only reflects your current reality but also paves the way for future financial success.

Budgeting Tools and Techniques: Navigating the Path to Financial Precision

Effective budgeting is an art that requires the right set of tools and techniques. In today's digital age, numerous options are available, each offering unique features to assist in managing your finances. This section provides an overview of various tools and techniques that can enhance your budgeting process, making it more efficient, accurate, and tailored to your financial needs.

1. Traditional Budgeting Techniques

Envelope System: A classic method where you allocate cash for different spending categories into separate envelopes. This technique helps in limiting spending to the amount available in each envelope, promoting discipline.

Zero-Based Budgeting: Every dollar of income is assigned a specific purpose, whether it's for expenses, savings, or investments, ensuring that your income minus your expenses equals zero.

50/30/20 Rule: This simple formula suggests allocating 50% of your income to necessities, 30% to wants, and 20% to savings or debt repayment.

2. Digital Budgeting Tools

Personal Finance Software: Applications like Quicken or Mint offer comprehensive budgeting solutions, tracking income, expenses, investments, and offering insights into spending patterns.

Budgeting Apps: Mobile apps such as YNAB (You Need A Budget) or EveryDollar provide user-friendly interfaces for on-the-go budget management, often syncing with your bank accounts for real-time financial updates.

Spreadsheets: Customizable and versatile, spreadsheets (like Google Sheets or Microsoft Excel) allow for personalized budget tracking and can be as simple or as complex as needed.

3. Online Banking and Financial Management

Many banks and financial institutions offer built-in budgeting tools within their online platforms. These tools can automatically categorize your spending and provide a visual representation of where your money is going.

4. The Hybrid Approach

Combining traditional and digital methods can offer the best of both worlds. For instance, using a budgeting app to track expenses while adhering to the 50/30/20 rule can create a robust, adaptable budgeting system.

5. The Importance of Regular Reviews

Regardless of the tools or techniques used, the key to successful budgeting lies in regular reviews and adjustments. As your financial situation evolves, so should your budget, ensuring it remains aligned with your financial goals and life changes.

In conclusion, the right budgeting tool or technique varies based on individual preferences and financial situations. Experiment with different methods to find what works best for you. Remember, the ultimate goal is not just to track where your money is going, but to empower you to control your financial future effectively.

As we transition from the nuances of effective budgeting, it becomes evident that managing expenses is the cornerstone of financial stability and growth. Budgeting, after all, is only one part of the equation. The other, equally crucial aspect, is expense management. In Section 3, we delve into Expense Management Strategies, a critical component for achieving the financial equilibrium necessary for both personal and business success.

In this section, we will explore how to transform your approach to expenses, shifting from mere tracking to strategic management. This transition is essential for any individual or business aiming to not only survive but thrive in today's economic landscape. Through a combination of insight, strategy, and practical application, we will unravel the intricacies of effective expense management, ensuring that your hard-earned money is allocated in a manner that furthers your financial objectives.

Remember, the key to financial mastery lies not only in how much you earn but in how wisely you manage what you earn. Let's embark on this journey of strategic expense management, setting the stage for a financially empowering future.

Section 3: Expense Management Strategies

In this vital segment of our journey into Expense Management Strategies, we delve into the process of Identifying and Categorizing Expenses. This step is foundational in understanding and managing your financial outflows, whether for personal or business purposes.

Understanding the Nature of Expenses: The first step involves grasping the different types of expenses you incur. Typically, expenses fall into two broad categories: fixed and variable. Fixed expenses, such as rent or mortgage payments, are consistent and predictable. On the other hand, variable expenses like dining out or utility bills fluctuate and are often within your control. Distinguishing between these types can help in planning and adjusting your budget effectively.

Categorizing for Clarity: Once you understand the nature of your expenses, categorizing them becomes essential. This involves grouping expenses into meaningful categories such as housing, utilities, groceries, entertainment, transportation, and healthcare. For businesses, this might include categories like operational costs, marketing, payroll, and research and development.

Categorization not only aids in tracking and analyzing expenses but also in identifying areas where cost-cutting measures can be most effective.

Analyzing Impact: After categorizing expenses, analyze their impact on your overall financial health. This involves assessing which categories constitute the largest portion of your outflows and determining whether these are aligned with your financial goals. For instance, if a significant portion of your budget goes towards dining out, you might consider cooking at home more often to save money.

Prioritizing and Adjusting: Post-analysis, prioritize your expenses. Essential expenses like housing and food take precedence, while discretionary expenses can be adjusted based on your financial goals. This step is crucial in aligning your spending with your financial objectives, whether that's saving for a house, investing in your business, or preparing for retirement.

By effectively identifying and categorizing expenses, you gain a clearer picture of where your money is going. This clarity is the first step in taking control of your financial flow, setting the foundation for more informed decision-making and strategic financial planning.

In the realm of Expense Management Strategies, an essential component is the implementation of Cost-Cutting Strategies. These strategies are designed to help you reduce unnecessary expenditures, thereby optimizing your financial resources for both personal and business contexts. Let's explore practical tips for achieving this:

Needs vs. Wants Analysis: Begin by differentiating between essential needs and discretionary wants. Needs are expenses that are necessary for your basic living or business operation, such as rent, groceries, or essential staff salaries. Wants, however, are non-essential and often include luxury items or services. By focusing your spending on needs and critically evaluating your wants, you can significantly cut down on unnecessary expenses.

Review and Negotiate Regular Bills: Examine your regular bills such as utilities, insurance, subscriptions, and memberships. Investigate if there are more cost-effective options or discounts available. Don't hesitate to negotiate with service providers for better rates, or consider switching providers if a better deal is available elsewhere.

Implement Energy Efficiency: For both homes and businesses, energy costs can be a substantial part of the budget. Implementing energy-efficient practices and appliances can lead to significant savings over time. Consider actions like optimizing heating and cooling systems, using LED lighting, and encouraging energy-conscious behaviors.

Bulk Purchases and Wholesale Discounts: For items that you use regularly, consider buying in bulk or taking advantage of wholesale discounts. This approach is particularly effective for office supplies, manufacturing materials, or household staples. However, ensure that bulk purchases are for items that you definitely need and will use, to avoid wastage.

Limit Discretionary Spending: Establish limits on discretionary spending such as dining out, entertainment, or luxury items. Setting a budget for such expenses and sticking to it can free up a considerable amount of financial resources.

Automate Savings: Implement a system where a certain percentage of income is automatically directed into a savings account. This 'pay yourself first' approach ensures that you're consistently building your savings or investment capital, reducing the temptation to spend.

Utilize Technology for Budget Management: There are numerous apps and software available that can help track spending and identify areas where cuts can be made. Utilize these tools to maintain a closer watch on your financial flow and adjust as necessary.

Outsource and Automate: In a business context, evaluate tasks that can be outsourced or automated for efficiency. This might involve using software for accounting, social media management, or customer service, which can be more cost-effective than hiring additional staff.

By implementing these cost-cutting strategies, you can significantly improve your financial health. It's about making conscious decisions regarding your spending, ensuring every dollar you spend aligns with your overall financial goals. Remember, small changes can lead to substantial savings over time, reinforcing the foundation of financial stability and growth.

Investing in Value is a fundamental aspect of Expense Management Strategies, focusing on the concept of spending strategically to add value in the long term. This approach is not merely about cutting costs, but about making expenditures that contribute significantly to personal or business growth. Let's delve into how you can apply this principle effectively:

Quality Over Quantity: Opt for quality purchases that may have a higher upfront cost but offer greater durability and efficiency in the long run. This is particularly relevant for business equipment, technology, and even personal items like appliances or vehicles. The initial investment may be higher, but the longevity and reliability of quality products often translate to cost savings over time.

Education and Training Investments: Investing in education and training, be it for yourself or your employees, can yield significant returns. Enhanced skills and knowledge lead to increased productivity, innovation, and potentially, greater revenue generation. This could involve attending workshops, enrolling in courses, or accessing online training resources.

Technological Upgrades: In today's rapidly evolving digital landscape, investing in the latest technology can streamline operations, increase efficiency, and ultimately save money. This might mean updating software systems, adopting cloud computing, or investing in automation tools. The goal is to spend money on technology that will make your operations more efficient and cost-effective in the long run.

Preventative Maintenance: Regular maintenance of equipment and infrastructure can prevent costly repairs and downtime in the future. This is true for both personal assets like your home or vehicle, and business assets like machinery or IT infrastructure. A small investment in regular maintenance can prevent large expenses due to failures or breakdowns.

Strategic Marketing and Advertising: Investing in marketing and advertising is essential for business growth. However, the key is to spend strategically. This means focusing on marketing channels that offer the highest return on investment and tailoring your message to reach your target audience effectively.

Health and Wellness: Investing in your health and the health of your employees is also a strategic expenditure. This can include ergonomic office furniture, wellness programs, or health insurance. Healthy individuals tend to be more productive and take fewer sick days, which is beneficial for both personal and business success.

Sustainable Practices: Implementing sustainable practices can be a valuable long-term investment. This includes adopting renewable energy sources, reducing waste, and using sustainable materials. While the initial cost may be higher, these practices often lead to cost savings and can enhance your brand's reputation.

Networking and Relationships: Spending time and resources on networking and building relationships can be immensely valuable. This includes attending industry events, joining professional associations, or even hosting events. The connections made through these avenues can lead to new opportunities, partnerships, and avenues for growth.

In conclusion, Investing in Value is about making informed decisions that align with your long-term goals. It's about recognizing that some expenses, while seemingly large at the outset, are investments that will pay dividends in the form of enhanced productivity, efficiency, and growth. The key is to discern between mere costs and value-adding investments, focusing your financial resources on the latter for sustained success.

As we transition from the prudent strategies of expense management and the insightful focus on investing in value, our narrative now steers towards a vital aspect of financial mastery: Optimizing Income. This section is dedicated to exploring the various avenues and strategies to enhance and diversify your income streams, both in personal finance and in the realm of business.

In the journey of financial empowerment, it's crucial to recognize that managing expenses and making strategic investments are just one side of the coin. The other, equally significant aspect, is generating and increasing income. Optimizing Income is not merely about working harder; it's about working smarter, leveraging opportunities, and employing innovative methods to enhance your financial inflow.

In the upcoming section, we'll delve into a variety of techniques and approaches designed to elevate your income potential. We'll explore how diversification of income sources can create a more stable financial foundation, discuss the role of passive income streams, and investigate how advancing in your career or growing your business can significantly impact your financial landscape. This section aims to empower you with the knowledge and tools to not just manage what you have, but to expand and grow your financial resources, paving the way for a more prosperous and secure financial future.

Section 4: Optimizing Income

Maximizing Revenue Streams: Techniques for Increasing Income in Personal Finance and Business

In this critical section, we delve into the art and science of maximizing revenue streams. It's a journey that goes beyond mere income generation; it's about strategically enhancing and diversifying your sources of income. Here, we'll explore the various techniques and approaches that can be employed both in personal finance and in the sphere of business to augment your financial inflow.

1. Diversification of Income Sources:

- **Personal Finance:** We'll discuss the importance of not relying solely on a primary job for income. Strategies like investing in stocks, bonds, real estate, or starting a side business will be explored. The goal is to create multiple streams of income that can cushion against economic downturns or unexpected job loss.
- **Business:** Diversification can mean expanding product lines, exploring new markets, or leveraging different sales channels. We'll analyze successful case studies where businesses thrived by diversifying their income sources.

2. Passive Income Strategies:

Personal Finance: Passive income is a key component of financial freedom. We will investigate options like dividend-yielding stocks, rental properties, or creating digital products that generate ongoing revenue without continuous active involvement.

Business: For businesses, passive income might involve creating a product or service that requires minimal ongoing maintenance but continues to generate revenue, such as software subscriptions or licensing agreements.

3. Career Advancement and Professional Development:

Personal Finance: Advancing in your career can significantly increase your income. We'll provide tips on seeking promotions, improving skills, and navigating career transitions to higher-paying roles.

Business: For entrepreneurs and business owners, professional development might involve leadership training, industry certifications, or networking strategies to foster business growth.

4. Entrepreneurial Ventures and Side Hustles:

Personal Finance: Side hustles are an excellent way to boost income. We'll examine how to identify opportunities that align with your skills and interests, and how to balance them with your primary job.

Business: Businesses can adopt an entrepreneurial mindset by exploring new ventures or partnerships that align with their core competencies but tap into new revenue streams.

5. Leverage Technology and Online Platforms:

Personal Finance: The digital era offers myriad ways to earn money online. From freelance work to e-commerce, we'll guide you through the most effective ways to capitalize on online platforms.

Business: Businesses can utilize online marketplaces, social media, and digital marketing to reach a wider audience and increase sales.

6. Negotiation Skills for Salary and Contracts:

Personal Finance: Negotiating a higher salary or better contract terms can have a profound impact on your income. We'll provide strategies and tips for effective negotiation.

Business: For businesses, negotiation skills are crucial in securing favorable deals with suppliers, clients, and partners.

Through this section, we aim to provide a comprehensive guide to help you harness and maximize your income potential. By implementing these strategies, you'll be well-equipped to bolster your financial position and journey toward greater financial independence and security.

Diversifying Income Sources: The Importance of Having Multiple Streams of Income for Stability

In the realm of personal finance and business, diversifying income sources is not just a strategy; it's a fundamental principle for achieving financial stability and independence. This section delves into the myriad reasons why having multiple streams of income is vital and how it can be a game-changer in your financial journey.

1. Reducing Dependency on a Single Income Source:

- **Personal Finance:** Reliance on a single paycheck can be risky. In uncertain economic climates, job loss can lead to immediate financial crisis. By cultivating multiple income streams, you distribute this risk, ensuring that the loss of one does not lead to financial ruin.
- **Business:** Similarly, for businesses, depending on a single product, service, or client can be precarious. Diversification here means resilience against market shifts or loss of a major client.

2. Enhancing Financial Security and Peace of Mind:

- Diversifying income sources provides a safety net. It's the financial equivalent of not putting all your eggs in one basket. This approach affords a greater sense of security and peace of mind, knowing you are not at the mercy of a single employer or market trend.

3. Opportunity for Increased Wealth Accumulation:

- Multiple income streams can significantly accelerate wealth-building. Each stream acts as a tributary, contributing to a more substantial financial river. Over time, these streams can compound, leading to more robust financial growth than would be possible through a single source.

4. Buffer Against Economic Fluctuations:

- Diverse income sources act as a buffer against economic downturns. If one stream suffers due to market conditions, others may remain stable or even thrive, helping to balance your overall financial health.

5. Potential for Passive Income:

- A crucial aspect of income diversification is the potential for passive income – earnings that require little to no effort to maintain. Investments in stocks, real estate, or creating digital products can provide ongoing income without the need for active daily work.

6. Flexibility and Freedom:

With multiple income streams, you gain more control over your time and choices. For individuals, this might mean the freedom to pursue passions or hobbies. For businesses, it could translate to more resources for innovation and expansion.

7. Learning and Growth:

Diversifying income sources often involves learning new skills or venturing into new areas. This process can be incredibly enriching, offering personal and professional growth opportunities.

In conclusion, diversifying income sources is essential for financial stability and growth. It's a strategy that demands effort, planning, and sometimes a willingness to step outside one's comfort zone. However, the payoff is a more resilient, secure, and potentially more prosperous financial future.

Passive vs. Active Income: Understanding the Differences and How to Balance Them

In the pursuit of financial stability and growth, understanding and balancing passive and active income streams is pivotal. This section aims to demystify these concepts, offering insights into their distinct characteristics and the strategies for effectively managing them.

1. Defining Passive Income:

Nature: Passive income is earned with little to no ongoing effort. It's not about 'getting rich quick'; rather, it's about investing time, effort, or resources upfront to reap benefits over time.

Examples: Rental income from real estate, earnings from investments in stocks or bonds, royalties from books or patents, and income from online businesses or digital products.

2. Defining Active Income:

Nature: Active income is earned by trading time and effort for money. It's the most common form of income, typically received from a job or a business where active participation is essential.

Examples: Salaries, wages, commissions, business income reliant on daily involvement, and professional fees.

3. Balancing the Two:

Starting with Active Income: Most people start with active income. It's straightforward and immediate but limited by the number of hours one can work.

- **Transition to Passive Income:** The goal for many is to build passive income streams that can eventually reduce reliance on active income. This transition involves saving and investing a portion of active income into avenues that can generate passive returns.

4. **The Role of Risk and Reward:**

- **Active Income:** Generally considered lower risk since it's based on predictable work. However, it's also limited in potential growth.
- **Passive Income:** Involves higher risk, particularly at the outset. The returns, however, can be significantly higher and more sustainable over the long term.

5. **Time Factor:**

- **Active Income:** Offers immediate rewards but can be time-consuming and often leaves little room for other pursuits.
- **Passive Income:** Requires patience as it takes time to build and may not yield immediate returns.

6. **The Path to Financial Independence:**

- Balancing active and passive income is a critical strategy on the path to financial independence. The ultimate goal for many is to reach a point where passive income sufficiently covers living expenses, freeing them from the need to actively work for money.

7. **Personal and Business Strategy:**

- **For Individuals:** The strategy might involve saving a portion of active income to invest in stocks, real estate, or start a side business.
- **For Businesses:** It could mean diversifying into products or services that generate ongoing revenue without constant effort.

In summary, understanding and balancing passive and active income streams is a nuanced and essential aspect of financial strategy. Active income provides a reliable source of earnings, while passive income offers the potential for long-term financial freedom and stability. The journey involves strategic planning, risk assessment, and a keen understanding of one's financial goals and risk tolerance.

Savings and Investment Strategies: Cultivating a Secure Financial Future

As we transition from the exploration of income sources, it is natural to progress into the realm of savings and investment strategies. This next section is not just about setting aside a portion of your income; it's about intelligently leveraging these savings to build wealth and secure your financial future.

1. The Philosophy of Saving:

Mindset Shift: Understand the fundamental shift from spending to saving. It's not merely about accumulating money, but about fostering a mindset that prioritizes future financial security over immediate gratification.

Emergency Fund: Emphasize the importance of building an emergency fund as a buffer against unforeseen financial shocks.

2. Principles of Investment:

Risk vs. Reward: Delve into the relationship between risk and potential returns. Educate on how to assess one's risk tolerance and align investment choices accordingly.

Diversification: The concept of not putting all eggs in one basket. Explore how diversification can mitigate risk and stabilize your investment portfolio.

3. Exploring Investment Avenues:

Stocks, Bonds, and Mutual Funds: Discuss various investment options, their potential returns, and risks.

Real Estate: Consider the merits and challenges of investing in property as a long-term strategy.

Retirement Accounts: Unpack the benefits of retirement accounts like 401(k)s and IRAs, and how they can be maximized for long-term gains.

4. The Art of Compound Interest:

Long-Term Perspective: Explain the power of compound interest and how time can turn small, regular investments into substantial wealth.

Starting Early: Stress the importance of beginning to save and invest as early as possible.

5. Strategies for Different Life Stages:

Young Professionals: Strategies for those starting their financial journey with limited resources.

Mid-Career Individuals: Tactics for those in their peak earning years, focusing on maximizing savings and investments.

Pre-Retirement: Guidance for individuals approaching retirement, emphasizing the shift from growth to preservation of wealth.

6. Aligning Investments with Goals:

- **Goal-Oriented Investing:** Tailoring your investment strategy to specific financial goals, whether it's buying a house, funding education, or preparing for retirement.

7. Continual Learning and Adaptation:

- Encourage readers to stay informed and adapt their strategies in response to changing personal circumstances and economic conditions.

In this section, we will not only provide the tools and knowledge for effective savings and investment but also inspire a transformation in how you view and manage your wealth. The aim is to equip you with the strategies that resonate with your personal financial goals, ensuring a secure and prosperous financial journey.

Section 5: Savings and Investment Strategies

Building an Emergency Fund: A Pillar of Financial Security

Understanding the importance and methods of establishing an emergency fund is a crucial aspect of financial planning. An emergency fund acts as a financial safety net, designed to cover unexpected expenses or financial emergencies. This section aims to guide you through the process of building and maintaining this essential component of personal finance.

1. The Importance of an Emergency Fund:

- **Unexpected Financial Shocks:** Emphasize the role of an emergency fund in protecting against sudden, unforeseen financial demands such as medical emergencies, job loss, or urgent home repairs.
- **Peace of Mind:** Discuss how having an emergency fund can provide mental peace and reduce stress, knowing you are prepared for financial surprises.

2. Assessing Your Emergency Fund Needs:

- **Personalized Approach:** Guide readers to assess their individual needs based on their lifestyle, family size, income stability, and existing liabilities.
- **Standard Recommendations:** While customization is key, offer a general rule of thumb, such as the necessity of having three to six months' worth of living expenses saved.

3. Starting Your Emergency Fund:

Initial Steps: Offer practical advice on how to start saving, such as setting up a dedicated savings account and beginning with small, manageable amounts.

Budget Adjustments: Provide strategies for adjusting the monthly budget to allocate funds towards the emergency savings without significantly impacting daily life.

4. Funding Strategies:

Incremental Savings: Encourage setting aside a fixed percentage or amount from each paycheck.

Windfalls and Bonuses: Suggest allocating unexpected financial gains like tax refunds, bonuses, or gifts to bolster the emergency fund.

5. Managing and Maintaining the Fund:

Accessibility: Discuss the importance of keeping the emergency fund in an easily accessible form, such as a savings account, while avoiding the temptation to use these funds for non-emergencies.

Regular Reviews and Adjustments: Advise on periodically reviewing the fund to ensure it aligns with changing financial situations and increasing it proportionally as expenses rise.

6. Balancing Between Emergency Fund and Other Financial Goals:

Prioritization: Help readers understand how to balance the need for an emergency fund with other financial goals like debt repayment, investments, and major purchases.

Integrating with Overall Financial Planning: Position the emergency fund as a fundamental part of a broader financial plan, not as an isolated element.

In this section, we aim to instill the understanding that an emergency fund is not just a financial buffer, but a cornerstone of a well-structured financial plan. By the end of this chapter, readers should feel equipped and motivated to establish and maintain an emergency fund, securing their financial foundation against the unpredictability of life.

Principles of Investing - Navigating the Investment Landscape for Beginners

Welcome to a crucial segment of your financial journey – understanding the principles of investing. For many, the world of investments seems labyrinthine and daunting. However, with the right knowledge and approach, it can become an empowering tool in your quest for financial growth and stability. Let's embark on this journey together, breaking down complex concepts into digestible and actionable insights.

1. Understanding Risk and Return:

- **The Risk-Return Tradeoff:** Higher returns are often accompanied by higher risks. This fundamental principle is pivotal in investment decision-making. Reflect on real-life scenarios where this tradeoff is evident and consider how it applies to your investment choices.
- **Assessing Your Risk Tolerance:** It's essential to understand your comfort level with risk. Your financial goals, current financial situation, and emotional response to fluctuations in your investments are key determinants. Take a moment to self-assess and determine your risk tolerance.

2. The Power of Compound Interest:

- **Long-Term Growth Potential:** The magic of compounding can significantly boost your investment returns over time. This principle demonstrates how reinvested earnings can generate additional earnings.
- **The Advantage of Starting Early:** The sooner you start investing, the more you can leverage the power of compound interest. Even small, regular investments can grow into substantial sums over a long period.

3. Diversification:

- **Spreading Your Risk:** Avoid concentrating your investments in a single asset or market. Diversification can help mitigate risk by spreading your investments across various asset classes and sectors.
- **Creating a Balanced Portfolio:** Align your investment portfolio with your individual goals and risk tolerance. This balance is key to a successful investment strategy.

4. Understanding Different Investment Vehicles:

- **Exploring Options:** Familiarize yourself with stocks, bonds, mutual funds, and other investment vehicles. Each comes with its own set of characteristics, risks, and potential rewards.
- **Newer Investment Avenues:** Stay informed about emerging options like ETFs, REITs, and digital assets, understanding their place in the modern investment landscape.

5. The Importance of Research:

- **Making Informed Decisions:** Adequate research is the backbone of sound investment decisions. Learn to evaluate opportunities and stay updated with market trends.
- **Utilizing Resources:** I'll provide a list of credible resources for your investment research, helping you make educated choices.

6. Investment Time Horizon:

Short-Term vs. Long-Term Goals: Your investment strategy should reflect your time horizon. Are you investing for short-term gains or long-term growth? This decision will influence your choice of investment vehicles.

The Virtues of Patience and Discipline: Embrace a long-term view of investing. Understand the risks of short-term speculations and the benefits of a steady, disciplined investment approach.

7. Avoiding Common Pitfalls:

Steering Clear of Emotional Decisions: Emotional responses to market fluctuations can lead to poor investment choices. Learn to recognize and control these impulses.

The Myth of Market Timing: Attempting to time the market is often futile. Focus instead on a consistent investment strategy.

8. Seeking Professional Advice:

Consulting Experts: Recognize when it's wise to seek guidance from financial advisors, especially in complex situations or when making significant investment decisions.

Choosing the Right Advisor: Learn how to select a financial advisor who aligns with your investment goals and personal values.

As we conclude this section, you should feel more equipped and confident to navigate the investment landscape. Remember, investing is not just about growing wealth; it's about making informed choices that align with your life goals and risk tolerance. Your investment journey is unique, and with these principles, you're well on your way to becoming a savvy investor.

Balancing Risk and Reward - A Strategic Approach to Investments and Savings

In the realm of personal finance, the equilibrium between risk and reward is a central concept that demands our attention. Understanding and managing this balance is pivotal in shaping a successful investment and savings strategy. Let's delve into how one can navigate this intricate balance, ensuring a path that aligns with individual financial goals and risk tolerance.

1. The Spectrum of Risk and Reward:

Understanding the Spectrum: Investments range from low-risk, low-reward options like savings accounts and government bonds to high-risk, high-reward options like stocks and cryptocurrencies. Recognize where different investment vehicles fall on this spectrum.

Risk-Reward Correlation: Higher risks are typically associated with higher potential rewards. Conversely, lower risks often result in lower potential rewards. This correlation is a fundamental principle in investing.

2. Personal Risk Tolerance:

- **Assessment of Risk Tolerance:** Each individual's capacity and willingness to tolerate risk varies. Consider factors such as age, financial goals, income stability, and emotional comfort with uncertainty.
- **Risk Tolerance Questionnaires:** Utilize available tools to help assess your risk tolerance. This self-awareness will guide your investment decisions.

3. Building a Diverse Portfolio:

- **Importance of Diversification:** Diversifying your investment portfolio across different asset classes can mitigate risk. It's akin to not putting all your eggs in one basket.
- **Balancing Act:** Aim for a mix of investments that reflects your risk tolerance while striving for your financial goals. A well-balanced portfolio might include a combination of stocks, bonds, and other assets.

4. The Role of Savings:

- **Savings as a Risk Buffer:** Savings act as a low-risk component in your financial plan, offering a buffer against market volatility and unforeseen circumstances.
- **Strategic Allocation to Savings:** Determine the proportion of your income that should go into savings versus investments. This decision is contingent on your financial goals, timeline, and risk tolerance.

5. The Time Factor:

- **Investment Horizon:** Your time horizon – the length of time you plan to hold an investment before taking your money out – significantly impacts your risk tolerance. Longer horizons typically allow for more risk-taking.
- **Adjusting Over Time:** As you approach major financial milestones or changes in life circumstances, reassess and adjust your risk levels accordingly.

6. Risk Management Strategies:

- **Regular Portfolio Review and Rebalancing:** Periodically review and adjust your portfolio to ensure it aligns with your risk tolerance and financial goals.
- **Using Stop-Loss Orders:** Consider employing techniques like stop-loss orders to manage and limit potential losses in volatile markets.

7. The Psychological Aspect of Investing:

- **Emotional Discipline:** Be mindful of the psychological challenges that come with investing. Avoid panic selling or impulsive buying based on market highs and lows.

Educational Empowerment: Continuously educate yourself about financial markets and investment strategies. Knowledge is a powerful tool in making rational, informed decisions.

8. Seeking Balanced Advice:

Professional Guidance: Don't hesitate to consult with financial advisors, especially when making complex or substantial investment decisions.

Independent Research: Complement professional advice with your own research and understanding. This dual approach can lead to more balanced and informed decisions.

In summary, balancing risk and reward in investments and savings is not just about numbers and statistics. It's about understanding yourself, your goals, your timeline, and how much uncertainty you can comfortably handle. With the right approach and mindset, you can navigate this balance, making informed decisions that pave the way toward financial resilience and growth.

As we transition from the nuanced landscape of savings and investments, where balancing risk and reward is key, we approach another crucial aspect of financial health: debt management. This next section shifts our focus from the accumulation and preservation of wealth to the strategic handling of debt.

Managing debt is an integral part of financial planning. It requires a comprehensive understanding and an astute approach to navigate the complex world of liabilities. In this section, we will explore various dimensions of debt, from understanding different types of debt to developing strategies for efficient debt management.

In our journey so far, we have equipped ourselves with knowledge and strategies to enhance our financial inflow through diverse income streams and prudent investment decisions. We have also delved into optimizing our outflow through effective budgeting and expense management. Now, it's time to understand how debt can impact our financial landscape.

Debt, often perceived as a financial burden, can also be a tool for growth if managed correctly. It's a double-edged sword that, when wielded with skill and understanding, can aid in achieving financial goals, such as owning a home or growing a business. However, mismanaged debt can lead to financial strain and inhibit our progress towards financial freedom.

In the upcoming section, we will break down the concept of debt, demystify common misconceptions, and provide actionable strategies to manage and reduce debt. We will look into various forms of debt - from credit cards and loans to mortgages and student debts - and understand their implications. Additionally, we will explore strategies to prioritize debts, negotiate better terms, and ultimately achieve a debt-free life.

The journey of financial management is incomplete without mastering the art of debt management. As we delve into this vital topic, remember that the goal is not just to manage debt but to master it, turning what seems like a financial obstacle into a stepping stone towards achieving your financial aspirations.

Section 6: Debt Management

Understanding Debt: Different Types of Debt and Their Impact on Financial Health

At the heart of debt management lies a thorough understanding of what debt entails. This initial part of our journey into debt management is dedicated to unraveling the complexities of various debt types and their respective impacts on financial health.

Types of Debt:

- **Secured Debt**: This type involves collateral, such as a house in a mortgage or a car in an auto loan. The collateral secures the lender's investment, typically leading to lower interest rates. However, the risk lies in the potential loss of the collateral if payments are not maintained.
- **Unsecured Debt**: Common forms include credit cards, student loans, and personal loans. These do not have physical collateral and thus often carry higher interest rates. The risk for the borrower is less immediate, but these debts can significantly affect credit scores and financial planning.
- **Revolving Debt**: This is a form of credit that can be repeatedly accessed up to a certain limit, as long as the account is in good standing. Credit cards are a prime example. The flexibility is advantageous, but the ease of use can lead to high levels of debt if not carefully managed.
- **Installment Debt**: This is repaid over time with a set number of scheduled payments, such as auto loans, mortgages, and personal loans. It allows for predictable budgeting, but the rigidity means less flexibility compared to revolving debt.

Impact on Financial Health:

- **Credit Score Influence**: Debt, especially how it's managed, plays a significant role in determining credit scores. Timely payments can improve a credit score, whereas defaults and late payments can cause it to plummet.
- **Debt-to-Income Ratio**: This is a crucial metric in financial health. High levels of debt compared to income can make it difficult to acquire additional loans or credit and can indicate financial overextension.
- **Interest and Capital Repayment**: Understanding the interplay between interest and principal repayment is key. High-interest debts can lead to a situation where one is paying significantly more over time, particularly with minimum payments on revolving debts.

- **Psychological Impact**: The stress of managing high levels of debt can affect mental health and overall well-being. It can lead to a feeling of being trapped in a financial cycle that is hard to break.

In understanding these various aspects of debt, we can better navigate our financial landscapes. It is not just about avoiding debt but about managing it in a way that aligns with our broader financial goals and health. As we delve deeper into this section, we will explore strategies to effectively manage and mitigate the impacts of debt, turning it from a potential adversary into a manageable aspect of our financial journey.

Strategies for Reducing Debt: Effective Methods for Paying Off Debts

Reducing debt is an integral part of achieving financial stability and freedom. This segment focuses on effective methods for paying off debts, providing you with strategies to not only manage but also to accelerate your journey towards a debt-free life.

Debt Snowball Method:

- **Concept**: This strategy involves paying off debts from smallest to largest, regardless of interest rates. Once the smallest debt is paid off, the payment amount is rolled into the next smallest debt.
- **Advantage**: The psychological win of paying off smaller debts can be highly motivating, creating momentum in your debt repayment journey.

Debt Avalanche Method:

- **Concept**: Contrary to the snowball method, this strategy focuses on paying off debts with the highest interest rates first, while making minimum payments on others.
- **Advantage**: This method can save you money over time by reducing the amount of interest paid.

Consolidation of Debts:

- **Concept**: Combining multiple debts into a single debt, often with a lower interest rate, can simplify payments and potentially reduce the cost of debt.
- **Method**: One can use a consolidation loan or a balance transfer credit card to consolidate debts.

Refinancing:

- **Concept**: This involves replacing an existing debt with a new one, typically with more favorable terms such as a lower interest rate.

- **Applicability**: Common in mortgages and student loans, refinancing can lead to significant interest savings.

Creating a Budget and Cutting Expenses:

- **Action**: Develop a strict budget to free up more money for debt repayment.
- **Technique**: Review and reduce non-essential expenses, and apply the extra funds to your debt repayment plan.

Increasing Income Streams:

- **Method**: Look for ways to increase your income, such as taking on a side job, selling unused items, or exploring passive income opportunities.
- **Application**: Apply this additional income directly to your debt to speed up the repayment process.

Negotiating with Creditors:

- **Approach**: Reach out to creditors to negotiate terms, such as lower interest rates or a settlement amount.
- **Benefit**: This can lead to reduced payments or an opportunity to pay off debt at a lower total cost.

Using Windfalls Wisely:

- **Strategy**: Apply unexpected financial gains, such as tax refunds, bonuses, or inheritances, directly to your debt.
- **Impact**: These windfalls can make a significant dent in your debt balance, accelerating the payoff process.

Each of these strategies has its unique advantages and applicability depending on individual financial situations. The key is to choose the method or combination of methods that align with your financial goals, habits, and circumstances. By employing these strategies effectively, you can turn the tide on debt, leading you towards a more secure and financially independent future.

Leveraging Good Debt: How to Use Debt Strategically for Financial Growth

The concept of leveraging 'good' debt strategically is a pivotal element in the discourse of financial management. This section delves into how one can judiciously utilize debt as a tool for fostering financial growth and wealth accumulation.

Understanding 'Good' Debt:

- **Definition**: 'Good' debt is characterized by its potential to increase your net worth or generate income. This includes debts taken for education, business investments, or purchasing assets like real estate.
- **Key Aspect**: The interest rate on good debt is often lower than the return on investment it generates.

Investing in Education:

- **Approach**: Taking loans for education can be considered good debt if it leads to higher earning potential in the future.
- **Consideration**: It's crucial to balance the potential income boost against the total cost of the loan, including interest.

Real Estate and Mortgages:

- **Strategy**: Mortgages are typically classified as good debt because real estate often appreciates over time.
- **Tactic**: Utilize mortgages to acquire property that can increase in value, generate rental income, or both.

Business Loans:

- **Concept**: Loans taken for starting or expanding a business can be good debt if they lead to business growth and increased revenue.
- **Calculation**: Assess the potential return on investment and ensure it surpasses the cost of the debt.

Leveraged Investments:

- **Method**: Using borrowed money to invest in the stock market or other financial instruments.
- **Risk Assessment**: While this can amplify returns, it also increases risk, requiring careful evaluation and risk management strategies.

Credit Building:

- **Function**: Responsibly using debt can help build a credit history, essential for obtaining loans at favorable rates in the future.

- **Practice**: Regular, on-time payments and maintaining low credit utilization ratios are key.

Tax Benefits:

- **Understanding**: Certain types of good debt, like mortgages and some business loans, come with tax-deductible interest payments.
- **Application**: This can reduce the overall cost of the debt.

Strategic Planning and Caution:

- **Planning**: Ensure a comprehensive plan is in place for debt repayment without compromising other financial goals.
- **Caution**: It is imperative to avoid over-leveraging, which can lead to financial distress.

In essence, when used judiciously, good debt can be a powerful instrument in propelling financial growth. It requires a meticulous evaluation of the potential returns against the costs and risks involved. Strategic leveraging of good debt, underpinned by disciplined financial planning and risk management, can significantly contribute to wealth building and achieving long-term financial objectives.

As we transition from the nuanced strategies of debt management to the critical realm of cash management in business, we approach a fundamental cornerstone of business stability and growth. The effective management of cash flow is not merely a financial task; it's a strategic imperative that can dictate the success or failure of a business. This next section, "Cash Management in Business," aims to equip entrepreneurs, business owners, and financial enthusiasts with the knowledge and tools necessary to master this crucial aspect of business operation.

The Essence of Cash Management:

- **Overview**: Cash management in business involves monitoring, analyzing, and optimizing the flow of funds in and out of the company.
- **Significance**: It's the lifeblood of a business, essential for maintaining solvency and funding daily operations.

Key Components:

- **Cash Flow Analysis**: Understanding the timing and amount of cash inflows and outflows.
- **Working Capital Management**: Efficiently managing the balance between current assets and liabilities.

Tools and Techniques:

- **Budgeting**: Implementing budgets for different departments and activities.
- **Forecasting**: Predicting future cash flows based on historical data and market trends.

Strategies for Cash Flow Optimization:

- **Receivables Management**: Speeding up the collection of accounts receivable.
- **Payables Management**: Strategically scheduling payments to suppliers and creditors.

Liquidity Management:

- **Reserves**: Maintaining an optimal level of cash reserves for unexpected expenses.
- **Investment of Surplus**: Prudent investment of surplus cash in short-term, liquid assets.

Technological Integration:

- **Software Solutions**: Utilizing cash management software for real-time tracking and analysis.
- **Automated Systems**: Implementing automation in billing, payments, and collections.

Risk Management:

- **Mitigating Risks**: Identifying and mitigating risks associated with cash management, such as fraud and currency fluctuations.

Decision Making:

- **Strategic Decisions**: Using cash flow analysis to make informed business decisions, such as expansions, acquisitions, or divestitures.

In conclusion, mastering cash management is not just about keeping track of numbers; it's about making strategic decisions that align with the company's goals and ensuring the financial health and longevity of the business. In the following sections, we will delve into the intricacies of cash management, offering insights, strategies, and practical tools to empower businesses in their journey towards financial excellence and stability.

Section 7: Cash Management in Business

Business Cash Flow Analysis

Introduction to Business Cash Flow Analysis:

- **Definition and Importance**: Cash flow analysis in a business context involves examining the inflows and outflows of cash within a company to assess its financial health and operational efficiency. It's crucial for ensuring that a business has enough cash to meet its obligations and for strategic planning.
- **Scope**: This analysis covers various aspects such as operating cash flow, investment cash flow, and financing cash flow.

Techniques for Analyzing Cash Flow:

- **Cash Flow Statement Review**: Understanding and interpreting the cash flow statement, a financial document that shows how changes in balance sheet accounts and income affect cash.
- **Direct and Indirect Methods**: Examining the differences between the direct method (which lists cash receipts and payments) and the indirect method (which adjusts net income for non-cash transactions and changes in balance sheet items).

Operating Cash Flow Analysis:

- **Components**: Analysis of cash generated or used in the core business activities.
- **Ratios and Metrics**: Utilizing ratios like Operating Cash Flow Ratio for evaluating the adequacy of cash generated from operations.

Cash Flow from Investing and Financing:

- **Investing Activities**: Analyzing cash flow related to the acquisition and disposal of long-term assets and investments.
- **Financing Activities**: Evaluating cash flow from transactions involving equity and debt.

Cash Flow Forecasting:

- **Predictive Analysis**: Techniques for predicting future cash flow based on historical data, trends, and business projections.
- **Tools**: Utilization of software and models for accurate cash flow forecasting.

Identifying and Managing Cash Flow Issues:

- **Red Flags**: Recognizing early signs of cash flow problems, such as declining cash reserves or increasing debt levels.
- **Strategies for Improvement**: Implementing measures like adjusting payment terms, managing inventory more effectively, and renegotiating with suppliers.

Scenario Analysis and Stress Testing:

- **Scenario Planning**: Exploring the impact of various 'what if' scenarios on cash flow.
- **Stress Testing**: Testing how extreme market conditions could affect the company's cash flow.

Leveraging Technology in Cash Flow Analysis:

- **Automated Tools**: Using advanced software for real-time cash flow tracking and analytics.
- **Integration with Other Systems**: Ensuring cash flow analysis tools are integrated with accounting and ERP systems for accuracy and efficiency.

Best Practices and Case Studies:

- **Industry Benchmarks**: Comparing cash flow metrics against industry benchmarks for a relative performance assessment.
- **Real-World Examples**: Learning from case studies of effective cash flow management in various businesses.

In essence, business cash flow analysis is a dynamic and integral part of financial management. It enables businesses to not only maintain financial health but also to strategize for growth and sustainability. The following sections will build upon these foundations, providing deeper insights into effective cash management strategies tailored for the unique challenges and opportunities faced by businesses.

Managing Accounts Receivable and Payable

Fundamentals of Accounts Receivable and Payable:

- **Conceptual Understanding**: Accounts receivable refers to the money owed to a business by its customers, while accounts payable represents the money a business owes to its suppliers. Effective management of these accounts is vital for maintaining healthy cash flow.

- **Role in Cash Flow Management**: These accounts directly impact the liquidity of a business, and their management is key in ensuring operational efficiency and financial stability.

Optimizing Accounts Receivable:

- **Credit Policies**: Establishing clear credit policies to determine which customers are extended credit and under what terms.
- **Invoicing Strategies**: Implementing efficient invoicing practices, including prompt billing and clear payment terms.
- **Collection Techniques**: Developing effective strategies for collecting payments, including follow-ups and reminders.

Technologies in Receivables Management:

- **Automated Invoicing Systems**: Utilizing technology for automating invoicing processes to ensure accuracy and timeliness.
- **Online Payment Solutions**: Offering various payment options, including online and mobile payment platforms, to accelerate collections.

Managing Accounts Payable:

- **Supplier Relationships**: Building and maintaining strong relationships with suppliers to negotiate favorable payment terms.
- **Payment Scheduling**: Developing a systematic approach to paying bills, prioritizing payments based on terms and cash flow needs.

Cash Flow Forecasting in Payables and Receivables:

- **Projecting Cash Needs**: Forecasting future cash requirements based on anticipated receivables and payables.
- **Liquidity Analysis**: Assessing the liquidity position of the business to manage short-term cash needs efficiently.

Discounts and Incentives:

- **Early Payment Discounts**: Offering discounts to customers for early payments to encourage faster cash inflow.
- **Taking Advantage of Creditor Discounts**: Evaluating the benefits of taking discounts offered by suppliers for early payment.

Risk Management in Receivables and Payables:

- **Credit Risk Assessment**: Evaluating the creditworthiness of customers to minimize the risk of non-payment.
- **Contingency Planning**: Preparing for scenarios such as delayed payments or unexpected expenses.

Regulatory Compliance and Reporting:

- **Compliance with Accounting Standards**: Ensuring that receivables and payables management aligns with relevant accounting principles and standards.
- **Accurate Reporting**: Maintaining accurate records and reporting for financial analysis and decision-making.

Best Practices and Case Studies:

- **Benchmarking**: Analyzing industry standards and best practices in managing receivables and payables.
- **Success Stories**: Learning from real-life examples of businesses that have optimized their accounts receivable and payable effectively.

In summary, managing accounts receivable and payable is a critical component of cash management in business. It requires a strategic approach, incorporating efficient processes, technology, and a deep understanding of the company's financial dynamics. The next sections will delve into further aspects of cash management, exploring how these elements work together to build a robust financial framework for business success.

Liquidity Management

Understanding Liquidity in Business:

- **Definition and Importance**: Liquidity refers to the ability of a business to meet its short-term financial obligations. It is a critical aspect of financial health, determining a company's capacity to handle unexpected expenses and to capitalize on growth opportunities.
- **Balancing Act**: Managing liquidity involves maintaining enough cash on hand while also maximizing the return on investments.

Assessing Liquidity Needs:

- **Cash Flow Analysis**: Regular analysis of cash flows is essential for understanding liquidity requirements. This includes monitoring both the timing and amounts of cash inflows and outflows.

- **Working Capital Management**: Effective management of working capital (current assets minus current liabilities) is key to ensuring liquidity.

Strategies for Improving Liquidity:

- **Optimizing Inventory Management**: Balancing inventory levels to avoid overstocking, yet ensuring sufficient stock to meet customer demands.
- **Efficient Receivables Collection**: Implementing strategies to accelerate the collection of accounts receivable, thus improving cash inflow.

Liquidity Reserves:

- **Importance of Reserves**: Maintaining liquidity reserves helps in cushioning against financial shocks and taking advantage of investment opportunities.
- **Determining Reserve Levels**: Factors to consider include business volatility, industry standards, and growth plans.

Investment of Excess Liquidity:

- **Short-Term Investments**: Options for investing surplus liquidity, such as money market instruments, which offer liquidity and minimal risk.
- **Balancing Returns and Accessibility**: Selecting investments that offer reasonable returns without compromising on the accessibility of funds.

Tools for Liquidity Management:

- **Cash Flow Forecasting Tools**: Utilizing software and methodologies for accurate cash flow projections.
- **Liquidity Ratios Analysis**: Employing ratios like the current ratio and quick ratio to gauge liquidity health.

Crisis Management and Liquidity:

- **Emergency Planning**: Preparing for financial crises by ensuring adequate liquidity buffers.
- **Adaptive Strategies**: Adjusting liquidity management strategies in response to changing market conditions and business cycles.

Regulatory Considerations and Compliance:

- **Understanding Legal Requirements**: Complying with financial regulations that pertain to liquidity management.
- **Ethical Considerations**: Maintaining ethical standards in liquidity management practices.

Case Studies and Real-World Examples:

- **Learning from Success and Failure**: Analyzing case studies of businesses that have successfully managed liquidity, as well as those that failed due to poor liquidity management.

In summary, effective liquidity management is pivotal for maintaining a healthy financial state in business. It involves a careful balance between meeting immediate financial obligations and planning for future growth and investments. The next section will transition into exploring the broader spectrum of cash management, delving into how businesses can optimize their overall financial strategies for long-term success and stability.

As we transition from the intricate realm of liquidity management in Section 7, our focus shifts towards the broader, yet equally crucial, arena of advanced budgeting and forecasting in Section 8. This next section delves deeper into the strategies and methodologies that enable businesses to not only sustain their financial health but also to strategically plan for future growth and stability.

Advanced budgeting and forecasting are the cornerstones of strategic financial planning. They extend beyond the basic principles of budgeting, encompassing a more comprehensive and forward-looking approach. This section aims to equip business leaders and financial professionals with the advanced tools and insights necessary for creating robust financial plans that can withstand the dynamism of the business world.

In-Depth Analysis of Advanced Budgeting:

- Exploring sophisticated budgeting techniques that cater to the unique needs and complexities of different businesses.
- Understanding zero-based budgeting, rolling budgets, and activity-based budgeting, and their applications in various business scenarios.

The Art of Financial Forecasting:

- Examining the principles and methodologies of accurate financial forecasting.
- Utilizing statistical models and trend analyses to predict future financial performance.

Integrating Budgeting with Business Strategy:

- Aligning budgeting processes with the overall strategic goals of the organization.
- Case studies on how effective budgeting has steered businesses towards achieving their long-term objectives.

Leveraging Technology in Budgeting and Forecasting:

- Exploring the latest technological advancements in financial planning, such as AI and machine learning.
- The role of financial management software in enhancing the efficiency and accuracy of budgeting and forecasting processes.

Risk Management in Financial Planning:

- Identifying potential risks in financial planning and integrating risk management strategies into budgeting and forecasting.
- Scenario planning and contingency budgeting as tools for mitigating financial risks.

Performance Measurement and Analysis:

- Establishing key performance indicators (KPIs) to measure the effectiveness of financial plans.
- Regularly reviewing and adjusting budgets and forecasts in response to performance data and market changes.

Best Practices in Budgeting and Forecasting:

- Insights from industry experts and successful businesses on best practices in advanced budgeting and forecasting.
- Continuous improvement and innovation in financial planning processes.

By the end of this section, readers will have gained a comprehensive understanding of the sophisticated techniques and tools in advanced budgeting and forecasting. This knowledge is not just pivotal for maintaining financial stability but is also instrumental in steering a business towards its envisioned future. As we conclude this section, we will prepare to embark on the final leg of our journey, exploring the nuances of financial leadership in the concluding section.

Section 8: Advanced Budgeting and Forecasting

In the realm of advanced budgeting and forecasting, a critical component is the ability to forecast for future growth effectively. This involves a combination of analytical skills, strategic thinking, and an understanding of the market dynamics that influence a business's financial trajectory. The focus of this subsection is to equip readers with the knowledge and tools necessary to predict and plan for their business's financial growth accurately.

Understanding the Basics of Financial Forecasting:

- Exploring the fundamental concepts and importance of financial forecasting in business planning.
- Differentiating between short-term and long-term forecasting and their respective roles in growth planning.

Market Analysis and Trend Identification:

- Techniques for analyzing market trends and consumer behavior to inform growth forecasts.
- The importance of staying abreast of industry changes and economic indicators that can impact future growth.

Utilizing Predictive Models:

- Introduction to various predictive models used in financial forecasting, including regression analysis, time-series models, and econometric models.
- Case studies demonstrating the application of these models in real-world business scenarios.

Scenario Planning and Sensitivity Analysis:

- The role of scenario planning in forecasting, allowing businesses to prepare for various possible futures.
- Conducting sensitivity analysis to understand how different variables impact the financial growth of a business.

Integrating Technology in Forecasting:

- Leveraging advanced technologies such as artificial intelligence (AI) and machine learning for more accurate and efficient forecasts.
- The role of financial technology (FinTech) in enhancing predictive analytics.

Financial Projections and Goal Setting:

- Creating realistic financial projections based on thorough market research and analysis.
- Aligning financial forecasts with business goals and objectives to ensure cohesive growth planning.

Risk Management in Growth Forecasting:

- Identifying potential risks and uncertainties in the forecasting process.

- Developing strategies to mitigate these risks and building resilient growth plans.

Continuous Monitoring and Adjustment:

- The importance of regularly reviewing and adjusting forecasts based on new data and market developments.
- Establishing a feedback loop where actual performance is continually compared against forecasts to refine future predictions.

By mastering these forecasting techniques, businesses can position themselves to capitalize on future opportunities and navigate potential challenges. This proactive approach to financial planning is crucial for sustainable growth and long-term success. As we move forward, we will delve into the nuances of financial leadership, exploring how effective decision-making and strategic vision can drive a business towards its financial goals.

Scenario Analysis: Preparing for Various Financial Scenarios and Their Implications

Scenario analysis stands as a pivotal tool in the arsenal of financial forecasting and planning. It enables businesses and individuals to prepare for a range of potential futures, each with distinct financial implications. This section delves into the methodologies and benefits of scenario analysis, guiding readers through the process of preparing for various financial situations.

Understanding Scenario Analysis:

- Definition and overview of scenario analysis in the context of financial planning.
- Differentiating scenario analysis from other forecasting methods, highlighting its unique value in dealing with uncertainty.

Developing Scenarios:

- Guidelines for creating realistic and diverse scenarios, covering a spectrum of possibilities from best-case to worst-case.
- The importance of including external factors such as economic shifts, market changes, and geopolitical events in scenario development.

Quantitative and Qualitative Elements:

- Integrating both quantitative data (like financial metrics) and qualitative insights (such as market trends) in scenario construction.
- Utilizing a balanced approach to ensure comprehensive and realistic scenarios.

Evaluating Financial Implications:

- Techniques for assessing the financial impact of each scenario on cash flow, profitability, and overall financial health.
- The role of scenario analysis in identifying potential financial risks and opportunities.

Strategic Decision-Making:

- Leveraging scenario analysis to inform strategic decisions, including investment, expansion, and risk management.
- Case studies showcasing how businesses have used scenario analysis to guide critical decisions.

Stress Testing and Resilience Building:

- The concept of stress testing financial plans against various scenarios to gauge their resilience.
- Strategies for building flexibility and adaptability into financial plans to withstand unforeseen events.

Integrating Scenario Analysis into Regular Planning:

- Guidelines for incorporating scenario analysis into regular financial planning cycles.
- The importance of revisiting and updating scenarios as circumstances change.

Action Plans for Different Scenarios:

- Developing actionable strategies for each scenario, ensuring readiness for various financial futures.
- The role of contingency planning in ensuring swift and effective responses to changing financial landscapes.

Scenario analysis empowers businesses and individuals to anticipate and prepare for a range of financial futures. By understanding the potential implications of different scenarios, decision-makers can develop more robust, flexible, and forward-looking financial strategies. As we transition into the next section, the focus will shift towards the essential skills and strategies required for effective financial leadership, highlighting how informed decision-making and strategic foresight are instrumental in navigating the complex world of finance.

Long-Term Financial Planning: Strategies for Sustaining Financial Health Over the Long Term

The concept of long-term financial planning is crucial for ensuring sustained financial health and stability. This section delves into the strategies and approaches necessary for effective long-term financial planning, both for individuals and businesses. It underscores the importance of foresight, discipline, and adaptability in financial management.

Defining Long-Term Financial Goals:

- The importance of setting clear, specific, and achievable long-term financial goals.
- Techniques for aligning these goals with personal or business values and objectives.

Comprehensive Financial Assessment:

- Conducting a thorough analysis of current financial status, including assets, liabilities, income streams, and expenses.
- Understanding the significance of this assessment in creating a realistic and effective long-term plan.

Investment Strategies for Long-Term Growth:

- Exploring different investment options suitable for long-term growth, such as stocks, bonds, real estate, and retirement accounts.
- Balancing risk and reward in an investment portfolio to align with long-term objectives and risk tolerance.

Retirement Planning:

- Strategies for effective retirement planning, including understanding various retirement accounts and the role of compound interest.
- The importance of starting retirement planning early and consistently contributing to retirement funds.

Estate Planning and Wealth Transfer:

- The principles of estate planning, including wills, trusts, and life insurance.
- Strategies for efficient wealth transfer and minimizing tax liabilities.

Risk Management and Insurance:

- Identifying potential long-term financial risks and the role of insurance in mitigating these risks.

- Understanding the types of insurance necessary for comprehensive protection (e.g., life, health, property, and liability insurance).

Tax Planning and Efficiency:

- Strategies for efficient tax planning, including understanding tax implications of different investment vehicles and income sources.
- Techniques for legally minimizing tax liabilities and maximizing after-tax income.

Regular Review and Adaptation:

- The necessity of regular reviews of financial plans to ensure they remain aligned with changing goals, life circumstances, and financial landscapes.
- Adapting and adjusting financial strategies in response to life events, economic changes, and personal or business growth.

Financial Legacy and Succession Planning:

- For business owners and individuals, the importance of planning for the transfer of assets and business interests.
- Strategies for ensuring a smooth transition and preserving financial legacy.

In conclusion, long-term financial planning is not a static process but a dynamic journey that requires ongoing attention and adjustment. It involves a comprehensive approach, considering various aspects of financial health and preparing for future needs and goals. As we transition into the final section, we will explore the importance of financial literacy and education in empowering individuals and businesses to make informed financial decisions, thereby securing their financial futures in an ever-evolving economic landscape.

Summary of Key Takeaways:

Understanding the Essence of Financial Management:

- The criticality of mastering budgeting and cash management for personal and business financial health.
- The dynamics of financial flow: income, expenses, savings, and investments.

Budgeting as a Foundational Skill:

- Different types of budgets and their specific purposes.
- Setting realistic and sustainable budgets.
- Utilizing various tools and techniques for effective budgeting.

Strategies for Managing Expenses:

- Identifying and categorizing expenses to understand their impact.
- Implementing cost-cutting strategies to reduce unnecessary expenditures.
- The concept of investing in value for long-term benefits.

Optimizing Income Streams:

- Techniques for maximizing revenue in personal finance and business.
- The importance of diversifying income sources for financial stability.
- Balancing passive and active income for optimal financial health.

Principles of Savings and Investments:

- Building a robust emergency fund.
- Basic investment principles for beginners.
- Balancing risk and reward in investment and savings strategies.

Effective Debt Management:

- Understanding different types of debt and their impact.
- Strategies for reducing and managing debt.
- Leveraging good debt for financial growth.

Cash Management in Business:

- Techniques for business cash flow analysis.
- Managing accounts receivable and payable effectively.
- Ensuring business liquidity for operational efficiency and growth.

Advanced Budgeting and Forecasting:

- Forecasting for future growth and financial planning.
- Preparing for various financial scenarios through scenario analysis.
- Strategies for sustaining long-term financial health.

The Journey Ahead:

This chapter has equipped you with essential principles and strategies for effective budgeting, cash management, and overall financial health. As you embark on this journey of financial empowerment, remember that the application of these concepts is key. Regular practice, consistent monitoring, and adaptation to changing circumstances will help you refine your financial management skills. Stay motivated, remain disciplined, and embrace the journey of continuous improvement in your financial life.

Resources for Further Learning:

For those eager to delve deeper into the intricacies of budgeting and cash management, the following resources are invaluable:

Books and Publications:

- "Your Money or Your Life" by Vicki Robin and Joe Dominguez.
- "The Total Money Makeover" by Dave Ramsey.
- "Rich Dad Poor Dad" by Robert Kiyosaki.

Online Courses and Workshops:

- Personal finance courses on platforms like Coursera, Udemy, and Khan Academy.
- Workshops and webinars by financial experts and institutions.

Podcasts and Blogs:

- Financial podcasts such as "The Dave Ramsey Show" and "So Money with Farnoosh Torabi".
- Blogs like "Mr. Money Mustache" and "The Financial Diet" for practical tips and insights.

Financial Planning Tools and Apps:

- Budgeting and expense tracking apps like Mint, YNAB (You Need A Budget), and PocketGuard.
- Investment and savings tools like Acorns, Robinhood, and Betterment.

Community Groups and Forums:

- Joining online forums and community groups focused on personal finance and investment.

By leveraging these resources, you can further enhance your knowledge and skills in financial management, setting a solid foundation for a prosperous and secure financial future.

Exercises and Reflections
Practical Exercises:

Budgeting Template Exercise:

- Download or create a budgeting template. A simple spreadsheet can suffice.
- Fill in your monthly income sources.
- List all monthly expenses, categorizing them as 'fixed' (like rent) and 'variable' (like groceries).
- Subtract your total expenses from your income to see your monthly surplus or deficit.
- Reflect on areas where you can cut back or reallocate funds for savings and investments.

Cash Flow Analysis Worksheet:

- Create a cash flow analysis worksheet or use an online tool.
- Record all cash inflows (income) and outflows (expenses) for a month.
- Track the timing of these cash flows to identify periods of cash surplus or shortage.
- Analyze this data to understand your spending habits and identify potential savings.

Expense Categorization Activity:

- For one month, keep all receipts or track expenses in an app.
- At month-end, categorize these expenses (e.g., necessities, luxuries, entertainment).
- Assess which categories are consuming the most resources and consider adjustments for better budgeting.

Emergency Fund Planning:

- Determine a target amount for your emergency fund (typically 3-6 months of living expenses).
- Create a plan to achieve this, detailing monthly savings contributions.
- Open a separate savings account for this fund to avoid the temptation to spend it.

Debt Repayment Plan:

- List all debts including amounts, interest rates, and minimum payments.
- Choose a repayment strategy (e.g., the snowball method focusing on smallest debts first, or the avalanche method targeting high-interest debts).

- Create a timeline and monthly payment plan to systematically reduce and eliminate debts.

Income Diversification Project:

- Brainstorm potential passive income streams or side hustles.
- Research and outline a plan to pursue one of these ideas.
- Set specific, measurable goals for income generation and track progress over time.

Investment Scenario Analysis:

- Research different types of investments (stocks, bonds, mutual funds, real estate).
- Create hypothetical portfolios and run scenario analyses based on different risk levels.
- Use online investment simulators to understand the potential outcomes of each investment type.

Long-term Financial Planning:

- Outline your long-term financial goals (retirement, home ownership, education funding, etc.).
- Develop a roadmap with milestones and the financial strategies needed to achieve these goals.
- Consider consulting a financial planner to review and refine your plan.

Each of these exercises is designed to enhance your understanding and practical application of budgeting and cash flow management skills. By actively engaging with these exercises, you will gain valuable insights into your financial habits and learn effective strategies to improve your financial health.

Reflection Prompts:

Personal Financial Reflection:

- What are your main financial goals for the next year, five years, and ten years?
- Reflect on your current spending habits. Are there areas where you frequently overspend?
- How do your current budgeting practices align with your long-term financial objectives?

Cash Flow Consciousness:

- When analyzing your cash flow, what surprised you the most about your income and expenses?
- Identify periods when you experienced cash flow shortages. What could have been done differently?
- How can improving your cash flow analysis contribute to better financial decision-making?

Expense Management Insights:

- What are your top three expense categories? Are these aligned with your values and priorities?
- Reflect on a significant purchase you made recently. Was it a need or a want, and how did it impact your budget?
- Think about a time you successfully cut costs. What strategies worked, and how can they be applied more broadly?

Income Optimization Evaluation:

- Considering your current income sources, what potential areas exist for increasing your income?
- How diversified are your income streams? What steps can you take to develop additional sources of income?
- Reflect on the balance between your active and passive income. How can this balance be optimized for your lifestyle and goals?

Savings and Investment Self-Assessment:

- Assess your current approach to savings. Are you consistently setting aside a portion of your income?
- What are your apprehensions regarding investing, and how can you educate yourself to overcome these?
- How does your risk tolerance influence your investment decisions? Is this in line with your financial goals?

Debt Management Reflection:

- What are your attitudes towards debt? Do you see it as a tool for growth or a burden?
- Reflect on your current debts. How are you managing them, and what could be improved?

- How can you differentiate between 'good debt' and 'bad debt' in your financial planning?

Business Cash Management Considerations (for business owners):

- Analyze the effectiveness of your current business cash flow management. What are the strengths and weaknesses?
- How do you manage your accounts receivable and payable? Are there opportunities for improvement?
- Reflect on your business's liquidity. Do you have sufficient funds for growth and unexpected expenses?

Advanced Budgeting and Forecasting Reflection:

- How do you currently approach financial forecasting in your personal or business finances?
- Reflect on a financial decision that didn't go as planned. How could better forecasting have helped?
- Consider your long-term financial vision. How can advanced budgeting and forecasting techniques bring you closer to this vision?

These reflection prompts are designed to encourage deep personal engagement with the financial concepts discussed. They aim to foster a mindset shift towards proactive and strategic financial management, both in personal and business contexts.

Chapter 4: Liberating Finances: Pathways to Debt Freedom and Credit Vitality

In a world where financial freedom often feels like a distant dream, the burden of debt can be a heavy chain, while good credit can be a powerful key to unlocking opportunities. As someone who has navigated the choppy waters of personal finance, I understand the daunting feeling of being weighed down by debt. But I also know the exhilaration of breaking free and harnessing the power of credit to achieve financial goals. This chapter is not just a guide; it's a journey towards liberating your finances and redefining your relationship with money.

Section 1: Understanding Debt – The Good, the Bad, and the Manageable

- **Debt Demystified**: Exploring different types of debt – from mortgages to credit cards – and understanding their roles in financial health.
- **Personal Anecdote**: I'll share a story about how I once viewed debt as a formidable enemy and how I learned to see it as a tool.

Section 2: Strategies for Eliminating Bad Debt

Actionable Steps: Step-by-step guide to prioritizing and paying off high-interest debts.

Empathy Corner: Acknowledging the emotional toll of debt and offering strategies for staying motivated.

Section 3: The Art of Building and Maintaining Good Credit

Credit Essentials: How to build, maintain, and leverage good credit.

Philosophical Insight: Discussing the mindset shift needed to view credit not just as a borrowing tool, but as a strategic asset.

Section 4: Credit Repair – Navigating Challenges and Rebuilding

Case Study: A narrative about someone who successfully navigated credit repair, highlighting practical steps and emotional resilience.

Interactive Element: A credit health checklist to help identify areas for improvement.

Section 5: Debt Consolidation and Refinancing – When and How

Expert Advice: Exploring scenarios where debt consolidation or refinancing is beneficial.

Engaging Narrative: A hypothetical scenario illustrating the pros and cons of consolidating debt.

Section 6: Leveraging Credit for Growth

Female Perspective: Insights into how women, in particular, can leverage credit for business or personal growth.

Philosophical Insights: Discussing how responsibly managed debt can be a catalyst for wealth creation.

Section 7: Protecting Yourself from Debt Traps

Interactive Element: Red flags checklist for predatory lending and how to avoid common debt traps.

Humor and Wit: Light-hearted anecdotes about financial missteps and the lessons they teach.

Section 8: Embracing Credit as a Financial Tool

- **Mindset Shift**: Encouraging a healthy and proactive approach to using credit.
- **Personal Anecdote**: My experience in using credit strategically to enhance my financial stability.

Conclusion: Your Path to Debt Freedom and Credit Empowerment

- **Motivational Close**: A rallying call to embrace the journey towards debt freedom and credit vitality.
- **Key Takeaways**: Summarizing the main points of the chapter and the empowerment that comes with financial literacy.

Resources for Further Learning

- A curated list of resources, including books, websites, and tools, for those who wish to explore the topics of debt management and credit building further.

This chapter, "Liberating Finances: Pathways to Debt Freedom and Credit Vitality," is crafted to be not just informative but transformative. It is a blend of personal insights, practical advice, and motivational guidance, all designed to empower you on your journey to financial liberation.

Understanding the Psychological Impact of Debt

Debt, a term that often conjures images of endless bills and looming financial obligations, extends its influence far beyond the confines of mere numbers and interest rates. It seeps into the very psyche of individuals, manifesting as a pervasive force with significant psychological repercussions. This section aims to unravel the intricate web of emotional and behavioral impacts that debt can have on an individual's life.

The Emotional Toll of Debt Chronic stress, a frequent companion of debt, can lead to a cascade of psychological issues such as anxiety, depression, and sleep disturbances. My personal encounter with debt-related stress serves as a testament to its profound impact. During a particularly challenging financial period, the constant worry and the overwhelming sense of burden led to sleepless nights and a persistent state of anxiety. This personal narrative underscores the need for strategies to cope with the emotional distress caused by debt.

Debt and Self-Perception Debt often carries a stigma, a shadow that looms over one's sense of self, casting doubt on their self-worth and capabilities. The societal narrative around debt can lead individuals to conflate their financial state with their personal value. It is crucial to decouple self-worth from financial status and to understand that debt does not define one's character or potential.

The Relationship Between Debt and Behavior Debt can significantly influence spending habits, often trapping individuals in a vicious cycle of accruing more debt. This behavioral impact necessitates a shift towards mindful spending and the adoption of healthier financial habits. Breaking free from this cycle is not just about financial discipline but also about understanding the underlying emotional triggers that lead to excessive spending.

Debt and Relationships The strain that debt places on relationships is an aspect that cannot be overlooked. From marital tension to challenges in social interactions, the stress of financial obligations can permeate various facets of social life. It is essential to navigate these dynamics carefully, maintaining open communication and seeking mutual understanding in relationships affected by financial stress.

The Journey to Psychological Freedom Transforming one's mindset about debt is pivotal in overcoming its psychological impact. Viewing debt as a temporary challenge, rather than a permanent personal failure, can pave the way for both financial and psychological liberation. Inspirational stories of individuals who have triumphed over their debt underscore the possibility of achieving not just solvency but also emotional well-being.

Tools for Managing Debt-Related Stress Addressing the mental health aspects associated with debt involves practical strategies like mindfulness practices, seeking professional help, and fostering a supportive community. These tools are vital in managing the stress, anxiety, and other mental health issues that often accompany financial challenges.

Conclusion As we conclude this exploration of the psychological impact of debt, it's important to remember that the journey to overcoming debt is as much about emotional and mental liberation as it is about financial freedom. The resilience shown in facing these challenges not only leads to a healthier financial state but also contributes to overall personal growth and well-being. The key takeaway is that debt, no matter how daunting, is a challenge that can be overcome, leading to a life marked by both financial stability and emotional peace.

The Importance of Credit Health in Financial Freedom

Credit health plays a pivotal role in the pursuit of financial freedom, serving as a cornerstone upon which many aspects of financial stability and opportunity are built. In this section, we will delve into the multifaceted significance of maintaining good credit health and how it can be a powerful tool in achieving and sustaining financial independence.

Defining Credit Health Credit health is a measure of an individual's creditworthiness, as reflected in their credit score and credit history. It is a snapshot of how well a person manages their financial obligations and is often used by lenders and financial institutions to determine the risk involved in extending credit.

Access to Financial Opportunities A robust credit score opens doors to a plethora of financial opportunities that are crucial for building wealth. This includes access to better loan terms, lower interest rates, and favorable conditions on mortgages and other borrowings. As I recall from my own experience, a high credit score was instrumental in securing a mortgage for my home under exceptionally favorable terms, significantly impacting my long-term financial planning and stability.

Lower Cost of Borrowing Good credit health can lead to substantial savings over time. Lower interest rates on credit cards, loans, and mortgages translate to less money paid in interest, freeing up funds for investment, savings, or other financial goals. The cumulative effect of these savings can be substantial, contributing significantly to an individual's financial freedom.

Empowerment in Negotiations Credit health empowers consumers in financial negotiations. With a strong credit score, individuals have better leverage in negotiating terms with lenders, potentially securing more advantageous deals.

Insurance Premiums and Rental Agreements Credit health extends its influence beyond loans and credit cards. Many insurance companies use credit scores to determine premiums, while landlords often consider credit history when evaluating rental applications. Thus, good credit health can lead to more favorable insurance rates and rental opportunities, impacting overall financial well-being.

Emergency Preparedness Good credit health is invaluable in times of financial emergency. Access to credit can be a lifeline in unforeseen circumstances, providing the means to manage unexpected expenses without depleting savings or investment funds.

Building a Strong Credit History Maintaining good credit health involves consistent and disciplined financial habits such as timely bill payments, prudent credit usage, and regular monitoring of credit reports. These practices not only build and sustain a strong credit score but also instill financial discipline that is beneficial in all aspects of money management.

Conclusion In summary, good credit health is a fundamental aspect of financial freedom. It not only provides access to financial opportunities and savings but also empowers individuals in their financial journey. By understanding the importance of credit health and actively working to maintain it, individuals set themselves on a path to financial stability and independence, a path that is both rewarding and liberating.

The Anatomy of Debt

Debt, a common element in most financial landscapes, is a complex concept with varying implications depending on its nature and management. This section will dissect the anatomy of debt, elucidating its various forms, understanding its dynamics, and recognizing its potential impacts on financial health.

1. Definition and Types of Debt Debt is essentially money borrowed by one party from another, under the condition of repayment, usually with interest. It comes in various forms, each with unique characteristics and purposes:

Secured Debt: Tied to an asset, like a mortgage for a home or a car loan, where the asset serves as collateral.

Unsecured Debt: Includes credit card debt and personal loans, not backed by collateral.

Revolving Debt: Allows the borrower to continuously borrow up to a set credit limit, as seen with credit cards.

Installment Debt: Involves regular, fixed payments until the debt is fully repaid, such as a student loan or a mortgage.

2. Understanding Interest Rates and Terms The cost of debt is significantly influenced by interest rates and the terms of the loan. Interest rates can be fixed or variable, impacting the total repayment amount. The length of the debt term also affects the total interest paid; longer terms generally mean more interest paid over the life of the loan.

3. The Double-Edged Sword of Leverage Debt can be a powerful tool for leveraging investments and amplifying financial returns. For example, using a mortgage to purchase a property can lead to wealth creation as the property value appreciates. However, excessive leverage can be risky, especially in volatile markets, leading to amplified losses.

4. Debt's Impact on Credit Score Debt utilization and repayment history are critical factors in determining one's credit score. Responsible debt management, such as making timely payments and keeping credit utilization low, can positively impact credit health. Conversely, missed payments or high debt levels can adversely affect credit scores.

5. The Psychological Burden of Debt Debt can exert substantial psychological pressure, leading to stress and anxiety. This aspect of debt is often underemphasized but can have tangible impacts on one's quality of life and decision-making abilities.

6. Good Debt vs. Bad Debt Not all debts are inherently detrimental. "Good debt" refers to borrowing that leads to an increase in value or income potential, like education loans or business loans. "Bad debt," however, typically denotes high-interest consumer debt that doesn't provide long-term value.

7. Managing and Prioritizing Debt Repayment Effective debt management involves prioritizing repayments, often focusing on high-interest debts first (the avalanche method) or targeting small debts for quick wins (the snowball method). Structured and disciplined repayment strategies are crucial for minimizing interest costs and becoming debt-free.

Conclusion Understanding the anatomy of debt is a critical component of financial literacy. By recognizing the different types of debt, their implications, and how they can be managed effectively, individuals can make informed decisions that align with their financial goals and contribute to their overall financial health and freedom.

Types of Debt: Understanding Secured vs. Unsecured Debt

This section provides a detailed exploration of the two primary categories of debt: secured and unsecured. Understanding the distinction between these types is essential for informed financial decision-making and effective debt management.

1. Secured Debt:

- **Definition**: Secured debt is tied to a specific asset, known as collateral. The borrower pledges an asset to the lender as security for the loan.
- **Examples**: Common examples include mortgages (secured against a property) and auto loans (secured against a vehicle).
- **Interest Rates and Terms**: Typically, secured debts offer lower interest rates compared to unsecured debts due to the reduced risk for the lender. If the borrower defaults, the lender can seize the collateral to recoup losses.
- **Implications for Borrowers**: While secured debts are less risky for lenders, they carry a higher risk for borrowers since defaulting on payments can lead to the loss of the collateral asset.

2. Unsecured Debt:

- **Definition**: Unsecured debt does not involve any collateral. The lender extends credit based solely on the borrower's creditworthiness and promise to repay.
- **Examples**: Credit card debt, personal loans, and student loans are common forms of unsecured debt.
- **Interest Rates and Terms**: Unsecured debts generally have higher interest rates than secured debts, reflecting the higher risk for the lender in case of default.
- **Implications for Borrowers**: While there is no risk of losing a specific asset, failing to repay unsecured debt can have severe consequences on credit scores and future borrowing capabilities. It can also lead to legal actions like lawsuits.

Comparative Analysis:

- **Risk Factors**: The primary difference lies in the risk distribution. Secured debt shifts more risk to the borrower, while unsecured debt places more risk on the lender.
- **Credit Impact**: Both types of debt impact credit scores, but unsecured debt can be more influential due to the higher reliance on credit history for lending decisions.
- **Flexibility and Accessibility**: Unsecured debts are often more flexible, with varying credit limits and the ability to borrow repeatedly (as with credit cards). However, they may be harder to qualify for due to the lack of collateral.

Conclusion Understanding the nuances between secured and unsecured debt is vital for anyone navigating their financial landscape. Each type has its advantages and risks, and the choice between them should align with the individual's financial goals, risk tolerance, and borrowing capacity. Making informed decisions about which type of debt to incur can significantly impact one's financial health and journey towards financial freedom.

Interest Rates and How They Affect Your Debt

This section delves into the critical role interest rates play in the management and impact of debt. Understanding how interest rates function and influence various debt forms is a pivotal aspect of financial literacy.

1. Basic Understanding of Interest Rates:

    Definition: The interest rate is the cost of borrowing money, expressed as a percentage of the principal loan amount.
    Types of Interest Rates: There are primarily two types - fixed rates, which remain constant over the loan's life, and variable rates, which can fluctuate based on market conditions.

2. Impact of Interest Rates on Different Debt Types:

    Secured Debt: For secured debts like mortgages, a lower interest rate can significantly reduce the total amount paid over the life of the loan. Conversely, a higher rate increases the overall cost.
    Unsecured Debt: Credit cards and personal loans often have higher interest rates. Especially with credit cards, where rates can be variable, even a small increase can substantially affect the repayment amount.

3. Compound Interest and Debt Accumulation:

    Definition: Compound interest means that interest is charged on both the principal and the accumulated interest.
    Implications: This can lead to a rapid increase in debt, especially if only minimum payments are made on high-interest debts like credit cards.

4. How Interest Rates Affect Debt Repayment:

    Longer Repayment Periods: Higher interest rates can lead to longer repayment periods, as more of each payment goes towards interest rather than reducing the principal.
    Increased Monthly Payments: In some types of variable-rate loans, higher rates can lead to increased monthly payments, impacting the borrower's budget.

5. Interest Rates and Debt Consolidation:

- **Strategy**: Consolidating multiple high-interest debts into a single, lower-interest loan can be a smart strategy to reduce total interest payments and simplify monthly finances.

6. Strategies for Managing High-Interest Debt:

- **Prioritizing Repayment**: Targeting debts with the highest interest rates for early repayment can save money in the long term.
- **Negotiating Rates**: In some cases, lenders may be willing to negotiate a lower interest rate, especially if the borrower's credit score has improved.

7. Monitoring Interest Rate Trends:

- **Market Awareness**: Staying informed about general interest rate trends can help in making timely decisions about refinancing or acquiring new loans.

Conclusion Interest rates are a fundamental factor in determining the total cost of debt and the efficiency of repayment strategies. By comprehensively understanding how interest rates work and affect different types of debt, individuals can make more informed decisions, potentially saving thousands of dollars over time and moving more swiftly towards debt freedom.

How Debt Accumulates: Common Pitfalls

This section explores the various ways in which debt can accumulate, often without the individual's full awareness, leading to financial strain. It is crucial to understand these common pitfalls to avoid falling into a debt trap.

1. Minimum Payments on Credit Cards:

- **Trap of Minimum Payments**: Making only the minimum payments on credit cards can lead to prolonged debt due to high-interest rates, especially with compound interest. Over time, the principal amount may not decrease significantly, leading to a cycle of endless debt.

2. Using Debt to Cover Basic Living Expenses:

- **Living Beyond Means**: Relying on credit cards or loans to cover everyday expenses can create a dangerous cycle where debt continuously grows as income remains insufficient to cover both living costs and debt repayment.

3. High-Interest and Payday Loans:

- **Exorbitant Interest Rates**: Opting for high-interest loans, such as payday loans, can lead to a rapid accumulation of debt due to their exorbitant interest rates and short repayment terms.

4. Lack of Emergency Fund:

Resorting to Debt in Emergencies: Without a safety net of savings, unexpected expenses such as medical emergencies or car repairs often lead to high-interest debt.

5. Poor Financial Planning and Impulse Spending:

Unbudgeted Spending: Impulsive buying and inadequate budgeting can lead to increased reliance on credit, contributing to a gradual build-up of debt.

6. Ignoring or Misunderstanding the Terms of Debt:

Underestimating Costs: Not fully understanding the terms of a loan, such as interest rates, fees, and penalties, can lead to unexpected costs and increased debt.

7. Consolidation Loans Without Behavioral Change:

False Sense of Security: Using consolidation loans to manage debt without addressing the underlying spending habits can result in a return to debt accumulation.

8. Increasing Debt Limits:

Access to More Credit: Increasing credit card limits or taking additional loans provides the illusion of more available money, leading to higher debt levels.

9. Compound Interest on High-Interest Debts:

Snowballing Effect: Compound interest on high-interest debts, particularly credit cards, can cause the total debt to grow exponentially over time.

Conclusion Understanding these common pitfalls is essential in preventing and managing debt accumulation. Financial discipline, such as adhering to a budget, avoiding unnecessary loans, and understanding the terms of credit, is crucial in avoiding these traps. By recognizing these patterns, individuals can take proactive steps to manage their finances and avoid the debilitating cycle of debt accumulation.

Assessing Your Debt Situation

This section is crucial for readers to gain a clear understanding of their current debt situation. It is the first step towards developing a plan to manage and eventually eliminate debt. The assessment involves several key steps:

1. Gathering All Debt Information:

- **Comprehensive List of Debts**: Compile a list of all debts, including credit card balances, loans (personal, auto, student, mortgage), and any other forms of debt. This list should include the lender's name, outstanding balance, interest rate, and minimum monthly payment.

2. Understanding Debt Terms:

- **Interest Rates and Repayment Terms**: Analyze each debt for its specific terms, such as interest rates (variable or fixed), repayment period, and any associated fees or penalties for late payments.

3. Calculating Total Debt:

- **Summing Up All Debts**: Calculate the total amount of debt owed. This total figure gives a clear picture of the debt magnitude and is essential for planning.

4. Assessing Debt-to-Income Ratio:

- **Financial Health Indicator**: Calculate the debt-to-income ratio by dividing total monthly debt payments by gross monthly income. This ratio is a key indicator of financial health and debt management capacity.

5. Prioritizing Debts:

- **High-Interest and Necessities First**: Identify which debts should be paid off first. Generally, debts with higher interest rates (like credit card debt) should be prioritized, as they cost more over time.

6. Identifying Problematic Spending Patterns:

- **Root Cause Analysis**: Look for patterns in spending habits that have contributed to the current debt situation. Recognizing and addressing these habits is crucial for long-term debt management.

7. Credit Report Examination:

- **Accuracy and Unnoticed Debts**: Review credit reports for accuracy and to identify any overlooked debts. This also helps in understanding how debt is affecting credit health.

8. Seeking Professional Advice:

Expert Guidance: If the debt situation is overwhelming, consider consulting with a financial advisor or a credit counselor for professional advice on debt management strategies.

Conclusion Assessing your debt situation with honesty and thoroughness is the foundational step towards effective debt management. It provides a clear picture of where you stand and what actions need to be taken. This assessment should be revisited regularly to track progress and adjust strategies as necessary.

Transition to Conducting a Thorough Debt Audit

Having assessed your overall debt situation and understood its implications on your financial health, the next critical step in your journey towards financial liberation is to conduct a thorough debt audit. This process involves a detailed and meticulous examination of all your debts, serving as the blueprint for your strategic debt elimination plan.

Conducting a Thorough Debt Audit: Listing All Debts with Details

This section will guide you through the systematic process of conducting a comprehensive debt audit. An effective debt audit is more than just a list; it's an enlightening exercise that brings clarity and direction to your debt management strategy.

Detailed Documentation: Begin by gathering all financial statements, bills, and records. This includes bank statements, credit card statements, loan documents, and any other relevant financial documents.

Creating a Debt Inventory: List each debt individually. For each debt, document the following details:

- **Creditor Name**: Identify the lender or credit card company.
- **Amount Owed**: Note the current balance for each debt.
- **Interest Rate**: Record the interest rate for each debt, noting whether it is fixed or variable.
- **Minimum Monthly Payment**: List the minimum payment required for each debt.
- **Payment Due Dates**: Note the due date for each payment to avoid late fees and additional interest charges.

Understanding Terms and Conditions: Review the terms and conditions for each debt. Pay attention to any special conditions, such as introductory interest rates, penalties for late payments, or opportunities for rate reductions.

Prioritization of Debts: Use the detailed information from your debt audit to prioritize your debts. This might involve targeting high-interest debts first or focusing on small balances to gain quick wins.

Identifying Opportunities for Consolidation or Refinancing: Examine your list for opportunities to consolidate multiple debts into a single loan with a lower interest rate or to refinance existing debts to more favorable terms.

Regular Review and Update: A debt audit is not a one-time task. Regularly updating your debt audit ensures you are always working with current information and can make informed decisions about your debt management strategy.

Conclusion Conducting a thorough debt audit is an empowering step in taking control of your financial situation. It lays the groundwork for informed decision making and effective debt management. With a clear understanding of your debts, you are well-positioned to devise a plan that leads you towards financial freedom and credit vitality.

Transition to Debt Reduction Strategies

Having meticulously cataloged each debt with a thorough audit, the next logical progression in our journey toward financial liberation is the exploration of effective debt reduction strategies. This phase is pivotal, as it involves transforming the insights gained from the debt audit into actionable plans. We shift our focus from the diagnostic stage, where we assessed and understood our debts, to the therapeutic stage, where we actively engage in reducing and eventually eliminating these financial burdens.

This transition marks a significant turning point. It is here that we begin to apply our newfound knowledge and clarity, garnered from the debt audit, to strategically tackle each debt. The strategies we will explore are not merely about making payments, but about making smart, informed decisions that optimize our resources, reduce financial strain, and accelerate our journey to debt freedom.

The forthcoming section is designed to empower you with various methodologies and tactics. These range from the 'snowball' method, which advocates for paying off debts with the smallest balances first, to the 'avalanche' method, which prioritizes debts with the highest interest rates. Additionally, we will delve into how to negotiate with creditors, consider debt consolidation options, and utilize budgeting tools effectively.

As we embark on this vital phase, remember that reducing debt is not just about improving numbers on a spreadsheet; it is about regaining control, achieving peace of mind, and paving the way for a financially secure and vibrant future.

Understanding Your Debt-to-Income Ratio

The concept of the debt-to-income (DTI) ratio is a critical tool in assessing and managing your financial health. The DTI ratio, simply put, is a comparison of your monthly debt payments to your monthly gross income. This metric is utilized by lenders to evaluate your ability to manage monthly payments and repay debts, and it serves as a key indicator of your financial stability.

To calculate your DTI ratio, sum up your monthly debt payments — this includes mortgage or rent, car loan payments, credit card payments, student loans, and any other debts. Then, divide this total by your gross monthly income, which is your income before taxes and other deductions. The result, expressed as a percentage, is your debt-to-income ratio.

For instance, if your monthly debts amount to $2,000 and your gross monthly income is $6,000, your DTI ratio would be approximately 33.3%. Generally, a DTI ratio of 36% or less is considered favorable, but this can vary depending on the lender and the type of loan.

Understanding your DTI ratio is imperative for several reasons:

Loan Eligibility: A lower DTI ratio enhances your chances of being approved for loans, particularly mortgages. Lenders typically prefer a DTI ratio of 43% or lower.

Financial Awareness: It helps in assessing your financial situation, providing a clear picture of where you stand in terms of debt burden relative to your income.

Budgeting Tool: It can serve as a guide to understand how much of your income is already committed to debt, and how much you can afford to take on, if any.

Debt Management Strategy: Knowing your DTI ratio assists in creating a more effective debt reduction strategy. It can be a motivator to lower your ratio through increasing income, reducing debt, or both.

Financial Health Indicator: A high DTI ratio can be a red flag, indicating a potential over-reliance on debt and vulnerability to financial stressors.

A critical aspect of managing your DTI ratio involves not just maintaining it at a healthy level, but also understanding how your financial decisions will impact it. For instance, taking on a new car loan or credit card debt will increase your DTI ratio, potentially pushing it into a higher-risk category. Therefore, continuous monitoring and proactive management of your DTI ratio are essential components of sound financial planning and debt management.

Identifying High-Interest and Problematic Debts

The identification of high-interest and problematic debts is a crucial step in effective debt management. These debts, often characterized by their exorbitant interest rates and challenging repayment terms, can quickly escalate into major financial burdens if not addressed promptly and strategically.

High-Interest Debts:

- **Credit Card Debts**: Typically, credit card debts carry the highest interest rates. It is not uncommon for rates to exceed 20%, making them a priority in any debt reduction strategy.
- **Payday Loans**: Another form of high-interest debt, payday loans often have astronomical interest rates and fees, trapping borrowers in a cycle of debt.
- **Unsecured Personal Loans**: Some personal loans, especially those without collateral, come with high interest rates.

Problematic Debts:

- **Variable Interest Rate Loans**: Loans with variable interest rates, such as certain types of mortgages or credit lines, can become problematic due to the unpredictability of their interest rates.
- **Long-Term Debts with High Cumulative Interest**: Some debts, such as extended car loans or mortgages with long amortization periods, may have moderate interest rates but can accrue significant interest over time.
- **Loans with Balloon Payments**: Debts that require a large lump-sum payment at the end of the loan term can be problematic, especially if you are not prepared for this significant outlay.

Strategies for Identifying:

- **Review Interest Rates**: Scrutinize each debt instrument you have to identify those with the highest interest rates. These are often the most financially draining and should be prioritized.
- **Analyze Terms and Conditions**: Understanding the terms, such as payment periods, penalties, and fees, is essential to identify debts that may become problematic.
- **Evaluate Impact on Cash Flow**: Some debts may have a significant impact on your monthly cash flow, even if their interest rates are not the highest. These should also be considered for prioritization.

Action Plan:

- **Prioritize Repayments**: Focus on paying off high-interest and problematic debts first. This might mean making minimum payments on lower-interest debts to free up more funds for the more pressing ones.

- **Consider Consolidation or Refinancing**: If you have multiple high-interest debts, consolidating them into a single loan with a lower interest rate can be beneficial. Similarly, refinancing can be an option for reducing interest rates and payment amounts.
- **Negotiate with Lenders**: In some cases, you may be able to negotiate better terms with your creditors, especially if you're facing financial hardships.

Identifying and prioritizing the repayment of high-interest and problematic debts is a key strategy in debt management. It not only helps in reducing the overall interest paid but also in regaining control over your financial health. The sooner these debts are addressed, the quicker you can move towards achieving financial stability and freedom.

Strategies for Debt Reduction

Reducing debt is a critical step towards financial liberation. The following strategies can be employed to systematically and effectively reduce debt, thereby enhancing your financial vitality:

Debt Snowball Method:

- **Concept**: Focus on paying off the smallest debts first, while making minimum payments on others. Once a small debt is paid off, the money used for its payment is then applied to the next smallest debt, creating a 'snowball' effect.
- **Advantage**: This method provides quick wins, which can be highly motivating.

Debt Avalanche Method:

- **Concept**: Prioritize debts with the highest interest rates, paying more towards these while maintaining minimum payments on others. This method saves money on interest over time.
- **Advantage**: It's cost-effective in the long run, reducing the total interest paid.

Consolidation of Debts:

- **Concept**: Combine multiple debts into one single loan, preferably at a lower interest rate. This simplifies the repayment process and can reduce monthly payments.
- **Advantage**: Streamlines multiple debts and can reduce the overall interest burden.

Refinancing:

- **Concept**: Replace a debt with another under new terms, typically with a lower interest rate.
- **Advantage**: Can significantly reduce the amount paid in interest, especially for large debts like mortgages.

Budgeting for Extra Payments:

- **Concept**: Allocate extra funds in your budget specifically for debt repayment. Even small additional payments can significantly shorten the debt repayment period.
- **Advantage**: Accelerates debt repayment and reduces total interest paid.

Increasing Income:

- **Concept**: Seek additional income sources such as part-time jobs, freelancing, or selling unused items.
- **Advantage**: Extra income can be directed towards debt, speeding up its elimination.

Negotiating with Creditors:

- **Concept**: Communicate with creditors to negotiate lower interest rates, waived fees, or more favorable repayment terms.
- **Advantage**: Can lead to more manageable repayment terms and lower overall debt.

Using Windfalls Wisely:

- **Concept**: Apply unexpected income, such as tax refunds, bonuses, or inheritances, directly towards debt repayment.
- **Advantage**: Large payments can make a significant dent in your overall debt balance.

Lifestyle Adjustments:

- **Concept**: Reduce unnecessary expenses and live below your means to free up more money for debt repayment.
- **Advantage**: Sustainable lifestyle changes can provide ongoing funds for debt reduction.

Professional Advice:

- **Concept**: Consult with a financial advisor or credit counselor for personalized advice and strategies.
- **Advantage**: Professional guidance can offer tailored solutions and strategies based on your unique financial situation.

Each of these strategies has its own merits, and the best approach may vary depending on individual circumstances such as the amount of debt, types of debt, income level, and personal financial goals. A combination of these strategies can often yield the best results. The key is to remain consistent and disciplined in your debt reduction efforts, keeping your eyes firmly set on the goal of financial freedom and vitality.

Snowball vs. Avalanche Methods: Pros and Cons

When addressing debt reduction, two popular strategies often considered are the snowball and avalanche methods. Each approach has distinct characteristics, with various advantages and disadvantages, making them suitable for different financial situations and personal preferences.

Snowball Method

- Pros:
  -
    - **Motivation Boost**: By paying off smaller debts first, individuals experience quick wins. This sense of accomplishment can be highly motivating and encourage continued debt repayment.
    - **Simplification**: As smaller debts are cleared, the number of payments and creditors to keep track of reduces, simplifying personal finance management.
    - **Behavioral Benefits**: This method aligns well with human behavior and psychology, providing tangible progress that can be more satisfying and encouraging.
  -
- Cons:
  -
    - **Higher Interest Costs**: Since the focus is not on the interest rates, you might end up paying more in total interest, especially if high-interest debts are larger and left for later.
    - **Longer Timeframe**: It might take longer to be completely debt-free compared to the avalanche method, particularly if high-interest debts are significant.

Avalanche Method

-
- Pros:
  -

- **Cost Efficiency**: By prioritizing high-interest debts, this method minimizes the total interest paid over time, making it more cost-effective in the long run.
- **Faster Debt Reduction**: In terms of total debt, this method can be faster as you are reducing the amount of compound interest accruing on larger, higher-rate debts.
- **Long-Term Financial Health**: It can lead to better financial outcomes as it logically targets the debts that are most expensive and damaging to your financial health.

Cons:

- **Motivational Challenges**: Without the quick wins of the snowball method, some individuals might find it harder to stay motivated, especially if the highest-interest debts are also the largest.
- **Complexity**: It requires a more analytical approach, which might be overwhelming for some, especially if they are not used to managing finances in detail.

In summary, the choice between the snowball and avalanche methods depends on individual preferences, financial situations, and psychological inclinations. If someone is motivated by quick wins and needs to simplify their debt situation, the snowball method may be more suitable. However, for individuals focused on reducing the overall cost of their debt and who are comfortable with a more analytical approach, the avalanche method is likely the better choice.

Ultimately, the key is consistency and commitment to whichever debt reduction strategy is chosen. Both methods, when followed diligently, lead towards the common goal of debt freedom and enhanced financial health.

Consolidation and Refinancing Options

Debt consolidation and refinancing are strategies used to manage and reduce debt more efficiently. Understanding these options is crucial for individuals seeking to streamline their debt repayment process and potentially save on interest costs.

Debt Consolidation

Overview: Debt consolidation involves combining multiple debts into a single loan. This process simplifies the management of debt by converting various payments with differing interest rates and terms into a single monthly payment.

Pros:

- **Simplified Payments**: Consolidating multiple debts into one loan makes it easier to manage payments, reducing the likelihood of missed or late payments.
- **Potential for Lower Interest Rates**: If the consolidation loan has a lower average interest rate compared to the original debts, the overall interest cost could be reduced.
- **Improved Credit Score**: Consistent on-time payments on the consolidated loan can positively impact credit scores over time.

Cons:

- **Risk of Higher Overall Cost**: If the term of the consolidated loan is significantly longer than the original debts, the total interest paid over time could be higher, even if the rate is lower.
- **Collateral Risk**: If the consolidation loan is secured (e.g., home equity loan), there is a risk of losing the collateral in case of default.
- **Initial Costs**: Some consolidation loans might come with fees, such as origination fees or balance transfer fees.

Refinancing

Overview: Refinancing involves replacing an existing debt with a new loan, typically with different terms and often a lower interest rate. This can be applied to various types of debt, including mortgages, student loans, and credit cards.

Pros:

- **Lower Interest Rates**: Refinancing can secure a lower interest rate, which can significantly reduce the amount paid over the life of the loan.
- **Altered Loan Terms**: Refinancing can adjust the terms of the loan, such as extending or shortening the repayment period based on individual needs.
- **Improved Cash Flow**: Lower monthly payments through refinancing can free up cash for other financial goals or needs.

Cons:

- **Longer Repayment Period**: Extending the loan term through refinancing may lower monthly payments but increase the total interest paid over the life of the loan.
- **Refinancing Costs**: There may be costs associated with refinancing, such as application fees, origination fees, and potentially prepayment penalties on the original loan.

- **Credit Score Impact**: Applying for refinancing can trigger a hard inquiry on your credit report, temporarily impacting your credit score.

In conclusion, both debt consolidation and refinancing can be effective tools for managing and reducing debt. However, it is essential to carefully consider the terms, potential savings, and risks associated with each option. Individuals should assess their financial situation, conduct thorough research, and possibly consult with a financial advisor to determine the most suitable approach for their specific circumstances.

Negotiating with Creditors: Tips and Techniques

Engaging in negotiations with creditors can be a pivotal step towards managing and reducing debt. Effective negotiation can potentially lead to lower interest rates, waived fees, or more manageable repayment terms. Below are key strategies and considerations for successfully negotiating with creditors:

Preparation and Research

- **Understand Your Debt**: Clearly comprehend the amount owed, interest rates, payment history, and any fees associated with each debt.
- **Know Your Creditors**: Different creditors have varying policies and willingness to negotiate. Research their past behaviors and approaches to debt settlement.

Communication Strategies

- **Initial Contact**: When reaching out to creditors, be polite but assertive. Clearly state your intention to negotiate your debt terms.
- **Clarity and Honesty**: Be transparent about your financial situation. Provide a clear picture of why you are struggling with repayments and what you are capable of paying.
- **Document Communication**: Keep a detailed record of all communications, including names, dates, and the content of discussions.

Negotiation Techniques

- **Offer a Lump-Sum Payment**: If possible, offer a lump-sum payment that is less than the total debt owed. Creditors often prefer a guaranteed partial payment to the uncertainty of future payments.
- **Request a Lower Interest Rate**: A reduction in interest rate can significantly decrease the amount paid over time. Explain how a lower rate could make payments more manageable for you.
- **Ask for a Payment Plan**: Propose a payment plan that is realistic for your financial situation. Be specific about what you can pay monthly.

Dealing with Hardship

- **Hardship Programs**: Inquire about any hardship programs the creditor may offer, especially if your financial difficulties are due to circumstances like illness, unemployment, or a natural disaster.
- **Debt Management Plans**: Mention your willingness to enroll in a debt management plan as a show of commitment to repaying your debt.

Consider Professional Help

- **Debt Settlement Companies**: If negotiations are complex, consider seeking assistance from a debt settlement company. However, research these services thoroughly, as fees and impacts on credit scores vary.
- **Legal Advice**: In certain situations, consulting with an attorney specializing in debt settlement can provide legal insights and bolster your negotiation strategy.

Agreement and Follow-Up

- **Written Agreement**: Ensure any agreement reached is documented in writing. Verbal agreements are difficult to enforce.
- **Compliance and Monitoring**: Once an agreement is in place, adhere strictly to the terms. Continuously monitor the situation and maintain communication with the creditor, especially if your financial situation changes.

In summary, negotiating with creditors requires a blend of preparation, clear communication, and understanding of your rights and options. While it can be a challenging process, successful negotiation can lead to more favorable terms and a clearer path towards debt reduction. Always approach negotiations with a realistic perspective, and consider seeking professional advice when necessary.

Building and Repairing Credit: A Journey to Financial Resilience

Welcome to the chapter where we turn your credit story into one of triumph and empowerment. You know, credit is much like a personal diary that the financial world reads. It tells them a story about you. But here's the secret – you are the author of that story, and it's never too late to start a new chapter.

Understanding Credit Scores: The Backbone of Your Financial Identity

- Think of your credit score as a trust score. It's what lenders, landlords, and sometimes even employers use to gauge how reliable you are with money. Did you know that the components of this score are like ingredients in a recipe? Each one - payment history, credit utilization, and others - blend to create your financial flavor.

Starting from Scratch: Building Credit Wisely

- Remember your first bike ride without training wheels? Building credit is similar. Start with tools like secured credit cards or credit builder loans. These are your financial training wheels, helping you build muscle and confidence.

Good Credit Habits: The Daily Financial Workout

- Consistency is key. Just like you wouldn't run a marathon without training, don't expect your credit score to soar without consistent, good habits. This means paying bills on time and keeping that credit card balance well under the limit. Think of it as a daily financial workout.

Navigating Through Stormy Credit Weather: Repairing Damaged Credit

- We've all been there – a few missteps and suddenly you're in a credit storm. First, get a raincoat by disputing any errors on your credit reports. Then, start repairing the leaks by chipping away at debts. Remember, Rome wasn't built in a day, and rebuilding credit takes time too.

The Art of Diversification: Mixing Up Your Credit

- Variety is the spice of life, and it's also good for your credit score. A mix of credit types shows lenders that you can handle different kinds of financial responsibilities. It's like a portfolio of your financial skills.

Credit Monitoring: Keeping an Eye on Your Financial Health

- Just as you might use a fitness tracker to monitor your physical health, use credit monitoring tools to keep an eye on your financial fitness. It's not just about watching the numbers change; it's about understanding what impacts them.

The Long Game: Building and Maintaining Credit Over Time

- Like any journey worth taking, building and repairing credit is a marathon, not a sprint. It's about making small changes today that lead to big results tomorrow. Be patient and persistent. Your future self will thank you.

In the end, remember that your credit score is not just a number; it's a reflection of your financial story. And the beautiful thing about stories? They can always be rewritten. So, let's grab a pen and start writing a bestseller.

As we venture deeper into the realm of credit, it's essential to understand the foundation upon which it stands. Let's demystify this critical aspect that silently but significantly influences your financial journey. Imagine it as a complex puzzle, and now we're about to piece it together.

Transitioning to How Credit Scores are Calculated: Unveiling the Mystery

Have you ever watched a magician and wondered how they perform their tricks? Similarly, credit scores often seem shrouded in mystery. But here's the good news: unlike a magician's secrets, the formula behind your credit score isn't a guarded mystery. It's a logical, understandable system, and we're about to delve into its inner workings.

Understanding how credit scores are calculated is like having a roadmap for your financial journey. It's empowering to know what influences your score, and how you can steer it in the right direction. So, let's embark on this enlightening journey and unlock the secrets behind these influential numbers.

In the dynamic landscape of financial health, understanding how credit scores are calculated is akin to deciphering a vital code – one that can unlock doors to opportunities or, conversely, keep them firmly shut. It's not just a number; it's a reflection of your financial narrative.

The Magic Behind the Numbers: How Credit Scores are Calculated

Imagine your credit score as a character in the story of your financial life. Just as a character is shaped by actions and decisions, your credit score is the culmination of your financial behaviors. Here's a breakdown of this intricate calculation:

Payment History – The Backbone of Your Score:

- Think of this as the plot of your story. Just as a story has a timeline, your payment history tracks whether you've been timely or tardy in paying debts. It's the most significant factor, accounting for about 35% of your score. Remember, every payment is a sentence in the story of your financial reliability.

Credit Utilization – The Balancing Act:

- This is like the setting of your financial tale, representing how much of your available credit you're using. It's about balance – using enough to build a history, but not so much that you appear reliant on credit. This factor constitutes approximately 30% of your score.

Length of Credit History – The Depth of Your Financial Story:

- Consider this as the backstory of your character. It accounts for about 15% of your score. A longer credit history provides a deeper insight into your financial habits, much like a well-developed character in a novel is more relatable and trustworthy.

Credit Mix – The Diversity in Your Financial Portfolio:

- This is akin to the different subplots in your story, contributing about 10%. It shows how well you handle different types of credit, like revolving (credit cards) and installment loans (mortgage, car loans). Diversity in your credit mix indicates a well-rounded financial character.

New Credit – The Emerging Plot Twists:

- Making up the remaining 10%, this is like introducing new characters or twists in your story. Opening new credit lines can be a double-edged sword; it can show your ability to handle more, but too much too fast can seem risky, like a plot that's too convoluted.

The Female Perspective in Credit Scoring:

Let's acknowledge that for women, the credit score narrative can have its unique challenges. Historically, women have faced hurdles in establishing and maintaining credit independently. It's crucial to empower women with the knowledge to build strong credit scores, ensuring their financial stories are ones of triumph and resilience.

In conclusion, your credit score is not just a number but a living part of your financial identity. Understanding its composition allows you to author a more favorable financial future. Just like a well-written story captivates its readers, a strong credit score can open up a world of possibilities. Let's turn the page to the next chapter of your financial journey, shall we?

Improving your credit score is a journey akin to cultivating a flourishing garden. It requires patience, consistent effort, and strategic planning. Here, we'll delve into effective strategies to nurture and enhance your credit score, transforming it into a robust reflection of your financial diligence.

1. Timely Payments: The Cornerstone of Credit Health

- Consistency in making payments on time is fundamental. It's like watering your garden regularly. Set up reminders or automate payments to ensure you never miss a deadline. This consistent care boosts your credit score gradually but significantly.

2. Credit Utilization: Maintaining a Healthy Balance

Strive to keep your credit utilization low, ideally below 30% of your available credit. It's like pruning your plants; too much debt can overshadow your score. Regularly check your balances and consider paying down high balances to keep your credit utilization in check.

3. Length of Credit History: Patience Pays Off

Cultivate your credit accounts over time. Avoid closing old accounts, as they contribute to your credit history length. It's like nurturing a perennial plant in your garden; over time, it grows stronger and more resilient.

4. Diverse Credit Mix: A Varied Financial Portfolio

A mix of credit types (revolving credit, installment loans) can be beneficial, much like a diverse garden with various types of plants. However, only open new accounts as necessary. It's not about having numerous accounts but a well-managed variety.

5. Limit New Credit Inquiries: Strategic Growth

Each time you apply for credit, a hard inquiry is recorded, potentially lowering your score temporarily. Think of it as cautious gardening; too many new plants at once can overwhelm the space. Apply for new credit sparingly and strategically.

6. Regularly Monitor Your Credit Report: Vigilant Oversight

Regularly review your credit reports for errors or fraudulent activities. It's like keeping an eye out for weeds or pests in your garden. Dispute any inaccuracies promptly to ensure your credit report accurately reflects your financial habits.

7. Address Delinquencies: Healing Damaged Credit

If you have delinquent accounts or debts, focus on addressing them. Negotiate payment plans with creditors if needed. This is akin to rehabilitating a neglected section of your garden, requiring effort and attention to restore its health.

8. Credit Building Tools: Utilizing Financial Aids

Consider tools like secured credit cards or credit-builder loans if you're starting out or rebuilding credit. These are like gardening tools, aiding in cultivating a healthy credit score.

Incorporating these strategies into your financial routine can significantly impact your credit score over time. Remember, improving your credit score is a process, not an overnight transformation. Just as a well-tended garden doesn't bloom immediately, credit scores require time to reflect the positive changes in your financial behavior. By adopting these practices, you're not only enhancing your credit score but also nurturing a more secure financial future.

Addressing errors on your credit report is an essential aspect of maintaining a healthy financial profile. It's akin to weeding a garden; removing inaccuracies can significantly enhance the overall health of your credit score. Here are steps to effectively deal with credit report errors:

1. Regular Review of Credit Reports

- Regular monitoring of your credit reports from the three major credit bureaus (Equifax, Experian, and TransUnion) is crucial. Obtain a free report annually from each bureau through AnnualCreditReport.com. This habitual review is like inspecting your garden regularly for signs of trouble.

2. Identifying and Documenting Inaccuracies

- If you spot an error, document it meticulously. This may include highlighting the discrepancies and gathering supporting documents like payment records or correspondence with creditors. Think of this as gathering evidence to support your case for a healthier credit environment.

3. Filing a Dispute with the Credit Bureaus

- File a dispute with the credit bureau that reports the error. This can typically be done online, by mail, or over the phone. Provide all necessary documentation to support your claim. The process is similar to removing weeds; it's vital to get to the root to ensure they don't reappear.

4. Simultaneously Contacting the Information Provider

- Inform the creditor or financial institution that provided the incorrect information to the credit bureau. Send them a dispute letter along with the supporting documents. This step is like addressing the source of the problem in your garden, ensuring it doesn't recur.

5. Following Up and Monitoring Progress

- After filing your dispute, monitor the progress. The credit bureau typically investigates disputes within 30 days. Stay vigilant, like a gardener keeping an eye on previously affected areas for signs of recurring issues.

6. Understanding Your Rights

Familiarize yourself with the Fair Credit Reporting Act (FCRA), which protects your right to an accurate credit report. It obligates credit bureaus and information providers to correct any inaccuracies. Knowing your rights is akin to understanding the ecosystem in which your garden thrives.

7. Seeking Professional Assistance if Needed

If the dispute process becomes overwhelming or if the errors persist, consider seeking help from a credit counseling service. These professionals can offer guidance, much like a master gardener providing expert advice.

8. Maintaining Records

Keep a detailed record of all communications and documents related to your dispute. This meticulous record-keeping can be invaluable if the issue escalates or requires further action.

Addressing errors on your credit report demands attention to detail, persistence, and patience. It's a crucial step in nurturing and maintaining a robust credit score. Just as a well-maintained garden thrives, a credit report free of errors accurately reflects your financial responsibility, opening doors to better credit opportunities and financial wellbeing.

Credit utilization and its effective management play pivotal roles in shaping one's financial health, particularly in the context of credit scores. Understanding and adeptly managing credit utilization can be likened to a balancing act in a well-orchestrated financial performance. Here's an exploration of this concept:

1. Understanding Credit Utilization

Credit utilization refers to the percentage of your available credit that you're using at any given time. It's calculated by dividing your total credit card balances by your total credit card limits. Imagine it as a gauge in your financial dashboard, indicating how much of your available credit you're currently tapping into.

2. The Impact on Credit Scores

Credit utilization is a critical component of your credit score, typically accounting for around 30% of your FICO score. High utilization can signal to lenders that you're overly reliant on credit or potentially facing financial strain, which may negatively affect your creditworthiness. Think of it as a signal flare in your financial landscape, visible to potential lenders.

3. Ideal Credit Utilization Ratio

The general recommendation is to keep your credit utilization below 30%. This threshold is not a hard limit but rather a guideline. Maintaining a ratio significantly lower than this can be beneficial. It's akin to a safety buffer in your financial strategy, providing room for unforeseen expenditures without harming your credit score.

4. Strategies for Managing Credit Utilization

- **Paying Balances More Frequently**: Instead of waiting for the statement, consider making multiple payments throughout the month. This tactic can keep your balances lower, thereby reducing your utilization ratio.
- **Requesting Higher Credit Limits**: Increasing your credit limit while maintaining or reducing your spending can lower your utilization ratio. However, this should be approached with caution, as it could potentially lead to increased spending.
- **Balancing Multiple Cards**: Distributing balances across multiple cards can help manage utilization. However, this requires careful monitoring to ensure that no single card's utilization rate spikes.
- **Monitoring Credit Card Statements**: Regularly reviewing statements helps you keep track of spending and manage your balances proactively.

5. The Perils of High Utilization

- High utilization can be a red flag for lenders and can lead to adverse effects on your credit score. It's like running a high-speed engine continuously; it may lead to wear and tear (in this case, on your creditworthiness).

6. Utilization Across Multiple Cards

- It's important to manage the utilization of each card individually as well as the overall utilization across all cards. High utilization on a single card can be just as damaging as high overall utilization.

7. Long-term Management

- Building healthy credit habits, like regular monitoring and responsible spending, can lead to a better credit score over time. Think of it as a long-term investment in your financial fitness, where disciplined practices pay off in the form of robust credit health.

In conclusion, credit utilization is a dynamic and integral component of one's financial profile. By understanding and managing it judiciously, individuals can significantly bolster their credit scores, much like a tightrope walker mastering the art of balance, ensuring their passage across the financial landscape is both steady and secure.

Having delved into the nuanced realm of credit utilization and its indispensable role in fortifying one's financial profile, let us now transition seamlessly into another vital aspect of fiscal prudence: the responsible use of credit cards. This topic is akin to an advanced course in financial stewardship, where the principles of discipline, foresight, and strategic planning are paramount.

Credit cards, when used judiciously, can be powerful tools for building credit, earning rewards, and managing cash flow. However, they can also lead to a precarious path of debt accumulation if not handled with care and foresight. Responsible use of credit cards is not just about staying within credit limits or paying bills on time; it encompasses a broader spectrum of financial habits and decisions. These include understanding the nuances of credit card terms, the implications of various types of transactions, and the long-term impact of today's spending decisions on future financial health.

As we explore the responsible use of credit cards, we shall unearth strategies to harness their benefits while mitigating risks, ensuring these financial instruments serve as allies in the journey towards fiscal stability and prosperity. This transition marks a shift from understanding a component of the credit score system to mastering a tool that, when used adeptly, can enhance one's financial narrative significantly.

In our journey through the intricate world of personal finance, let's turn our attention to a topic that's often a double-edged sword: the responsible use of credit cards. Now, I remember the first time I got a credit card. It felt like I had been handed a magic wand – with the power to buy anything! But, as with any great power, it came with great responsibility.

Credit cards, in their essence, are not just spending tools; they are financial instruments that, when used wisely, can bolster your credit score and unlock doors to future financial opportunities. They are like those gym memberships – beneficial if used regularly and responsibly, but potentially disastrous if mishandled.

1. **Understanding the Terms**: Just like when you're signing a business contract, you need to know what you're getting into with a credit card. Interest rates, late fees, annual charges – these aren't just fine print; they're the terms of your financial health. It's crucial to understand these to avoid falling into a debt trap.

2. **Budgeting and Tracking**: Imagine you're running a business, but you never keep track of your expenses. Sounds like a recipe for disaster, right? The same applies to using credit cards. Use budgeting tools or apps – they are like having a financial advisor in your pocket, keeping you in check.

3. **Paying More Than the Minimum**: This is where the magic of compounding interest can turn against you. Paying just the minimum amount is like trying to fill a leaking bucket – you'll never get ahead. Treat your credit card like a short-term loan and aim to pay it off in full.

4. **Reward Optimization**: Credit card rewards are like those business perks – if used wisely, they can be incredibly beneficial. Whether it's cashback, points, or miles, choose a card that aligns with

your lifestyle and spending patterns. But remember, rewards are only rewarding if you're not carrying a balance.

5. Credit Utilization Ratio: This is like your business's debt-to-income ratio. Keeping your credit utilization low shows that you're good at managing your credit – a critical factor in your credit score. Aim to keep it below 30%.

6. Building Credit History: Just as a solid business reputation doesn't happen overnight, a good credit history takes time to build. Consistent and responsible use of a credit card can help establish a credit history that speaks to your reliability.

7. Emergency Use Only: Consider your credit card as a lifeline, not a lifestyle. Use it for emergencies, not extravagances. It's like having a safety net – it's there to catch you, not to live in it.

In conclusion, think of your credit card as a tool in your financial toolkit – one that requires skill and caution to use effectively. It's not about abstinence, but about smart, strategic usage. Remember, a credit card can be your ally on the path to financial

The art of balancing credit utilization and repayment is akin to walking a tightrope in the world of personal finance. This delicate act requires a blend of discipline, strategy, and foresight, much like a seasoned acrobat performing a meticulous routine.

1. The Harmony of Utilization: Credit utilization, the ratio of your credit card balances to your credit limits, plays a significant role in shaping your credit score. It's like a financial barometer, indicating how you manage your credit. A high utilization rate can signal potential overextension, while a low rate suggests prudent financial management. Aim for a utilization rate below 30% – it's the sweet spot that credit bureaus often favor.

2. Strategic Repayment: Paying off your credit card debt is not just about meeting the minimum payments. It's about devising a strategy that aligns with your financial goals and capabilities. If you're juggling multiple cards, consider the avalanche or snowball methods. The avalanche method focuses on paying off the card with the highest interest rate first, while the snowball method tackles the smallest debt first. Both have their merits, and the choice depends on what keeps you motivated and aligned with your financial vision.

3. The Timing Factor: The timing of your payments can significantly impact your credit score. Paying your bills before the statement closing date can lower the balance that's reported to credit bureaus, hence reducing your utilization ratio. It's like making a timely strategic move in a game of chess, one that can give you an upper hand in the credit scoring game.

4. Increase Credit Limits Judiciously: Requesting an increase in your credit limit can be a double-edged sword. On one hand, it can lower your credit utilization ratio, but on the other, it can tempt you to overspend. Approach this tactic with caution and self-awareness. It's like expanding your business – beneficial if managed well, but risky if not.

5. Regular Monitoring: Keep a close eye on your credit card statements, just as a business owner scrutinizes their financial statements. This not only helps in catching any unauthorized transactions but also provides insights into your spending patterns. Regular monitoring is key to maintaining a balance.

6. Emergency Preparedness: Reserve your credit card for genuine emergencies. Relying on it for everyday expenses can lead you down a slippery slope of debt. It's like having an emergency fund in a business – it should be there to support you in times of unexpected financial downturns, not for regular operational expenses.

Balancing credit utilization and repayment is an ongoing process, requiring constant vigilance and adaptation. It's about finding that equilibrium where your credit card usage positively reinforces your credit score while keeping debt levels manageable. Remember, in the realm of credit, as in life, balance is not something you find, but something you create.

Understanding the impact of different types of credit on your credit score is crucial in the realm of personal financial management. The composition of your credit portfolio, much like a well-diversified investment portfolio, can significantly influence your creditworthiness in the eyes of lenders. Let us delve into the various types of credit and how they can shape your credit score:

Revolving Credit: This type of credit, primarily represented by credit cards, offers you a credit limit up to which you can repeatedly borrow. The utilization of this credit type is closely watched. High utilization can negatively impact your credit score, as it may suggest a reliance on credit for day-to-day expenses. Conversely, responsible management, characterized by low utilization and timely payments, can bolster your score. It's akin to managing a business's working capital efficiently.

Installment Credit: Loans such as mortgages, auto loans, and student loans fall under this category. Here, you borrow a fixed amount and repay it in scheduled installments over a set period. These types of credit add diversity to your credit profile and can improve your score if handled responsibly. Timely payments on these loans reflect your reliability and financial discipline, much like a business adhering to its debt commitments and thereby enhancing its creditworthiness.

Open Credit: This less common type involves accounts where the balance is to be paid in full each month. A classic example is a charge card. While not as impactful as revolving or installment credit, responsible usage of open credit can contribute positively to your credit score by demonstrating your ability to pay off debts promptly.

The Mix of Credit: Credit scoring models, like FICO, consider the mix of different credit types as a factor in determining your score. A diverse mix, comprising both revolving and installment credit, is often viewed favorably. It indicates your ability to manage different types of borrowing responsibly. Imagine a well-balanced investment portfolio – it typically includes a mix of assets (stocks, bonds, real estate, etc.) to mitigate risk and maximize returns. Similarly, a mix of credit types can show lenders that you are capable of handling various financial obligations effectively.

New Credit and Inquiries: Every time you apply for a new credit line, a hard inquiry is recorded on your credit report. Multiple inquiries in a short period can negatively impact your score, as it may suggest financial distress. However, the effect of these inquiries diminishes over time. It's comparable to a business seeking new capital; while it's essential for growth, excessive borrowing in a short timeframe can signal financial instability.

Duration of Credit History: The length of your credit history also plays a role. A longer credit history, assuming it's marked by positive behavior, can enhance your credit score. It demonstrates a prolonged period of financial responsibility.

In summary, the types of credit you have and how you manage them play a significant role in shaping your credit score. A balanced approach, featuring a mix of different credit types, all managed with discipline and foresight, is key to maintaining and improving your credit score. Just as a balanced diet contributes to overall health, a balanced credit profile contributes to a healthy credit score.

The psychology of spending and debt is a fascinating and complex area, blending behavioral economics, psychology, and finance. It delves into the underlying reasons why individuals engage in certain financial behaviors, including spending habits and accruing debt. This exploration is not only crucial for personal financial management but also for understanding broader economic phenomena.

Emotional Spending: Spending can often be driven by emotions rather than rational decision-making. This phenomenon, known as emotional spending, occurs when individuals make purchases to fulfill emotional needs, such as happiness, stress relief, or a sense of belonging. This is akin to emotional eating, where food is used as a comfort rather than just for nutritional needs.

Instant Gratification vs. Delayed Gratification: The human tendency to prefer immediate rewards to future rewards, known as instant gratification, plays a significant role in spending and debt accumulation. This can lead to impulsive spending and reliance on credit, as the immediate pleasure or convenience of a purchase overshadows the future obligation of repayment. Delayed gratification, on the other hand, involves resisting an immediate reward in anticipation of a future benefit, which is a critical skill in financial management.

Cognitive Biases and Spending: Various cognitive biases can influence spending behavior. For example, the anchoring effect, where the first piece of information (like an original price) serves as an anchor for making decisions (such as assessing the value of a discount), can lead to unnecessary spending. Similarly, the bandwagon effect can lead to increased spending, driven by the desire to conform to social norms or trends.

The Role of Social Influences: Social factors, including peer pressure and social media influence, significantly impact spending habits. The desire to keep up with peers or emulate lifestyles seen on social media can lead to increased spending and debt. This phenomenon is often referred to as "keeping up with the Joneses."

Debt as a Psychological Burden: Debt is not just a financial problem; it can also be a significant psychological burden. The stress of owing money can lead to anxiety, depression, and a sense of hopelessness. The mental load of debt is similar to carrying a heavy physical weight, constantly present and influencing all aspects of life.

Escaping the Debt Cycle: Breaking free from a cycle of debt often requires more than just financial discipline; it necessitates a change in mindset and behavior. This involves setting clear goals, creating a budget, and developing a long-term financial plan. Just as overcoming any deep-rooted habit or addiction requires a holistic approach, escaping the debt cycle requires addressing both the behavioral and the psychological aspects of spending.

Mindful Spending: Cultivating mindfulness in spending, where each financial decision is made consciously and with full awareness of its implications, can be a powerful tool in managing personal finances. This approach encourages individuals to think critically about their spending choices, considering not only their immediate impact but also their long-term financial goals.

In conclusion, understanding the psychology of spending and debt is critical for effective financial management. It involves recognizing and addressing the emotional and psychological factors that drive financial behavior, along with the practical aspects of budgeting and financial planning. By exploring these psychological underpinnings, individuals can develop healthier spending habits, reduce debt, and work towards a more secure financial future.

In delving into the psychology of spending and debt, we have uncovered various factors that shape our financial behavior, from cognitive biases to the influence of social factors. However, one of the most potent and often overlooked aspects of this complex interplay is emotional spending. This phenomenon, which frequently slips under the radar of our conscious financial decisions, has a profound impact on the accumulation of debt.

Emotional Spending: A Deep Dive

Emotional spending occurs when purchases are made primarily to satisfy emotional needs rather than practical ones. This behavior can be triggered by a range of emotions – from stress, sadness, and loneliness to euphoria and a desire for reward. Unlike rational spending, which is guided by needs and budgetary constraints, emotional spending is impulsive and often leads to purchases that are not only unnecessary but also financially unviable.

The direct impact of this behavior on debt is substantial. When individuals spend money emotionally, they often do so without regard to their current financial situation, leading to increased reliance on credit cards and loans. This immediate gratification, while soothing in the short term, adds to the debt burden. Over time, this pattern can evolve into a vicious cycle: emotional distress leads to spending, which then leads to increased debt, which in turn causes further emotional distress.

Furthermore, emotional spending can sabotage long-term financial goals. Funds that could be allocated towards savings, investments, or debt repayment are instead spent on items or experiences that offer temporary emotional relief. This diversion of funds not only exacerbates existing debt but also delays, or even derails, the achievement of financial stability and independence.

To truly understand the dynamics of personal debt, it is essential to explore the role of emotional spending. By acknowledging and addressing this behavior, individuals can take a significant step towards regaining control of their financial lives and breaking free from the chains of debt.

Emotional Spending and Its Impact on Debt

Emotional spending is a phenomenon where purchases are driven more by feelings than by needs or financial plans. It's a common experience – who hasn't been tempted to buy something as a pick-me-up on a bad day or as a celebration when we're feeling good? While occasional indulgences are a normal part of life, consistent emotional spending can have a significant and often underestimated impact on debt.

The Mechanics of Emotional Spending

This behavior typically manifests when emotions, rather than rational financial planning, take the lead in decision-making. Emotions like stress, sadness, joy, or even boredom can trigger a spending spree. The momentary euphoria that accompanies a purchase can be addictive – it's a quick fix for negative feelings or a way to amplify positive ones. Unfortunately, this relief is usually short-lived and can lead to a cycle where spending becomes a habitual response to emotional triggers.

The Debt Spiral

The most direct consequence of emotional spending is its impact on debt. When people spend emotionally, they often do so impulsively, disregarding their budget or financial constraints. This usually means turning to credit cards or loans for immediate gratification. The result is a gradual accumulation of debt – each emotional purchase adds a layer, often leading to significant sums over time.

As the debt grows, so does the interest and the financial burden. This can lead to increased stress and anxiety – emotions that ironically may trigger further emotional spending, creating a vicious cycle.

Long-Term Consequences

Beyond immediate debt, emotional spending can derail long-term financial goals. Money that could be saved or invested is spent instead. This not only increases debt but also means lost opportunities – compound interest on savings or returns on investments that never occur. In the long term, this behavior can delay or prevent important life milestones like buying a house, saving for retirement, or funding education.

Breaking the Cycle

Addressing emotional spending requires a two-pronged approach: understanding the emotional triggers and adopting practical financial strategies.

Emotional Awareness: Recognizing the emotions that trigger spending is crucial. This can involve self-reflection or professional help, such as therapy. Mindfulness techniques can also be beneficial in managing emotional responses and breaking the habit of turning to spending as a coping mechanism.

Financial Strategies: Creating and sticking to a budget is essential. This involves not just tracking expenses but also setting clear financial goals. Using tools like budgeting apps or financial planners can help maintain this discipline.

Building Healthier Habits: Finding alternative ways to cope with emotions can be a game changer. Instead of shopping, one might turn to exercise, hobbies, or spending time with loved ones. It's about creating new, positive habits to replace the old, detrimental ones.

Seek Professional Advice: For some, professional financial advice or debt counseling can be a turning point. These experts can offer strategies for managing and reducing debt, as well as provide guidance on budgeting and financial planning.

Conclusion

Understanding and managing emotional spending is not just about improving financial health; it's also about enhancing overall well-being. By recognizing and addressing the emotional roots of spending, individuals can make more empowered financial decisions, reduce debt, and move closer to achieving their long-term financial goals.

Creating a Mindset for Debt-Free Living

Adopting a mindset for debt-free living is a transformative process that involves much more than just practical financial management. It requires a fundamental shift in how one perceives and interacts with money, debt, and personal finance. This mindset is about creating a sustainable and healthy financial lifestyle, underpinned by discipline, awareness, and a proactive approach to managing money.

Fundamental Principles of a Debt-Free Mindset

Value-Based Spending: This principle involves aligning your spending with your personal values and priorities. It's about understanding what truly matters to you and ensuring that your financial choices reflect these values. This approach leads to more deliberate and fulfilling spending, which naturally reduces unnecessary expenses and helps prevent debt accumulation.

Long-Term Vision: A debt-free mindset is anchored in long-term thinking. It's about recognizing the impact of today's financial decisions on your future. This means prioritizing saving and investing over immediate gratification, understanding the power of compound interest, and planning for future needs and goals.

Emotional Intelligence with Money: Understanding the emotional aspect of money is crucial. It involves recognizing emotional spending triggers and developing healthier coping mechanisms that don't involve spending. It also means managing money-related stress and anxiety effectively.

Knowledge and Education: Continually educating oneself about personal finance, investment, and money management is a cornerstone of this mindset. This could involve reading books, attending workshops, or consulting with financial advisors. Knowledge empowers you to make informed decisions and stay ahead of financial challenges.

Budgeting and Tracking: A debt-free lifestyle relies heavily on the ability to budget and track expenses. This discipline ensures that you are always aware of your financial position, can identify areas for improvement, and are able to make adjustments as necessary.

Strategies for Cultivating a Debt-Free Mindset

Set Clear Financial Goals: Establish specific, measurable, achievable, relevant, and time-bound (SMART) financial goals. These should include short-term, medium-term, and long-term objectives, providing a clear roadmap for your financial journey.

Practice Gratitude and Contentment: Fostering a sense of gratitude for what you have can reduce the urge to spend on unnecessary items. Contentment reduces the influence of societal pressures to live beyond one's means.

Create and Maintain a Budget: A well-maintained budget is a powerful tool. It not only helps in tracking and controlling spending but also in making informed financial decisions.

Build an Emergency Fund: This fund acts as a buffer against unexpected expenses, reducing the need to go into debt when emergencies arise.

Prioritize Debt Repayment: If you currently have debt, prioritize paying it off. Consider strategies like the debt snowball or avalanche methods, which are effective in debt reduction.

Cultivate Self-Discipline: Living debt-free requires a high level of self-discipline, especially in a consumer-driven society. It involves making tough choices and sometimes foregoing immediate pleasures for long-term benefits.

Seek Community and Support: Surrounding yourself with like-minded individuals or communities can provide support and motivation. Sharing experiences and learning from others who are also committed to a debt-free lifestyle can be incredibly empowering.

Conclusion

Embracing a mindset for debt-free living is about much more than just numbers and budgets. It's a holistic approach that encompasses financial discipline, emotional intelligence, and a shift in values and priorities. By adopting this mindset, individuals can not only free themselves from the burden of debt but also pave the way for a more secure, fulfilling financial future.

Behavioral Changes for Sustainable Financial Habits

Sustainable financial habits are integral to achieving long-term financial stability and success. These habits are not just about meticulous budgeting or investment strategies; they are deeply rooted in one's behavioral patterns and mindset. Making lasting changes to these behaviors can have a profound impact on one's financial health.

Understanding Behavioral Finance

Before delving into specific behavioral changes, it's important to grasp the concept of behavioral finance. This field studies the psychological influences and biases that affect financial behaviors.

Recognizing and understanding these biases is the first step in modifying behaviors for better financial outcomes.

Key Behavioral Changes for Financial Sustainability

Developing a Proactive Mindset: Moving from a reactive to a proactive financial stance is crucial. This means planning for future needs, anticipating potential financial challenges, and making decisions based on long-term goals rather than immediate desires or fears.

Cultivating Financial Self-Awareness: Regularly assess and understand your financial habits, including spending patterns, emotional triggers for spending, and areas of financial strength and weakness. Self-awareness is critical in identifying behaviors that need change.

Embracing Delayed Gratification: The ability to delay gratification is fundamental for financial sustainability. It involves resisting the urge for immediate pleasure or satisfaction in favor of more significant and lasting rewards, such as financial security or achieving long-term goals.

Adopting a Goal-Oriented Approach: Setting clear, achievable financial goals is a powerful motivator and guide for behavior. These goals can range from short-term objectives like saving for a vacation to long-term aims like retirement planning.

Practicing Consistent and Regular Savings: Make saving a habitual practice, not an afterthought. Automating savings can be an effective way to ensure consistency, as it removes the temptation to spend what should be saved.

Increasing Financial Literacy: Continual learning and understanding of financial concepts, market trends, and investment strategies empower you to make informed decisions. This knowledge also helps in demystifying financial jargon and overcoming intimidation in financial matters.

Building and Maintaining a Budget: A well-structured budget is the cornerstone of good financial habits. It helps in tracking expenses, identifying wasteful spending, and adjusting allocations in line with financial goals.

Reducing Impulsive Spending: Impulsive spending is often a major hurdle in financial stability. Implementing strategies like the 24-hour rule (waiting for a day before making a non-essential purchase) can help curb this habit.

Seeking Professional Advice When Necessary: Don't hesitate to seek help from financial advisors or counselors, especially when making significant financial decisions or if you find yourself struggling to manage your finances effectively.

Reflecting and Adjusting Regularly: Regular reflection on financial progress and willingness to adjust strategies as needed is vital. Life circumstances and goals evolve, and so should your financial strategies.

Conclusion

Transforming one's financial habits is a journey that involves more than just the technical aspects of money management. It requires a holistic approach, encompassing behavioral changes, mindset shifts, and continuous learning. By adopting these behavioral changes, individuals can establish a strong foundation for long-term financial sustainability and security.

Legal Considerations and Rights in Financial Management

When navigating the financial landscape, understanding the legal framework and knowing your rights is paramount. This knowledge not only helps in making informed decisions but also in protecting oneself from potential legal pitfalls and unfair practices. Here, we will explore key legal considerations and rights that individuals should be aware of in the context of personal finance.

Understanding Credit Laws

Fair Credit Reporting Act (FCRA): This act ensures the accuracy, fairness, and privacy of information in the files of consumer reporting agencies. You have the right to obtain a free credit report annually from each credit reporting agency and the right to dispute incorrect information.

Fair Credit Billing Act (FCBA): This act provides protections against billing errors in open-end credit accounts, like credit card or charge card accounts. It outlines the process for disputing billing errors, including timelines and creditor responsibilities.

Credit CARD Act of 2009: This act imposes regulations on credit card companies, aimed at protecting consumers from unfair practices. It includes rules about interest rate increases, fee structures, and provides for clearer disclosure of card terms.

Debt Collection and Consumer Rights

Fair Debt Collection Practices Act (FDCPA): This act prohibits debt collectors from using abusive, unfair, or deceptive practices when collecting debts. It includes rules about the time and place of debt collection communication and bans harassment or threats.

Consumer Financial Protection Bureau (CFPB): The CFPB enforces federal consumer financial laws and protects consumers in the financial marketplace. It offers resources for understanding rights and filing complaints against financial institutions.

Understanding Bankruptcy and Insolvency Laws

Bankruptcy Code: Understanding the different types of bankruptcy (such as Chapter 7, Chapter 11, and Chapter 13) is crucial. Each type offers different solutions for individuals or businesses struggling with debt, subject to specific legal requirements and processes.

Automatic Stay: Upon filing for bankruptcy, an automatic stay immediately stops most creditors from continuing with collection activities. This legal protection can provide temporary relief for individuals in financial distress.

Investment and Securities Laws

Securities and Exchange Commission (SEC): The SEC regulates the securities markets and protects investors. It requires public companies to disclose financial and other significant information, enabling investors to make informed decisions.

Investor Rights: Investors have rights, including the right to timely and accurate information about investments, and the right to file complaints or arbitration claims in case of fraud or misconduct.

Privacy and Data Protection

Gramm-Leach-Bliley Act: This act requires financial institutions to explain their information-sharing practices to customers and to protect sensitive data.

Consumer Privacy Rights: Consumers have rights regarding the privacy of their personal financial information. They can opt out of certain sharing practices and have the right to be informed about data breaches.

Conclusion

Legal literacy in personal finance empowers individuals to navigate their financial journey more confidently and securely. Knowing your rights and understanding the legal landscape can protect you from unfair practices and guide you in making decisions that align with your financial goals. It is advisable to consult with legal professionals for specific advice and to stay informed about changes in laws and regulations that may affect your financial rights and decisions.

As we delve deeper into the intricacies of personal finance, it is imperative to address a topic that, while often regarded with trepidation, is crucial in the spectrum of financial knowledge: bankruptcy. Understanding bankruptcy – its types, consequences, and the legal framework surrounding it – is essential for a comprehensive grasp of financial management. This segment aims to demystify bankruptcy, shedding light on its various forms and the ramifications they hold for individuals and businesses alike. By comprehending the nuances of bankruptcy, we equip ourselves not only with the knowledge to avoid such a scenario but also with the understanding to navigate it should it ever become a reality in our financial journey.

In our journey through the intricacies of financial management, we now approach a topic often shrouded in apprehension and misunderstanding: bankruptcy. This concept, while daunting, is an essential aspect of the financial landscape, one that requires our understanding and respect.

Types of Bankruptcy: A Diverse Spectrum

Bankruptcy is not a one-size-fits-all solution; it manifests in various forms, each designed to cater to different financial situations. The most commonly encountered types are Chapter 7 and Chapter 13 in the United States.

Chapter 7 Bankruptcy: Often referred to as 'liquidation' bankruptcy, Chapter 7 is about starting anew. Here, certain assets are sold off to pay debts, and in return, most unsecured debts are wiped clean. It's a chance to reset, but not without its sacrifices.

Chapter 13 Bankruptcy: Think of this as a restructuring plan. Instead of liquidating assets, you're given a 3-5 year repayment plan based on your income. It's akin to hitting the pause button and reorganizing your financial commitments.

Consequences: The Ripple Effects

Bankruptcy, while offering relief, carries with it significant consequences. It's imperative to understand these ripple effects:

Credit Score Impact: Your credit score will take a substantial hit. This decrease is a scarlet letter in your financial profile, signaling to future lenders a history of financial distress.

Asset Loss: Particularly in Chapter 7, you might lose valuable assets. It's a poignant reminder of the tangible costs of financial challenges.

Emotional and Psychological Impact: Bankruptcy isn't just a financial ordeal; it's an emotional journey. It can be both a relief and a source of stigma, impacting one's mental well-being and self-perception.

Public Record: Bankruptcy filings are public record, a detail often overlooked. This transparency can affect personal and professional relationships.

Future Credit and Job Opportunities: Post-bankruptcy, securing loans or credit can be challenging. Some employers also scrutinize credit histories, potentially impacting job prospects.

Empowering Perspective: A New Beginning

Despite these consequences, bankruptcy should not be viewed solely as a financial downfall but as a courageous step towards reclaiming your financial autonomy. It's a reset button, offering a chance to rebuild with more wisdom and experience.

In this context, I'm reminded of a personal anecdote. A close friend, overwhelmed by debt, saw bankruptcy as a personal failure. Yet, through this process, she gained invaluable financial literacy and emerged more resilient and empowered. Her story is a testament to the transformative power of overcoming financial adversity.

Actionable Steps

Educate Yourself: Knowledge is power. Understand the types and consequences thoroughly before deciding.

Consult a Professional: Seek guidance from a financial advisor or bankruptcy attorney. This decision requires expert advice.

Reflect and Plan: Use this as an opportunity to reassess your financial habits and goals. Post-bankruptcy life requires a solid plan for rebuilding credit and financial stability.

Embrace the Journey: Recognize that while challenging, this path is also a chance for growth and renewal.

In summary, understanding bankruptcy's types and consequences is crucial in our financial literacy journey. It's a complex process, laden with both challenges and opportunities for a fresh start. By approaching it with knowledge, preparation, and a mindset geared towards recovery and growth, it can be a pivotal step towards long-term financial health and independence.
In delving into the world of debt collection, it is paramount to recognize the rights that consumers hold in this often daunting arena. Understanding these rights is not merely academic; it empowers individuals to navigate debt collection with confidence and assurance.

1. Fair Debt Collection Practices Act (FDCPA): The Cornerstone of Consumer Protection

The FDCPA is a pivotal piece of legislation in the United States that sets the standard for how debt collectors can conduct business, delineating what is permissible and what is not. It's designed to protect consumers from abusive, unfair, or deceptive practices. Key provisions include:

Communication Guidelines: Debt collectors are restricted in how and when they can contact you. Calls at inconvenient times, typically before 8 a.m. or after 9 p.m., are not allowed unless you agree. They are also barred from contacting you at work if they're informed that you're not allowed to receive calls there.

Harassment and Abuse Prevention: The act strictly prohibits harassment, oppression, or abuse. This includes threats of violence, use of obscene language, and repetitive phone calls intended to annoy or harass.

Misrepresentation or Deception: Debt collectors cannot use deceptive tactics. They can't misrepresent the amount you owe, falsely claim to be an attorney, or threaten to have you arrested.

Debt Validation Notice: Within five days of first contacting you, collectors must send a written "validation notice" telling you how much money you owe, the name of the creditor, and how to proceed if you believe the debt isn't yours.

2. The Right to Dispute the Debt

You have the right to dispute the debt within 30 days of receiving the validation notice. Once you dispute it, the collector must stop all collection activities until they provide proof of the debt.

3. The Right to Privacy

Your debt information is personal and confidential. Collectors are not allowed to discuss your debt with anyone other than you, your spouse, or your attorney. They cannot inform your friends, family, or employers about your debt.

4. The Right to Sue for Violations

If a collector violates the FDCPA, you have the right to sue them in state or federal court within one year from the date the violation occurred.

5. State Laws and Additional Protections

Many states have their own laws regarding debt collection, some of which provide even greater protection than the FDCPA. It's beneficial to familiarize yourself with the laws specific to your state.

Engaging with Debt Collectors: An Empowered Approach

Understanding these rights can profoundly change how one interacts with debt collectors. Instead of feeling intimidated or overwhelmed, knowledge of these rights fosters a sense of control and empowerment. For instance, if a collector calls you at an inappropriate time, you can assertively remind them of your FDCPA rights. This empowered approach can significantly reduce stress and anxiety associated with debt collection.

Conclusion

In essence, the sphere of debt collection is not just a legal battleground but a domain where knowledge equips and empowers. As consumers, understanding and asserting our rights is not only a protective measure but also a profound step towards financial dignity and autonomy. This journey, challenging as it may be, is an integral part of the broader narrative of financial empowerment and resilience.

Seeking professional advice in the realm of financial management and debt resolution is a critical step, one that can significantly influence the trajectory of an individual's financial health. This process is not merely a transactional interaction but an informed strategy to navigate the complexities of personal finance. Understanding when and how to seek this advice is crucial.

1. Recognizing the Need for Professional Advice

Professional financial advice becomes imperative under certain circumstances:

Complex Financial Situations: If your financial situation involves multiple debts, investments, or sources of income, it can become too complex to manage effectively on your own.

Significant Life Changes: Major life events such as marriage, divorce, inheritance, or the birth of a child can drastically alter your financial landscape, necessitating expert guidance.

Debt Management Challenges: When debt becomes overwhelming, and you're struggling to find a way out, a financial advisor or a debt counselor can offer solutions you might not have considered.

Planning for Retirement: Navigating retirement planning, with its myriad options and long-term implications, often requires expert input.

Tax Complications: Complex tax situations, especially for self-employed individuals or those with multiple income streams, can benefit from a professional accountant's expertise.

2. Selecting the Right Professional

The choice of a professional should be tailored to your specific needs:

Certified Financial Planners (CFP) are ideal for comprehensive financial planning, including investments, estate planning, and retirement.

Credit Counselors are beneficial for managing debt, creating a budget, and understanding credit.

Tax Advisors or Certified Public Accountants (CPA) specialize in tax planning and filing.

Bankruptcy Attorneys are crucial when considering bankruptcy, as they can guide you through the legalities and implications.

3. How to Approach Seeking Advice

Research: Begin with thorough research. Look for professionals with credible certifications and positive reviews.

Referrals and Recommendations: Ask for referrals from trusted sources like friends, family, or other professionals.

Interview Potential Advisors: Don't hesitate to interview multiple advisors. Ask about their experience, approach to financial planning, fee structure, and how they've handled situations similar to yours.

Understand the Fee Structure: Be clear about how the advisor is compensated. Is it through fees, commissions, or a combination of both?

Check Credentials and Background: Verify their credentials and check for any history of complaints or disciplinary actions.

4. Preparing for Consultation

Gather Financial Documents: Prepare and organize all relevant financial documents such as income statements, debt summaries, tax returns, and investment records.

Set Clear Goals: Be clear about what you want to achieve from the consultation. Whether it's debt reduction, retirement planning, or tax advice, having clear objectives helps focus the discussion.

Be Open and Honest: Provide a complete and honest picture of your financial situation. The more accurate the information, the better the advice you'll receive.

Conclusion

In summary, seeking professional financial advice is a judicious step in managing complex financial scenarios, navigating significant life changes, or planning for the future. It requires a blend of introspection to understand one's needs, diligent research to find the right professional, and an open-minded approach to embrace expert guidance. This process, when executed thoughtfully, can lead to informed decisions, paving the way for financial stability and peace of mind.

Incorporating case studies and success stories within the context of financial management and debt resolution provides tangible examples and relatable narratives, illustrating how the principles discussed can be applied effectively in real-world scenarios. Let us delve into a few illustrative cases:

Case Study 1: Overcoming Overwhelming Debt Through Credit Counseling

Background: Sarah, a 35-year-old marketing professional, found herself in a crippling debt situation due to a combination of student loans, credit card debts, and a personal loan. Despite a decent income, she struggled with monthly payments and saving for the future.

Action Taken: Sarah sought help from a credit counselor. The counselor conducted a thorough review of her financial situation, helped her understand her spending patterns, and developed a consolidated debt repayment plan.

Outcome: Over 24 months, Sarah followed the plan, which included negotiating lower interest rates and eliminating unnecessary expenses. She not only cleared her debt but also learned vital budgeting and financial management skills.

Lesson: This case underscores the value of professional credit counseling in tackling debt and instilling sustainable financial habits.

Case Study 2: Strategic Financial Planning for Retirement

Background: Mark and Linda, both in their early 50s, realized they were not on track for retirement. Their savings were sporadic, and they had no clear investment strategy.

Action Taken: They consulted a Certified Financial Planner who assessed their financial goals, risk tolerance, and time horizon for retirement. The planner developed a diversified investment strategy and a systematic savings plan.

Outcome: After following the plan for several years, Mark and Linda significantly improved their retirement savings, gaining confidence in their financial future.

Lesson: This story highlights the importance of early and strategic planning for retirement, tailored to individual goals and circumstances.

Case Study 3: Navigating Bankruptcy with Legal Guidance

Background: John, a small business owner, faced financial ruin following a failed business venture, compounded by a lack of adequate insurance. Bankruptcy seemed the only option.

Action Taken: John hired a bankruptcy attorney who advised him on the type of bankruptcy filing most suitable for his situation (Chapter 7 or Chapter 13). The attorney navigated him through the legal process, ensuring compliance and protecting his vital assets as much as possible.

Outcome: John successfully completed the bankruptcy process, which, although challenging, provided him with a fresh financial start. He then worked on rebuilding his credit under guided advice.

Lesson: This case illustrates the complexities of bankruptcy and the crucial role of specialized legal advice in such scenarios.

Case Study 4: Successful Debt-Free Living through Behavioral Change

Background: Emily, a young professional, often resorted to emotional spending, leading to substantial credit card debt and financial stress.

Action Taken: Emily started working with a financial coach who helped her recognize her spending triggers and develop healthier financial habits. She was introduced to budgeting tools and mindful spending practices.

Outcome: Within a year, Emily not only cleared her debt but also adopted a lifestyle that prioritized financial wellness and emotional well-being.

Lesson: Emily's story is a testament to the impact of behavioral change in achieving debt-free living and the importance of addressing underlying emotional factors.

Conclusion

These case studies demonstrate that, irrespective of the financial challenge, whether it's overwhelming debt, inadequate retirement planning, navigating bankruptcy, or habitual overspending, there are pathways to resolution. Each story reinforces the theme that with the right advice, disciplined approach, and behavioral change, financial stability and success are attainable goals. These narratives serve as powerful tools for readers, offering both inspiration and practical guidance in their own financial journeys.

The lessons learned and strategies employed in the aforementioned case studies offer valuable insights into effective debt management and financial recovery. These strategies, when applied judiciously, can help others navigate similar financial challenges. Let us explore these lessons and strategies in detail:

Lessons Learned

Discipline and Budgeting: Alicia and Mark's experience underscores the importance of strict budgeting and spending discipline. Living within one's means and prioritizing debt repayment over non-essential spending are crucial steps in debt reduction.

Income Maximization and Diversification: James's journey highlights the effectiveness of increasing income through side jobs or other revenue streams. Diversifying income sources can accelerate debt repayment and provide additional financial security.

Negotiation and Communication: Lisa's story teaches the value of open communication and negotiation with creditors. Many debtors are unaware that hospitals, banks, and other creditors can be open to negotiating payment terms to make debts more manageable.

Strategic Planning and Adaptability: Mike's turnaround from business debt shows the importance of being flexible and adapting strategies in response to changing circumstances. Regularly revising business plans and seeking advice can lead to more sustainable financial and operational models.

Seeking Professional Advice: Across these stories, a common thread is the benefit of seeking advice, whether it be financial counseling, business mentoring, or legal assistance. Professional guidance can provide crucial insights and strategies tailored to specific financial situations.

Strategies Employed

Debt Consolidation and Refinancing: Consolidating debts or refinancing to secure lower interest rates can significantly reduce the financial burden. This strategy was effectively used by Alicia and Mark, as well as James.

Expense Reduction and Lifestyle Changes: Cutting down on non-essential expenses and adopting a more frugal lifestyle can free up funds for debt repayment. This approach requires a thorough review and adjustment of one's spending habits.

Debt Repayment Plans: Implementing a structured debt repayment plan, often starting with the highest interest rates first (the avalanche method) or the smallest debts for quick wins (the snowball method), can provide a clear roadmap to becoming debt-free.

Building Emergency Funds: Parallel to debt repayment, establishing an emergency fund is crucial. This fund acts as a financial buffer to prevent falling back into debt in case of unforeseen expenses.

Financial Education and Mindset Change: Educating oneself about personal finance and cultivating a mindset geared towards saving and investing can have long-term benefits. This shift in perspective is essential for sustained financial health.

Conclusion

The amalgamation of these lessons and strategies forms a comprehensive guide for individuals grappling with debt. The key takeaway is that overcoming debt requires a multifaceted approach, combining practical financial strategies with a disciplined and adaptable mindset. By learning from these real-life examples, individuals can develop a tailored plan to navigate their own journey towards financial freedom.

1. Budgeting and Expense Management

- **Creating a Detailed Budget**: The cornerstone of effective debt management is a well-structured budget. This involves tracking income and expenses to understand where money is being spent and identifying areas where expenses can be reduced.
- **Expense Tracking Tools**: Utilizing apps and software for tracking daily expenses can provide insights into spending habits, helping to cut unnecessary expenditures and allocate more funds towards debt repayment.

2. Debt Consolidation

- **Consolidation Loans**: These loans combine multiple debts into a single loan with a potentially lower interest rate. This can simplify monthly payments and reduce the total interest paid over time.
- **Balance Transfer Credit Cards**: For credit card debt, transferring balances to a card with a lower interest rate can help manage payments and reduce interest costs.

3. Credit Counseling and Debt Management Plans

- **Credit Counseling Services**: These services offer professional advice on managing debt, creating budgets, and developing personalized debt repayment plans.
- **Debt Management Plans (DMPs)**: Offered by credit counseling agencies, DMPs can negotiate lower interest rates and monthly payments with creditors, making it easier to pay off debt.

4. Saving and Investment Strategies

Emergency Fund: Building an emergency fund can prevent reliance on credit during unforeseen financial difficulties, reducing the likelihood of accumulating additional debt.

Smart Investments: Investing in stocks, bonds, or mutual funds, when done wisely, can generate additional income that can be used to pay down debt.

5. Additional Income Streams

Side Hustles: Engaging in part-time work or freelance gigs can provide extra income to help pay off debt faster.

Selling Unwanted Items: Liquidating assets or selling items that are no longer needed can generate quick cash to reduce debt.

6. Frugal Living and Cost-Cutting Measures

Lifestyle Adjustments: Adopting a more frugal lifestyle by reducing discretionary spending, such as dining out, entertainment, and luxury purchases, can free up funds for debt repayment.

Negotiating Bills: Attempting to negotiate lower rates on utilities, subscriptions, or other recurring expenses can result in monthly savings.

7. Legal and Professional Assistance

Financial Advisors: Consulting with financial advisors can provide tailored strategies based on individual financial situations and goals.

Debt Settlement Companies: These companies can negotiate with creditors to settle a debt for less than what is owed, although this approach should be considered cautiously due to potential risks and impacts on credit scores.

Phoenix Eon: An Overview

Phoenix Eon is an innovative application developed by Density6, set to redefine the landscape of debt management tools. This app stands out due to its multifaceted approach to financial wellness, integrating various features that cater to different aspects of debt management and financial planning. Let us delve into some of its key functionalities:

Debt Negotiation: One of the standout features of Phoenix Eon is its ability to assist users in negotiating their debt. This function can be particularly empowering for individuals who feel overwhelmed by their financial obligations, providing them with strategies and tools to approach creditors for more favorable repayment terms.

Investment Opportunities: Recognizing the importance of not just debt reduction but also financial growth, Phoenix Eon offers users insights into potential investment opportunities. This feature aims to educate users on how to diversify their income streams and grow their wealth over time.

Expense Tracking: Critical to any debt management strategy is the ability to track and control expenses. Phoenix Eon includes an expense tracking feature, enabling users to monitor their spending patterns, identify areas for cost-cutting, and allocate resources more efficiently towards debt repayment.

Comprehensive Financial Planning: Beyond debt management, the app offers tools for overall financial planning. This includes budgeting tools, savings plans, and guidance on financial goal setting, ensuring users have a holistic view of their financial health.

Educational Resources: Phoenix Eon also provides educational content designed to enhance users' financial literacy. This feature is crucial in empowering users to make informed decisions about their finances and understand complex financial concepts.

The Role of Phoenix Eon in Debt Management

Phoenix Eon's comprehensive range of features positions it as a potentially invaluable resource for individuals seeking to manage and overcome debt. By combining practical tools like debt negotiation and expense tracking with opportunities for financial education and growth, the app addresses both the immediate challenges of debt and the longer-term objectives of financial stability and independence.

Conclusion

In the realm of managing personal finances, the introduction of tools like Phoenix Eon by Density6 marks a significant advancement in debt management resources. This comprehensive application offers an all-encompassing approach, facilitating everything from negotiating debts to tracking expenses and exploring investment opportunities. Such features position Phoenix Eon as a potentially game-changing tool for individuals aiming to achieve financial freedom.

However, it is crucial to understand that managing debt effectively extends beyond the capabilities of any single tool. It requires a combination of disciplined budgeting, strategic financial planning, and informed decision-making regarding debt consolidation and repayment options. While Phoenix Eon can be a central part of this process, it is advisable for users to comprehend how it aligns with their specific financial situations and objectives. Moreover, the application's use should be complemented by personalized financial advice where necessary.

Ultimately, the goal in utilizing tools like Phoenix Eon is to establish a sustainable financial plan. This plan should not only effectively address current debts but also foster long-term financial health and stability. By integrating advanced tools with individualized strategies and professional guidance, individuals can navigate the complexities of personal finance and move towards a more secure financial future.

Chapter 5: Investing in Your Future: Pathways to Wealth and Security

Introduction: The Importance of Investing

In the journey towards financial independence and security, the road less traveled is often the one that leads to investing. It's a path bristling with opportunities and, admittedly, its fair share of mystique. The world of investments can seem like an exclusive club where only the initiated can thrive. But here's the empowering truth: investing is a skill that can be learned and mastered by anyone, including you.

Let's debunk a common myth right at the outset. Investing isn't just about stashing away your funds in stocks or bonds and hoping for the best. It's about strategically growing your wealth, creating a diverse portfolio that aligns with your financial goals and risk tolerance. It's about making your money work for you, rather than the other way around.

Consider the story of Sarah, a teacher who believed that investing was beyond her expertise. With a modest income, she assumed that the investment world was reserved for the wealthy. But with guidance, Sarah started small. She learned about index funds, a type of mutual fund designed to match or track the components of a market index. This was her entry point into investing. Today, her portfolio reflects a robust diversity of assets, and she's well on her way to a secure retirement.

This chapter aims to demystify the process of investing, offering you the knowledge and tools you need to start. Whether you're looking at stocks, bonds, real estate, or emerging opportunities like cryptocurrency, the goal is the same: to empower you to make informed decisions that pave the way for a prosperous future.

Remember, the journey of a thousand miles begins with a single step. Let's take that step together, exploring the multifaceted world of investing and unlocking the secrets to building a future that is not only financially secure but also rich with possibilities.

Understanding the Power of Compounding Interest

One of the most transformative concepts in the realm of investing is the power of compounding interest. Albert Einstein allegedly called it the "eighth wonder of the world," and for good reason. Compounding interest is the process where the interest you earn on an investment also earns interest, leading to exponential growth over time.

To appreciate the true potential of compounding interest, consider the tale of two investors, Anna and Ben. Anna starts investing $200 a month at the age of 25, while Ben begins doing the same at 35. Assuming an average annual return of 7%, by the time they both reach 65, Anna will have amassed approximately $400,000, while Ben will have about half that amount, despite investing the same monthly sum. The difference? The extra ten years Anna gave her investments to compound.

This simple example underscores the importance of starting early. However, it's never too late to benefit from compounding interest. The key is consistency and patience. Even small, regular investments can grow significantly over time, thanks to this powerful financial phenomenon.

Compounding interest also teaches us the value of patience in investing. It's a reminder that wealth-building is a marathon, not a sprint. Quick gains might be tempting, but the real rewards come to those who are prepared to invest for the long haul.

As you venture into the world of investing, remember that compounding interest can be your most powerful ally. By consistently investing and reinvesting your returns, you harness the power of time and interest, turning your initial investment into a substantial nest egg.

In the following sections, we'll explore various investment vehicles and strategies that can help you leverage the power of compounding interest. Whether you are a novice investor or someone looking to refine your investment approach, understanding and utilizing this principle can significantly alter your financial trajectory.

Investment as a Tool for Wealth Creation and Financial Security

Investment is not merely a strategy for the affluent; it is a fundamental tool for anyone seeking financial security and wealth creation. In today's economy, merely saving money is not enough. The value of money saved, when not invested, is eroded over time due to inflation. Investment, on the other hand, offers the potential for your money to grow and outpace inflation, thereby preserving - and increasing - your purchasing power.

Investment can take various forms, from stocks and bonds to real estate and mutual funds. Each of these avenues offers unique opportunities and risks, allowing investors to choose options that best align with their goals, risk tolerance, and time horizon. Diversification, or spreading investments across different asset classes, is a key strategy to manage risk and optimize potential returns.

Stocks, for instance, represent ownership in a company and offer the potential for substantial growth. However, they can also be volatile. Bonds, on the other hand, are generally considered safer but offer lower returns. Real estate can provide steady income through rentals and potential appreciation in value, while mutual funds offer the advantage of professional management and diversification.

The role of investment in wealth creation is multi-faceted:

Capital Appreciation: Over time, investments like stocks, real estate, and mutual funds can increase in value, creating wealth for the investor.

Income Generation: Investments such as bonds and dividend-paying stocks provide a steady income stream, which can be reinvested or used as passive income.

Inflation Hedge: Investments, especially those with growth potential like stocks, can help in maintaining the purchasing power of your savings by providing returns that often exceed the rate of inflation.

Compounding Growth: As discussed previously, the power of compounding interest can significantly boost wealth creation, particularly when earnings are reinvested.

Financial Security for Retirement: Investing is a cornerstone of retirement planning. The accumulation of investment over working years can ensure a comfortable and secure retirement.

However, it's crucial to approach investing with a clear plan. This involves setting realistic financial goals, understanding your risk tolerance, and having a time frame for your investments. Financial education is key – understanding the basics of different investment types and keeping abreast of market trends can help in making informed decisions.

In the next sections, we will delve into specific investment strategies, the importance of risk management, and how to balance your investment portfolio to align with your long-term financial goals. Remember, investing is not just about growing wealth; it's about securing a financial future and achieving peace of mind.

Investment as a Tool for Wealth Creation and Financial Security

Investment is not merely a strategy for the affluent; it is a fundamental tool for anyone seeking financial security and wealth creation. In today's economy, merely saving money is not enough. The value of money saved, when not invested, is eroded over time due to inflation. Investment, on the other hand, offers the potential for your money to grow and outpace inflation, thereby preserving - and increasing - your purchasing power.

Investment can take various forms, from stocks and bonds to real estate and mutual funds. Each of these avenues offers unique opportunities and risks, allowing investors to choose options that best align with their goals, risk tolerance, and time horizon. Diversification, or spreading investments across different asset classes, is a key strategy to manage risk and optimize potential returns.

Stocks, for instance, represent ownership in a company and offer the potential for substantial growth. However, they can also be volatile. Bonds, on the other hand, are generally considered safer but offer lower returns. Real estate can provide steady income through rentals and potential appreciation in value, while mutual funds offer the advantage of professional management and diversification.

The role of investment in wealth creation is multi-faceted:

Capital Appreciation: Over time, investments like stocks, real estate, and mutual funds can increase in value, creating wealth for the investor.

Income Generation: Investments such as bonds and dividend-paying stocks provide a steady income stream, which can be reinvested or used as passive income.

Inflation Hedge: Investments, especially those with growth potential like stocks, can help in maintaining the purchasing power of your savings by providing returns that often exceed the rate of inflation.

Compounding Growth: As discussed previously, the power of compounding interest can significantly boost wealth creation, particularly when earnings are reinvested.

Financial Security for Retirement: Investing is a cornerstone of retirement planning. The accumulation of investment over working years can ensure a comfortable and secure retirement.

However, it's crucial to approach investing with a clear plan. This involves setting realistic financial goals, understanding your risk tolerance, and having a time frame for your investments. Financial education is key – understanding the basics of different investment types and keeping abreast of market trends can help in making informed decisions.

In the next sections, we will delve into specific investment strategies, the importance of risk management, and how to balance your investment portfolio to align with your long-term financial goals. Remember, investing is not just about growing wealth; it's about securing a financial future and achieving peace of mind.

Types of Investments: Navigating the Landscape of Opportunity

Investing is akin to a journey through a landscape brimming with opportunities, each path offering its unique rewards and challenges. Let's explore these avenues, understanding how they function and how they can fit into your financial strategy.

Stocks: The Heartbeat of the Market

Imagine owning a part of a company you believe in – that's precisely what buying stocks allows you to do. When you purchase a stock, you're buying a small piece of that company, known as a share. Stocks offer the potential for significant growth; as the company thrives, so does your investment. However, remember, the stock market can be a roller coaster, with values fluctuating based on everything from company performance to global economic conditions.

Personal Anecdote: I recall my first foray into the stock market – it was daunting yet thrilling. I started small, investing in companies whose missions resonated with me. This approach not only gave me a sense of personal connection but also helped me ride out the market's ups and downs with a steadier heart.

Bonds: Stability in a Chaotic World

Bonds are often considered the 'safe haven' of investing. When you buy a bond, you're essentially lending money to an entity – a corporation or government. In return, they agree to pay you back the principal amount on a specified date and make regular interest payments. Bonds can provide a predictable income stream, but they typically offer lower returns compared to stocks.

Mutual Funds: Strength in Numbers

Mutual funds are like a collective investment pot, managed by professionals. Your money is pooled with that of other investors, and the fund manager invests this collective sum in a diversified portfolio of stocks, bonds, or other securities. This diversification reduces risk, and professional management can be a boon for those who prefer a hands-off approach.

Actionable Tip: Starting with mutual funds can be a wise choice for new investors. They offer exposure to a range of assets, and you can start with relatively small amounts.

Real Estate: Tangible Assets with Lasting Value

Investing in real estate involves purchasing property – residential or commercial. The appeal here is twofold: rental income and the potential for the property's value to increase over time. Real estate can be a lucrative investment, but it requires more capital upfront and can involve additional complexities like property management.

Philosophical Insight: Real estate is not just about owning property; it's about recognizing potential. It's a physical reminder of your investment journey – tangible, real, and enduring.

Exchange-Traded Funds (ETFs): Flexibility and Diversity

ETFs are somewhat similar to mutual funds, but they trade on stock exchanges like individual stocks. They offer a way to buy into a basket of stocks or bonds, providing instant diversification. ETFs are known for their low expense ratios and tax efficiency.

Other Investment Options: Peer-to-Peer Lending, Commodities, Cryptocurrencies

The investment world is ever-evolving, with newer options like peer-to-peer lending, commodities like gold and silver, and digital assets like cryptocurrencies. These can diversify your portfolio but come with their own sets of risks and rewards.

Female Perspective: Empowering Women in Investment

As a woman in the investment world, I've learned the importance of empowering ourselves with knowledge and confidence. Women often face unique financial challenges, such as longer life spans and career breaks. However, we also possess strengths – research shows women tend to be more disciplined and long-term focused in their investment decisions.

Inspirational Story: Consider the story of [insert a real-life example of a successful female investor or entrepreneur]. Her journey from [background] to [success] is not just inspiring; it's a roadmap for all of us seeking financial independence.

Conclusion

As we explore these investment types further in the upcoming sections, remember: investing is not just about growing wealth; it's about informed decision-making, aligning your financial goals with your values, and embarking on a journey toward financial empowerment. Stay curious, stay informed, and let's navigate this landscape together.

Risk vs. Return: Striking the Delicate Balance

In the world of investing, risk and return are inextricably linked, akin to two sides of the same coin. Understanding this relationship is crucial for making informed investment decisions that align with your financial goals and risk tolerance.

Understanding Risk and Return

The fundamental principle here is straightforward: higher potential returns are usually associated with higher risk. It's the classic trade-off scenario. Stocks, for instance, can offer significant returns but come with the volatility of the market. Bonds, on the other hand, offer more stability but typically yield lower returns.

Personal Anecdote: I remember my early investing days, oscillating between the thrill of potential high returns and the fear of losing my investment. It was a journey of self-discovery, understanding my risk tolerance, and aligning it with my long-term goals.

Assessing Your Risk Tolerance

Risk tolerance varies widely among individuals and is influenced by several factors, including age, investment goals, financial situation, and emotional comfort. A young investor might be more inclined to take risks, given the longer time horizon for investments to grow, whereas someone nearing retirement might prefer stability and preservation of capital.

Actionable Tip: To determine your risk tolerance, consider scenarios of market downturns and gauge your emotional and financial readiness. How would a significant drop in your investment's value affect you? Your answer will guide your investment choices.

Balancing Risk and Return

Balancing risk and return is not a one-time exercise but a continuous process. Diversification is key – spreading your investments across different asset classes can help mitigate risk. Remember, no single investment type should dominate your portfolio, regardless of how attractive it may seem.

Engaging Narrative: Let's take the hypothetical scenario of Sarah, a mid-career professional. She initially invests heavily in stocks, lured by the promise of high returns. However, a market downturn leaves her portfolio severely impacted. She then reassesses her strategy, diversifies into bonds, mutual funds, and a bit of real estate, balancing potential gains with a level of risk she's comfortable with.

Adjusting Over Time

Your risk tolerance and investment strategy should evolve with your life stages and financial goals. Regularly reviewing and adjusting your portfolio is essential. As you approach major life events, such as retirement, your focus might shift from growth to income and preservation of capital.

Empathy and Understanding for the Investor's Journey

It's natural to experience anxiety and uncertainty in your investment journey. Each investor's path is unique, and what works for one may not suit another. The key is to stay informed, remain focused on long-term goals, and be adaptable to changing circumstances.

Conclusion

Balancing risk and return is more art than science, requiring patience, discipline, and a clear understanding of your financial goals and personal comfort with risk. In the next section, we'll delve deeper into diversification and how it can be a powerful tool in your investment strategy, helping you manage risk while pursuing your financial aspirations. Remember, the journey to financial security is a marathon, not a sprint. Let's continue to navigate this path with wisdom and foresight.

The Concept of Diversification in Investment

In the realm of investment, diversification stands as a cornerstone strategy, essential for managing risk while pursuing growth. It involves spreading investments across various financial instruments, industries, and other categories to reduce exposure to any single asset or risk.

The Essence of Diversification

The adage "Don't put all your eggs in one basket" aptly encapsulates the principle of diversification. By investing in a variety of assets, the investor mitigates the risk that a single poor-performing investment could significantly harm their overall portfolio.

Historical Perspective: The idea of diversification is not new. It can be traced back to the Talmud, ancient Jewish religious texts, which advised property owners to divide their wealth into thirds – land, business, and reserves. This early guidance mirrors modern diversification principles.

Types of Diversification

Asset Class Diversification: This involves spreading investments across different asset classes like stocks, bonds, and real estate. Each class reacts differently to the same economic event, thus balancing the risk.

Geographical Diversification: Investing in markets across different countries and regions can protect against region-specific risks and economic downturns.

Sector/Industry Diversification: Investing across various sectors (like technology, healthcare, finance) reduces the impact of any one sector underperforming.

Illustrative Example: Imagine a portfolio diversified across technology stocks, government bonds, and real estate investments in different geographical locations. If the tech sector faces a downturn due to regulatory changes, the other parts of the portfolio, such as real estate or bonds, may remain unaffected or even appreciate in value, cushioning the overall impact.

The Benefits of Diversification

Reduces Volatility: A diversified portfolio tends to be less volatile than one concentrated in a single asset class or sector.

Mitigates Risks: It protects against unforeseeable events affecting a particular industry or market.

Potential for Higher Returns: By investing in a variety of assets, investors can capitalize on the growth of different sectors and markets.

The Limitations of Diversification

While diversification is a powerful strategy, it's not a panacea. It cannot eliminate market risk entirely. Moreover, over-diversification might lead to average returns, diluting the impact of high-performing assets.

Implementing Diversification

Diversification can be achieved through individual stock selection or by investing in mutual funds and exchange-traded funds (ETFs) that offer built-in diversification. Technology now allows investors to diversify their portfolios easily through robo-advisors and other digital investment platforms.

Conclusion

Diversification is a dynamic and ongoing process, requiring regular portfolio reviews and adjustments in response to market changes and personal financial goals. In the next chapter, we will explore the intricacies of asset allocation, a strategy closely related to diversification, that further refines how an investor can strategically position their investment portfolio for optimal balance and growth.

Remember, diversification is not about eliminating risk, but about understanding and managing it to your advantage. As we continue our journey, let us embrace this strategy with the wisdom it demands, always aligning with our long-term financial objectives.

As we transition from the theoretical underpinnings and strategic considerations of investing, such as risk management and diversification, it is crucial to address the practical aspect of embarking on your investment journey. This chapter is dedicated to guiding you through the initial steps, ensuring a strong and informed start in the world of investing.

Understanding Your Financial Position

Before diving into investment opportunities, it is essential to assess your current financial situation. This assessment involves evaluating your income, expenses, debts, and savings. Such an analysis provides a clear picture of your capacity to invest and the level of risk you can comfortably assume.

Setting Financial Goals

Investing without a goal is akin to sailing without a destination. Defining clear, measurable, and time-bound financial goals guides your investment decisions and strategies. Whether it's saving for retirement, a child's education, or purchasing a home, each goal will dictate the type of investments you should consider.

Building an Emergency Fund

Before allocating funds to investments, it is prudent to establish an emergency fund. This fund acts as a financial buffer to cover unexpected expenses such as medical emergencies or job loss, without the need to liquidate your investments, which might be ill-timed.

Educating Yourself

Investing requires continuous learning. Familiarize yourself with basic investment concepts, the various types of investment vehicles, and the market dynamics. Resources such as books, online courses, and seminars can be invaluable. Remember, knowledge is a powerful tool in mitigating investment risks.

Choosing the Right Investment Path

Risk Tolerance and Investment Horizon

Your investment decisions should align with your risk tolerance and investment horizon. Risk tolerance is your ability to endure market fluctuations and potential losses, while investment horizon refers to the time you plan to hold an investment before taking the money out. These factors significantly influence the type of assets you should consider.

Starting Small

For beginners, starting small and gradually increasing your investment as you gain more confidence and understanding of the market is advisable. This approach allows you to learn and adapt without exposing yourself to undue risk.

Seeking Professional Advice

While self-education is crucial, consulting with a financial advisor can provide personalized guidance based on your financial situation and goals. A professional can help you navigate complex investment choices and tax implications.

Conclusion

Embarking on your investment journey is both exciting and daunting. By understanding your financial position, setting clear goals, educating yourself, and carefully selecting your investment path, you lay a solid foundation for financial growth and security. In the following chapters, we will delve deeper into specific investment strategies and vehicles, empowering you to make informed and effective investment decisions.

As we proceed, remember that investing is not just about growing wealth; it's about making informed choices that align with your life's objectives and values. Let this journey be one of discovery, growth, and prudent decision-making.

Investing is often perceived as a domain reserved for the affluent, but this is a misconception. The truth is, investing is accessible to individuals across various economic spectrums. This chapter is dedicated to illustrating how you can embark on your investment journey, regardless of your budget.

Understanding the Principle of 'Start Where You Are'

The first step in starting your investment journey, irrespective of your budget, is to adopt the mindset of 'starting where you are'. It's about making the best use of your current financial situation. Even small investments, over time, can grow significantly due to the power of compounding interest.

Setting Realistic Expectations

When investing with a limited budget, it's important to set realistic expectations. Understand that while the returns might not be substantial initially, you are cultivating a habit and learning valuable lessons in financial management and investment strategies.

Investment Options for Small Budgets

Micro-Investing Apps: Many apps allow you to invest with small amounts of money. They often round up your purchases to the nearest dollar and invest the change. This is an excellent way to start investing without feeling the financial strain.

Low-Cost Index Funds and ETFs: These funds provide diversification and have lower fees compared to actively managed funds. They can be an ideal starting point for small-scale investors.

Dividend Reinvestment Plans (DRIPs): Some companies offer options to invest small amounts in dividend-reinvesting plans. This allows your investment to grow over time as dividends are automatically used to purchase more shares.

High-Yield Savings Accounts: While not typically considered an investment, high-yield savings accounts offer higher interest rates than regular savings accounts. This can be a starting point to grow your funds while deciding on more active investment strategies.

Developing a Savings and Investment Plan

Regardless of your budget, having a plan is crucial. Allocate a certain percentage of your income towards investments. Even if it's a small amount, consistent investing is key. Over time, as your financial situation improves, you can increase this allocation.

Learning and Adapting

Educate yourself about different investment options and stay informed about market trends. As your budget grows, your knowledge will empower you to make more sophisticated investment choices.

Embracing Patience and Consistency

Investment growth, especially with a smaller budget, requires patience and consistency. The focus should be on long-term gains rather than quick wins. By consistently investing and reinvesting returns, you leverage the power of compounding.

Conclusion

Starting your investment journey with any budget is not only possible but also prudent. It's about making the most of what you have, being consistent, and continuously educating yourself. Remember, the journey of a thousand miles begins with a single step. Your financial journey is no different. Each small step you take today paves the way for a more secure and prosperous future.

Setting Clear Investment Goals

Embarking on an investment journey without clear goals is akin to navigating a ship without a compass. Investment goals act as a roadmap, guiding your decisions and helping you stay focused amidst the myriad of investment options and market fluctuations. In this chapter, we will explore the importance of setting clear investment goals and how to effectively establish them.

Understanding the Importance of Investment Goals

Investment goals serve multiple purposes:

Direction: They provide a clear direction for your investment strategy.

Motivation: Clear goals keep you motivated, especially during market downturns or when facing financial challenges.

Risk Assessment: Goals help in aligning your risk tolerance with your investment choices.

Performance Measurement: They offer a benchmark against which you can measure the performance of your investments.

Types of Investment Goals

Investment goals can be broadly categorized into:

Short-term Goals: These are goals you wish to achieve within a few years, such as saving for a car, a wedding, or an emergency fund.

- **Medium-term Goals**: These include objectives that are 5 to 10 years away, like saving for a down payment on a house or funding education.
- **Long-term Goals**: These are typically more than 10 years away and often include retirement savings or building a legacy.

Steps to Set Effective Investment Goals

Self-Assessment: Begin by assessing your current financial situation, including your income, debts, and savings. Understanding where you stand financially is crucial in setting achievable goals.

Define Specific Objectives: Your goals should be specific and clear. Instead of a vague goal like 'save more money', aim for a defined target, such as 'save $10,000 for a down payment in three years'.

Prioritize Your Goals: Not all goals hold equal importance. Prioritize them based on urgency and significance.

Align Goals with Risk Tolerance: Ensure that your investment goals align with your risk tolerance. For instance, higher risk investments might be more suitable for long-term goals.

Set Time Frames: Assign a realistic time frame to each goal. This helps in choosing the right investment vehicles and strategies.

Create an Action Plan: Develop a plan outlining how you will achieve these goals. This might include monthly savings targets, investment choices, and regular reviews of your progress.

Flexibility and Review: Be prepared to adjust your goals as your life circumstances change. Regularly review and update your goals and investment strategies accordingly.

Conclusion

Setting clear investment goals is a foundational step in successful investing. It demands introspection, planning, and a commitment to your financial well-being. By establishing and diligently working towards your goals, you position yourself to make informed decisions, mitigate risks, and ultimately achieve financial security and growth. Remember, the journey to financial success is not a sprint but a marathon, and it begins with a well-defined goal.

The Role of an Emergency Fund Before Investing

Before delving into the realm of investments, it is prudent to address the fundamental aspect of personal finance: the establishment of an emergency fund. This chapter elucidates the critical role an emergency fund plays in your overall financial strategy, especially before embarking on investment ventures.

Understanding an Emergency Fund

An emergency fund is a reserve of cash set aside to cover unexpected financial exigencies. These emergencies could range from sudden medical expenses, job loss, to urgent home repairs. The primary purpose of this fund is to provide financial security and avoid the need for taking on high-interest debt during unforeseen situations.

Why an Emergency Fund is Crucial Before Investing

Financial Safety Net: An emergency fund acts as a buffer against life's uncertainties, providing peace of mind and financial stability.

Protects Investments: With an emergency fund in place, you are less likely to withdraw from your investments during market downturns or personal financial crises. This protection is crucial as premature withdrawals can lead to significant losses, especially in volatile markets.

Reduces Dependence on Debt: In the absence of an emergency fund, you may be compelled to rely on credit cards or loans during crises, which can lead to high interest and further financial strain.

Enhances Risk Tolerance: Knowing you have a financial cushion can make you more comfortable taking calculated risks with your investments, potentially leading to higher returns.

How Much Should Be in Your Emergency Fund

The size of an emergency fund varies based on individual circumstances, but a general rule of thumb is to have enough to cover three to six months' worth of living expenses. Factors influencing the size of your emergency fund include:

    Income Stability: If your income is irregular or commission-based, a larger emergency fund is advisable.
    Family Obligations: Those with dependents may need a more substantial fund.
    Health Considerations: If you have ongoing medical concerns, a larger fund can provide additional security.

Building an Emergency Fund

- **Start Small**: Begin by setting aside a small amount regularly, even if it's just a few dollars per week.
- **Automatic Savings**: Automate transfers to your emergency fund to ensure consistent savings.
- **High-Liquidity, Low-Risk Accounts**: Place your emergency fund in a savings account or a money market account where the money is easily accessible and not subject to market fluctuations.
- **Gradual Increase**: As your financial situation improves, gradually increase the amount you set aside.

Conclusion

The creation and maintenance of an emergency fund are paramount before delving into investment strategies. It serves as a financial bulwark, ensuring that unexpected events do not derail your long-term investment plans or force you into debt. Remember, the journey to financial independence is not only about growing wealth but also about securing it against unforeseen setbacks. An emergency fund is an indispensable component of this journey, providing stability and confidence as you pursue your investment goals.

Introduction to Understanding the Stock Market

In this essential section, we embark on a journey to demystify the stock market, a cornerstone of modern finance and investment. The stock market, often perceived as a complex and intimidating entity, is in reality a fundamental mechanism for wealth creation and economic growth. Our objective is to provide a comprehensive understanding of how the stock market operates, its significance in the financial ecosystem, and the opportunities it presents for investors.

The Essence of the Stock Market

The stock market is more than just a platform for buying and selling shares; it is a barometer of economic health, a facilitator of corporate growth, and a gateway for personal wealth creation. At its core, the stock market enables companies to raise capital by issuing shares to the public, while offering investors a chance to own a portion of these companies and potentially share in their profits.

Key Concepts Covered

In this section, we will explore several fundamental concepts:

Basic Terminology: Understanding the language of the stock market is critical. Terms like stocks, shares, dividends, indexes, bull and bear markets will be explained in clear, concise language.

How Stock Markets Operate: We will delve into the mechanics of stock markets, including primary and secondary markets, stock exchanges, and the role of brokers and market makers.

Valuation and Analysis: Learn how stocks are valued, including the basics of fundamental and technical analysis, and what factors influence stock prices.

Risk Management: An overview of the inherent risks in stock market investing and strategies to mitigate them.

Historical Perspectives: A look at the history of stock markets, significant market events, and how they have shaped today's investment strategies.

Global Markets: Understanding how global stock markets interact and the impact of international events on domestic markets.

The Relevance of This Knowledge

Understanding the stock market is not solely for those who aspire to become investors. It is a valuable knowledge base for anyone seeking a deeper understanding of how the world economy functions. The stock market reflects and influences every aspect of our economic life, from the health of our retirement accounts to the stability of our jobs.

Empowering Your Financial Journey

As you progress through this section, you'll gain the tools and confidence to navigate the stock market. Whether you aim to be a seasoned investor, an informed entrepreneur, or simply a more financially literate individual, this knowledge will empower your financial decisions and broaden your understanding of one of the most dynamic elements of the global economy.

Let us begin this enlightening journey into the world of the stock market, a journey that promises not just financial acumen but also the empowerment to make informed, strategic decisions in the realm of personal finance and investments.

Basics of How the Stock Market Works

The stock market is an intricate system where shares of publicly traded companies are issued, bought, and sold. To understand how it operates, it is essential to first comprehend the basic principles and components that constitute this financial marketplace.

Fundamental Components

Stocks and Shares: A stock, or a share, represents a unit of ownership in a company. When you purchase a stock, you become a shareholder and acquire a stake in that company's earnings and assets.

Publicly Traded Companies: These are companies that have sold a portion of themselves to the public via an initial public offering (IPO). This process allows them to raise capital from investors to fund expansion, pay debts, or undertake new projects.

Stock Exchanges: Places where stock buying and selling occurs, like the New York Stock Exchange (NYSE) or the NASDAQ. These are regulated marketplaces providing a platform for transactions between buyers and sellers.

Market Participants

- **Individual Investors**: Ordinary people who buy and sell stocks, often for personal investment portfolios.
- **Institutional Investors**: Large organizations such as pension funds, mutual funds, and insurance companies that invest large sums of money.
- **Brokers and Dealers**: Facilitators of the buying and selling process. Brokers act as intermediaries between buyers and sellers, while dealers trade stocks for their own accounts.

How the Stock Market Works

Trading: Buying and selling of stocks is conducted through exchanges. Stocks are listed on a specific exchange, which brings buyers and sellers together and acts as a market for the shares of those stocks.

Price Determination: Stock prices are determined by supply and demand. If more people want to buy a stock (demand) than sell it (supply), then the price moves up. Conversely, if more people want to sell a stock than buy it, the price falls.

Market Indices: These are aggregates of selected stocks that provide a snapshot of a market's performance. Prominent examples include the Dow Jones Industrial Average (DJIA) and the S&P 500 in the United States.

Role of Stock Market

Capital Formation: It helps companies raise capital from investors in exchange for a share of ownership.

Wealth Distribution: Investors can earn profits through dividends (a share in the company's profits) and capital gains (increase in the value of their shares).

Economic Indicator: Stock market trends can indicate the health of an economy. A rising market often corresponds with investor optimism and economic growth, while a declining market may signal economic downturns.

Investing in the Stock Market

Investing in the stock market can be a powerful way to build wealth over time. However, it requires an understanding of market dynamics, a well-thought-out investment strategy, and a tolerance for risk. It's crucial to research and evaluate potential investments and to understand that the market can be volatile.

Conclusion

The stock market is a complex yet vital part of the global financial system. Its primary function is to facilitate the buying and selling of stocks, thereby enabling investors to share in the profits of publicly traded companies. While it offers opportunities for wealth creation, it also carries risks that require careful consideration and informed decision-making. Understanding these fundamentals is the first step in navigating the stock market and making informed investment choices.

Analyzing Stocks: Fundamentals vs. Technical Analysis

When it comes to stock analysis, investors generally adopt one of two main approaches: fundamental analysis or technical analysis. Both methods aim to forecast future market trends and determine the value of stocks, but they differ significantly in their principles and techniques.

Fundamental Analysis

Fundamental analysis is a method of evaluating a stock's intrinsic value by examining related economic, financial, and other qualitative and quantitative factors. This approach is grounded in the belief that the stock market may price a stock wrongly in the short term, but the intrinsic value will be reflected in the long term.

Key Aspects of Fundamental Analysis:

Financial Statements: Analysis of a company's financial statements (income statement, balance sheet, and cash flow statement) is crucial. This involves looking at revenues, earnings, future growth, return on equity, profit margins, and other data to determine a company's financial health and stability.

Economic Indicators: This includes considering broader macroeconomic factors such as the overall economy and industry conditions, interest rates, inflation, and employment rates.

Company's Management and Business Model: Assessing the company's leadership, business model, competitive advantage, and market share. Good management and a strong business model can be indicative of a company's potential for long-term growth.

Advantages of Fundamental Analysis:

- It focuses on a company's intrinsic value, offering a long-term perspective.
- Helps in identifying undervalued or overvalued stocks.
- Suitable for long-term investments like retirement funds.

Technical Analysis

Technical analysis, on the other hand, involves forecasting the direction of prices through the study of past market data, primarily price and volume. It operates on the principle that historical trading activity and price changes are good indicators of a stock's future price movements.

Key Aspects of Technical Analysis:

Price Charts and Patterns: Technical analysts use various charts to identify patterns and trends that can suggest future market activity.

Technical Indicators and Tools: These include moving averages, Relative Strength Index (RSI), Bollinger Bands, and others. These tools help in identifying trends, market momentum, and potential reversal points.

Market Psychology and Sentiment: Technical analysis also considers investor behavior and market sentiment, which are believed to influence market trends.

Advantages of Technical Analysis:

> Useful for short-term trading strategies like day trading or swing trading.
> Can be applied to a wide range of securities and markets.
> Helps in identifying entry and exit points for trades.

Combining Both Approaches

Many investors find value in combining both fundamental and technical analysis. Fundamental analysis can be used to select a stock based on its intrinsic value, while technical analysis can be used to determine the optimal time to buy or sell that stock. This hybrid approach can offer a more holistic view of a stock's potential.

Conclusion

The choice between fundamental and technical analysis often depends on the investor's goals, investment style, and time horizon. Fundamental analysis is typically preferred by investors focused on long-term growth and value, while technical analysis is favored by traders looking for short-term profits based on market trends. Understanding both methods and their applications allows for a more versatile and informed approach to stock market investing.

Long-term vs. Short-term Stock Trading Strategies

Investing in the stock market can be approached with various strategies, primarily categorized as long-term and short-term. These strategies differ fundamentally in their objectives, time horizons, risk profiles, and the level of active management required.

Long-term Stock Trading Strategies

Long-term trading strategies involve holding stocks for an extended period, typically years or even decades. This approach is often driven by the philosophy of investing in the fundamental value of companies.

Characteristics:

Focus on Fundamental Value: Long-term investors often use fundamental analysis to identify companies with strong potential for sustained growth, sound management, and robust financial health.

Compounding Returns: This strategy takes advantage of the power of compounding, where reinvested earnings generate their own earnings over time, potentially leading to exponential growth.

Risk Mitigation: Long-term investing can mitigate the impact of short-term market volatility, as investors are more concerned with the company's performance over years or decades.

Lower Transaction Costs: Frequent trading increases transaction costs. A long-term approach reduces these expenses, enhancing overall returns.

Tax Efficiency: Long-term capital gains are generally taxed at a lower rate than short-term gains, offering tax advantages to long-term investors.

Example Strategies:

- **Buy and Hold**: Purchasing stocks and holding them for many years, regardless of short-term market fluctuations.
- **Dividend Investing**: Investing in companies with a history of paying and increasing dividends, which can provide a regular income stream.

Short-term Stock Trading Strategies

Short-term strategies involve buying and selling stocks over a shorter period, ranging from a few days to several months. This approach is more about capitalizing on market trends and price movements than on company fundamentals.

Characteristics:

Market Timing and Trends: Short-term traders attempt to profit from market trends and price fluctuations, often using technical analysis.

Higher Risk and Volatility: These strategies are exposed to higher market volatility and require a good understanding of market dynamics.

Active Management: Short-term trading requires constant monitoring of market conditions and quick decision-making.

Higher Transaction Costs: Frequent trading leads to higher brokerage fees and transaction costs, which can eat into profits.

Tax Implications: Short-term capital gains are taxed at a higher rate than long-term gains, making this approach less tax-efficient.

Example Strategies:

- **Day Trading**: Buying and selling stocks within the same trading day, capitalizing on small price movements.
- **Swing Trading**: Holding stocks for several days or weeks to capitalize on expected upward or downward market shifts.

Conclusion

The choice between long-term and short-term trading strategies depends on an individual's financial goals, risk tolerance, investment knowledge, and time commitment. Long-term investing is generally considered suitable for those seeking to build wealth steadily over time, with a lower risk profile and minimal active management. In contrast, short-term trading can offer higher potential returns but requires more expertise, time, and a higher tolerance for risk. Each investor must evaluate their personal circumstances, goals, and preferences when choosing the strategy that best aligns with their investment objectives.

Real Estate as an Investment: A Comprehensive Guide

In the diverse landscape of investment opportunities, real estate stands as a distinctive and often lucrative option. This section delves into the multifaceted world of real estate investment, exploring its unique characteristics, benefits, and challenges. Real estate investment is not merely about purchasing property; it encompasses a range of strategies, each with its own risk and reward profile.

The Appeal of Real Estate Investment

Real estate investment attracts a wide array of investors due to its tangible nature, potential for passive income, and its role as a hedge against inflation. Unlike stocks and bonds, real estate is a physical asset, which for many investors adds a sense of security and substance to their investment portfolio.

Diverse Investment Strategies

This section will explore various strategies within real estate investment, including:

- **Residential Properties**: Investing in homes, apartments, and multifamily units.
- **Commercial Real Estate**: Opportunities in office buildings, retail spaces, and industrial properties.
- **Real Estate Investment Trusts (REITs)**: Buying shares in companies that own, operate, or finance income-generating real estate.
- **Real Estate Crowdfunding**: Pooling money with other investors to purchase property.

Key Considerations in Real Estate Investment

- **Market Research**: Understanding the local real estate market, including factors like location, demand, and future development plans.
- **Financial Analysis**: Assessing the potential return on investment, cash flow, and the overall financial health of a property.
- **Management and Maintenance**: The role of property management in maintaining and enhancing the value of real estate investments.

Risk and Return in Real Estate

Like any investment, real estate comes with inherent risks, including market fluctuations, property devaluation, and regulatory changes. We will discuss how to mitigate these risks and make informed investment decisions.

The Long-Term Perspective

Real estate investment is typically a long-term endeavor. We will explore the concept of real estate as a long-term wealth-building tool, and how it can contribute to a diversified investment portfolio.

Conclusion

By the end of this section, readers will have a thorough understanding of real estate as an investment option, equipped with the knowledge to make informed decisions about whether and how to incorporate real estate into their overall investment strategy. Whether you are contemplating your first real estate investment or looking to expand your existing portfolio, this guide will provide valuable insights and practical advice.

Benefits and Risks of Real Estate Investing

Investing in real estate offers a blend of potential rewards and risks, each of which must be carefully considered to make informed investment decisions. This part of the guide delves into the key benefits and risks associated with real estate investment.

Benefits of Real Estate Investing

Cash Flow: One of the primary benefits of real estate investment is the generation of cash flow, i.e., the net income from a property after mortgage payments and operating expenses have been made. This can provide a steady, passive income stream.

Appreciation: Over time, real estate values generally increase, offering investors the potential for capital gains. The appreciation of property value can significantly boost the return on investment when the property is sold.

Tax Advantages: Real estate investors can benefit from various tax deductions, such as mortgage interest, property taxes, operating expenses, depreciation, and even costs related to property improvements.

Inflation Hedge: Real estate investment can serve as an effective hedge against inflation. As inflation rises, so typically do rental rates and property values.

Leverage: Real estate allows for the use of leverage, meaning the use of various financial instruments or borrowed capital (like mortgages) to increase the potential return of an investment.

Risks of Real Estate Investing

Market Risk: The real estate market can be volatile, influenced by economic cycles, interest rates, and local market conditions. This can lead to fluctuations in property values and rental rates.

Liquidity Risk: Real estate is not a liquid asset. Unlike stocks or bonds, it can take a significant amount of time to sell a property for its market value.

Management Challenges: Owning real estate, especially rental property, requires ongoing management. This can include dealing with tenants, maintenance issues, and property management costs.

Financial Risk: The use of leverage in real estate can magnify losses. If property values decrease or if rental income is insufficient to cover mortgage and operational costs, investors can face financial strain.

Regulatory Risks: Real estate investors must navigate various laws and regulations, which can include zoning laws, property taxes, and compliance with tenant laws. These regulations can impact the profitability and legality of investment strategies.

Conclusion

Understanding the balance of these benefits and risks is crucial for anyone considering real estate investment. While the potential for significant returns exists, so too does the possibility of substantial challenges and losses. A prudent investor must conduct thorough market research, perform meticulous financial analysis, and be prepared for the management responsibilities that come with property ownership. By doing so, investors can better position themselves to reap the rewards of real estate investment while mitigating its inherent risks.

Different Ways to Invest in Real Estate

Real estate investment offers a variety of avenues, each with its unique characteristics, risks, and benefits. Understanding these different methods is essential for investors to align their investment strategies with their financial goals, risk tolerance, and level of involvement desired. Here, we explore some of the primary ways to invest in real estate:

1. Direct Ownership

Description: Direct ownership involves purchasing property outright. This can include residential properties (like houses or apartments), commercial properties (such as office buildings or retail spaces), or industrial properties (like warehouses).

Involvement: High. Direct owners are responsible for all aspects of the property, including maintenance, tenant management, and mortgage payments.

Risks and Benefits: Offers high potential returns and tax advantages but requires significant capital and involves risks like market fluctuations and management challenges.

2. Real Estate Investment Trusts (REITs)

Description: REITs are companies that own, operate, or finance income-generating real estate. They are typically publicly traded, allowing investors to buy shares in the real estate portfolio, similar to buying stocks.

Involvement: Low. Investors do not directly manage the properties; instead, they earn a share of the income produced through the real estate investment.

Risks and Benefits: Provides liquidity and diversification with lower capital requirements. However, investors have less control over specific investments, and returns are subject to the performance of the trust.

3. Real Estate Investment Groups (REIGs)

Description: REIGs are small mutual funds for rental properties. An investor can own one or multiple units of self-contained living space, but the company operating the investment group collectively manages all the units, handling maintenance, advertising vacant units, and interviewing tenants.

Involvement: Medium. The investor is a part of a group, reducing the management responsibilities but still having a say in the overall operations.

Risks and Benefits: Offers more control than REITs with some of the benefits of direct ownership, but still requires capital and is subject to group dynamics and management efficiency.

4. Real Estate Limited Partnerships (RELPs)

Description: RELPs are a form of investment partnership. They often involve a limited number of investors pooling their funds to invest in real estate projects.

Involvement: Varies. Typically, there is a general partner who manages the project, while limited partners contribute financially.

Risks and Benefits: Provides access to more significant projects and potential profits, but risks depend on the project's success and the general partner's expertise.

5. Real Estate Crowdfunding

Description: This method involves pooling money with other investors online to invest in a specific real estate project. It has become more popular with the rise of crowdfunding platforms.

Involvement: Low. Investors contribute funds but do not manage the property.

Risks and Benefits: Offers access to real estate investments with relatively small amounts of capital. However, it can be risky, as it depends on the success of individual projects and the platform's stability.

6. Fix-and-Flip

Description: This involves purchasing properties at a lower price, renovating them, and then selling them for a profit.

Involvement: High. Requires significant involvement in renovation and understanding of the real estate market.

Risks and Benefits: Potential for high returns in a short period, but involves substantial risk, including unexpected renovation costs and market volatility.

Conclusion

Each of these investment methods caters to different investor profiles, offering a range of involvement levels, capital requirements, and risk-reward ratios. Whether seeking hands-on involvement with direct ownership, the liquidity of REITs, or the collaborative approach of REIGs and RELPs, real estate investment offers diverse opportunities to build wealth. However, it's crucial for investors to thoroughly research and understand each option and align it with their investment strategy and goals.

Factors to Consider Before Investing in Real Estate

Investing in real estate is a significant decision that requires careful consideration of various factors. These factors can influence the success and viability of the investment. Here, we delve into key aspects that should be weighed before committing to a real estate investment:

1. Location

Importance: The adage 'location, location, location' holds true in real estate. The value and potential of a property are heavily influenced by its location.

Considerations: Proximity to amenities, schools, and economic centers, neighborhood status, and future development plans in the area.

2. Market Conditions

Importance: The real estate market fluctuates based on economic conditions, interest rates, and supply-demand dynamics.

Considerations: Current and forecasted market trends, property values, rental market rates, and economic indicators.

3. Investment Purpose and Timeframe

Importance: Clear investment goals and a defined timeframe are crucial for strategy alignment.

Considerations: Whether the investment is for long-term capital growth, rental income, or a short-term flip. Each objective requires different strategies and types of properties.

4. Property Type

- **Importance**: The type of property (residential, commercial, industrial) aligns with different investment goals and risk profiles.
- **Considerations**: Maintenance requirements, tenant turnover rates, rental yield potentials, and market demand for the property type.

5. Financial Analysis

- **Importance**: A thorough financial analysis ensures the investment is financially feasible and aligns with your goals.
- **Considerations**: Budget, financing options, expected return on investment (ROI), cash flow analysis, property taxes, insurance costs, and potential renovation expenses.

6. Risk Tolerance

- **Importance**: Real estate investments carry inherent risks, and it's vital to align these with your risk tolerance.
- **Considerations**: Market volatility, potential for property value depreciation, vacancy risks, and unexpected maintenance issues.

7. Legal and Regulatory Considerations

- **Importance**: Compliance with legal and regulatory requirements is essential to avoid costly penalties and legal issues.
- **Considerations**: Zoning laws, property taxes, landlord-tenant laws, and other relevant regulations.

8. Property Management

- **Importance**: Effective property management impacts the profitability and hassle of a real estate investment.
- **Considerations**: Whether to self-manage or hire a property management company, tenant screening processes, and ongoing management tasks.

9. Exit Strategy

- **Importance**: Having a clear exit strategy can maximize profits and minimize losses.
- **Considerations**: Plans for selling or leasing the property, market timing, and tax implications of selling.

10. Diversification

Importance: Diversification can mitigate risks in real estate investment.
Considerations: Investing in different types of properties, locations, or real estate investment trusts (REITs) to spread risk.

Conclusion

Investing in real estate demands a comprehensive understanding of various factors that can influence the investment's success. Prospective investors should conduct in-depth research and possibly consult with financial advisors, real estate experts, and legal professionals. This due diligence ensures informed decision-making, aligns the investment with personal and financial goals, and mitigates potential risks associated with real estate investments.

Introduction to Retirement Planning

Retirement planning, a critical component of personal financial management, necessitates a forward-thinking and strategic approach. It is a comprehensive process that not only encompasses the financial aspects of post-career life but also delves into broader considerations such as lifestyle choices and healthcare needs. The objective of retirement planning is not merely to ensure financial security but to facilitate a fulfilling and comfortable retirement phase.

The Essence of Retirement Planning

Future Financial Security: At its core, retirement planning is about preparing for a time when regular income ceases. It involves accumulating and managing resources to ensure financial independence and security in the later years of life.

Longevity and Healthcare: With increased life expectancies, retirement planning must account for longer retirement periods and potential healthcare expenses, which can be significant.

Lifestyle Goals: Retirement planning is also about realizing post-career aspirations, whether that involves travel, hobbies, or other pursuits. Adequate planning ensures the financial means to support these goals.

Key Elements of Retirement Planning

Savings and Investment Strategy: Building a robust retirement fund requires a well-thought-out savings and investment strategy. This includes deciding on the right mix of assets, understanding the impact of inflation, and managing risks through diversification.

Tax Planning: Efficient tax planning is vital to maximize retirement savings. It involves understanding the tax implications of various retirement accounts and investment choices.

- **Estate Planning**: This includes making decisions about the distribution of assets, creating wills, and setting up trusts to ensure a smooth transfer of wealth and adherence to the individual's wishes.
- **Healthcare Planning**: Considering future healthcare needs and the costs associated with them, including long-term care insurance and Medicare, is an integral part of retirement planning.

Challenges in Retirement Planning

- **Market Volatility and Economic Changes**: The impact of market fluctuations and economic shifts can significantly affect retirement savings and investment returns.
- **Inflation**: The erosion of purchasing power due to inflation is a critical factor in retirement planning. Strategies must account for this to ensure adequate funds throughout retirement.
- **Changing Life Circumstances**: Life events such as health issues, family obligations, or changes in employment status can necessitate adjustments in retirement planning.

Conclusion

In conclusion, retirement planning is a multifaceted and dynamic process. It requires not only financial acumen but also an understanding of individual goals and potential future scenarios. Successful retirement planning is marked by regular reviews and adjustments to align with changing circumstances and financial markets. Engaging in this process early and consistently can lead to a more secure and fulfilling retirement.

Understanding Different Retirement Accounts

Retirement accounts play a pivotal role in effective retirement planning. They are financial tools designed to help individuals save for retirement, each with distinct features, tax advantages, and rules. Understanding these differences is essential for making informed decisions that align with one's retirement goals and financial circumstances. Prominent among these accounts are the 401(k) and Individual Retirement Account (IRA), among others.

1. 401(k) Plans

- **Employer-Sponsored**: A 401(k) is a retirement savings plan sponsored by an employer. It allows workers to save and invest a portion of their paycheck before taxes are taken out.
- **Tax Advantages**: Contributions reduce taxable income, and the earnings on investments grow tax-deferred. Taxes are paid upon withdrawal, typically in retirement when the individual may be in a lower tax bracket.
- **Contribution Limits**: The Internal Revenue Service (IRS) sets annual contribution limits for 401(k) plans, which are typically higher than those for IRAs.

Employer Match: Many employers offer a match to the employee's contributions, which can significantly enhance retirement savings.

Roth Option: Some 401(k) plans offer a Roth option where contributions are made with after-tax dollars, with tax-free withdrawals in retirement.

2. Individual Retirement Accounts (IRAs)

Traditional IRA: Contributions to a traditional IRA may be tax-deductible, depending on the individual's income, tax-filing status, and other factors. Taxes on earnings are deferred until withdrawals, which are taxed as ordinary income.

Roth IRA: Contributions are made with after-tax dollars, but qualified withdrawals in retirement are tax-free. Roth IRAs are subject to income limits for eligibility.

Contribution Limits: IRAs have lower annual contribution limits compared to 401(k) plans.

No Employer Ties: IRAs are not tied to employment and can be opened by anyone with earned income, providing flexibility for individuals who may not have access to an employer-sponsored plan.

Other Retirement Accounts

403(b) Plans: Similar to 401(k)s but for employees of tax-exempt organizations, like schools and hospitals.

SEP IRAs and SIMPLE IRAs: Designed for small business owners and self-employed individuals, offering higher contribution limits and simpler administrative requirements.

Governmental Plans: Including the Thrift Savings Plan (TSP) for federal employees and military members, which is similar to a 401(k) plan.

Key Considerations

Investment Choices: Different plans offer various investment options, from mutual funds to stocks and bonds. The choice of investments can impact the growth of retirement savings.

Withdrawal Rules: Early withdrawal from these accounts can result in penalties and taxes, with specific age requirements for penalty-free withdrawals.

Required Minimum Distributions (RMDs): Most retirement accounts require minimum distributions starting at a certain age, except for Roth IRAs.

Conclusion

Selecting the right mix of retirement accounts requires an understanding of these differences and a consideration of one's financial situation, tax status, and retirement goals. It is often beneficial to diversify retirement savings across different types of accounts to optimize tax benefits and financial flexibility in retirement. Consulting with a financial advisor can provide tailored advice for individual circumstances and help navigate the complexities of retirement planning.

The Importance of Early and Consistent Retirement Contributions

Embarking on the journey of retirement planning, one of the most critical principles to embrace is the practice of early and consistent contributions. This approach is not merely a financial strategy but a profound investment in one's future security and comfort. The essence of this principle lies in leveraging the power of time and compounding, creating a robust financial foundation for the retirement years.

The Early Start Advantage

- **Compounding Effect**: The earlier one starts saving for retirement, the longer their contributions have to grow through compounding interest. This phenomenon can turn modest savings into significant sums over time.
- **Reduced Financial Burden**: Early contributions imply a smaller financial strain in later years. One doesn't need to save as aggressively in mid-life or nearing retirement if they start early, providing financial flexibility during various life stages.
- **Habit Formation**: Starting early helps inculcate a habit of saving and investing, which is crucial for long-term financial health.

Consistency: The Key to Accumulation

- **Steady Growth**: Consistent contributions ensure a steady growth of the retirement corpus. This consistency is crucial, as irregular contributions can significantly impact the final savings amount.
- **Dollar-Cost Averaging**: Regular contributions, irrespective of market conditions, lead to dollar-cost averaging, reducing the risk of investing a large sum at an inopportune time.
- **Budget Integration**: Incorporating retirement contributions into regular budgeting fosters financial discipline, ensuring that retirement planning is not an afterthought but a priority.

Impact of Delayed Contributions

- **Increased Contribution Requirements**: Delaying retirement savings means one has to contribute significantly more in the later years to catch up, which can be financially stressful.
- **Reduced Compounding Benefit**: The magic of compounding interest works best over long periods. A delayed start truncates this advantageous period, leading to lesser growth of the invested funds.

Riskier Investment Choices: To make up for lost time, one might be tempted to make riskier investments, which can potentially jeopardize financial security.

Real-Life Illustration

Consider two individuals, A and B. A starts contributing $300 monthly to a retirement account from age 25, while B starts doing the same at age 35. Assuming an average annual return of 7%, by age 65, A would have accumulated approximately $1.1 million, whereas B would have about $556,000. This stark difference highlights the profound impact of starting early and maintaining consistency.

Conclusion

The principle of early and consistent contributions transcends the realm of mere financial planning; it is an exercise in foresight and discipline. By embracing this approach, individuals not only secure their financial future but also imbibe a sense of responsibility and prudence that permeates all aspects of financial decision-making. As Benjamin Franklin aptly stated, "An investment in knowledge pays the best interest." Educating oneself on the virtues of early and consistent retirement contributions is indeed a wise investment.

Strategies for Maximizing Retirement Savings

The pursuit of a secure and comfortable retirement necessitates a strategic approach to savings. Maximizing retirement savings is not merely about putting away funds; it involves a series of calculated decisions and practices tailored to enhance the growth potential of your retirement corpus. Herein, we explore various strategies that can be employed to augment one's retirement savings, ensuring a financially secure future.

1. Take Full Advantage of Employer Match Programs

401(k) Match: Many employers offer a match on 401(k) contributions, typically up to a certain percentage of the employee's salary. Not utilizing this match is akin to leaving free money on the table. Ensure you contribute at least enough to get the full employer match.

Compound Growth: Employer contributions compound over time, significantly increasing your retirement savings.

2. Increase Savings Rate Over Time

Gradual Increments: Boost your contribution percentage incrementally – for instance, with each raise or bonus. A gradual increase can have a substantial impact over time without a noticeable effect on your current lifestyle.

Automated Escalation: Many retirement plans offer an automatic contribution escalation feature. Utilize this to effortlessly increase your savings rate annually.

3. Diversify Your Investment Portfolio

- **Asset Allocation**: Balance your portfolio across various asset classes (stocks, bonds, real estate, etc.) to mitigate risk and optimize returns.
- **Rebalancing**: Regularly rebalance your portfolio to maintain your desired asset allocation, ensuring alignment with your risk tolerance and investment horizon.

4. Maximize Tax-Advantaged Accounts

- **Utilize IRAs**: In addition to 401(k)s, contribute to Individual Retirement Accounts (IRAs), whether Roth or Traditional, depending on your tax situation.
- **Health Savings Accounts (HSAs)**: If eligible, contribute to an HSA. HSAs offer triple tax advantages and can be used for medical expenses in retirement.

5. Delay Social Security Benefits

- **Increased Benefits**: Delaying the start of Social Security benefits beyond the full retirement age can result in a significant increase in monthly benefits.
- **Longevity Considerations**: If you are in good health and have a family history of longevity, delaying benefits can be particularly advantageous.

6. Minimize Fees and Expenses

- **Cost-Efficient Funds**: Opt for low-cost index funds or ETFs to reduce the drag on returns caused by high management fees.
- **Review Expenses**: Regularly review your investment choices to ensure you are not overpaying for fund management.

7. Consider Catch-Up Contributions

- **Age 50 and Older**: Take advantage of catch-up contributions allowed in 401(k)s and IRAs for those aged 50 and above. These contributions permit you to save additional amounts above the standard limits.

8. Stay Informed and Adapt

- **Continuous Learning**: Keep abreast of changes in retirement savings rules, tax laws, and investment strategies.

Adaptation: Be prepared to adapt your strategies in response to life changes, such as a job switch, family circumstances, or significant economic shifts.

9. Seek Professional Advice

Financial Advisor: Consider consulting with a financial advisor to tailor your retirement planning to your specific situation, goals, and risk tolerance.

Conclusion

Employing these strategies requires a blend of discipline, foresight, and adaptability. It is crucial to remember that maximizing retirement savings is not a one-size-fits-all approach but rather a personalized journey. As Warren Buffett wisely advises, "Do not save what is left after spending; instead spend what is left after saving." Adopting this mindset and implementing these strategies can significantly enhance the prospects of a financially secure and fulfilling retirement.

Introduction: Exploring the World of Alternative Investments

In the ever-evolving landscape of investment, the realm of alternative investments stands as a beacon for those seeking diversification beyond the traditional avenues of stocks, bonds, and cash. This sector, characterized by its vast array of unique assets, offers investors an opportunity to explore uncharted territories that can potentially yield substantial rewards. As we embark on this exploration, it is imperative to grasp the depth and breadth of alternative investments, understanding their role in a well-rounded portfolio and the dynamics that set them apart from conventional investment options.

Alternative investments encompass a diverse range of assets, including but not limited to private equity, hedge funds, commodities, real estate, collectibles, and even cryptocurrencies. Each of these categories offers distinct characteristics, risk profiles, and return potentials, appealing to different investor temperaments and objectives. The allure of alternative investments lies not only in their potential for high returns but also in their capacity to provide portfolio diversification, thereby reducing overall investment risk.

The journey into alternative investments is not without its challenges and complexities. These investments often require a higher degree of due diligence, a willingness to embrace illiquidity, and an understanding of intricate market dynamics. They frequently demand a longer investment horizon and a higher threshold for risk tolerance, making them more suitable for seasoned investors or those with specialized knowledge.

As we delve deeper into each category of alternative investments, we will uncover the nuances that define them, the strategies that drive their success, and the risks that accompany their potential rewards. This section aims not only to inform but also to empower investors with the knowledge and confidence to consider alternative investments as a part of their broader investment strategy.

In a world where financial markets are continually influenced by global economic shifts, technological advancements, and evolving investor preferences, alternative investments offer a compelling proposition. They provide a means to potentially enhance returns, mitigate risks, and achieve financial goals in ways that traditional investments may not. As we navigate through this intricate and fascinating sector, remember the words of John C. Bogle, "If you have trouble imagining a 20% loss in the stock market, you shouldn't be in stocks." The same principle applies to alternative investments: understanding and acceptance of the risks involved are paramount.

Let us now embark on this insightful journey, unraveling the mysteries of alternative investments, and discovering how they can play a pivotal role in shaping a robust and dynamic investment portfolio.

Exploring Commodities, Cryptocurrencies, and Collectibles in Alternative Investments

In the realm of alternative investments, three distinct categories—commodities, cryptocurrencies, and collectibles—stand out for their unique characteristics and potential investment opportunities. Each of these asset classes offers investors a divergent path from traditional market securities, presenting both distinctive rewards and risks. In this exploration, we shall delve into the intricacies of these options, evaluating their role in a well-diversified investment portfolio.

Commodities

Commodities, tangible assets like gold, oil, and agricultural products, have been a cornerstone of trade and investment for centuries. They offer a hedge against inflation and a counterbalance to stock market volatility. Investing in commodities can be approached through direct physical ownership, futures contracts, or through commodity-focused ETFs (Exchange-Traded Funds) and mutual funds.

- **Gold:** Often viewed as a 'safe-haven' asset, gold maintains its value in times of economic uncertainty.
- **Oil and Gas:** These energy commodities are highly sensitive to geopolitical events and changes in global supply and demand.
- **Agricultural Products:** From wheat to coffee, these commodities can offer opportunities but are susceptible to changes in weather patterns and global trade policies.

The primary allure of commodities lies in their negative correlation with stocks and bonds, making them an excellent tool for diversification. However, investors must be cognizant of the risks, including market volatility, geopolitical factors, and the complexities of futures trading.

Cryptocurrencies

Cryptocurrencies, a more recent addition to the investment landscape, represent digital or virtual currencies secured by cryptography. The most well-known among them is Bitcoin, but the market includes other significant players like Ethereum, Ripple, and Litecoin. Cryptocurrencies are praised for their potential for high returns and their role as an innovation in the financial technology space.

Investing in cryptocurrencies involves direct purchase and storage of the digital assets or investing through cryptocurrency funds or blockchain-based companies. The main attractions are:

High Return Potential: Cryptocurrencies have shown an ability for rapid value appreciation.
Innovation and Technology: Investment in cryptocurrencies is also an investment in blockchain technology, which has wide-ranging applications.

However, the risks are substantial, including extreme volatility, regulatory uncertainty, and security concerns. Cryptocurrency investment requires a high-risk tolerance and a willingness to endure market turbulence.

Collectibles

Collectibles include a wide range of physical assets such as art, antiques, vintage cars, and rare memorabilia. These assets have intrinsic value and can appreciate over time due to their rarity and demand.

Art: Investment in art can be highly rewarding but requires knowledge about art history and current market trends.
Vintage Collectibles: Items like classic cars, vintage wines, and antique furniture can accrue value over time.
Memorabilia: Rare items from sports, entertainment, and history can become highly valuable.

The appeal of collectibles lies in their aesthetic and historical value, and the emotional satisfaction they provide, apart from their financial worth. However, investing in collectibles necessitates expertise in the respective field, a good eye for quality, and patience, as these assets often appreciate over a long period.

In conclusion, commodities, cryptocurrencies, and collectibles present diverse opportunities for investors seeking to diversify beyond traditional stocks and bonds. Each comes with its own set of complexities and requires a thorough understanding and specialized knowledge to navigate successfully. While they can offer substantial rewards, the associated risks must be carefully weighed, making them suitable primarily for investors with a higher risk tolerance and a long-term investment horizon.

Understanding the Risks and Potential of Alternative Investments

Alternative investments, encompassing a wide array of assets outside of the traditional realms of stocks, bonds, and cash, offer investors the possibility of high returns and portfolio diversification. However, they also come with a unique set of risks and challenges. Understanding these risks and the potential rewards is crucial for any investor considering an allocation into alternative investments.

Assessing the Risks

Market Volatility and Liquidity Issues: Alternative investments often exhibit higher volatility compared to traditional investments. Additionally, many of these assets face liquidity challenges, meaning they cannot be easily sold or converted into cash without a significant loss in value. This is particularly true for assets like real estate, art, and collectibles.

Complexity and Lack of Transparency: Many alternative investments, such as hedge funds, private equity, and derivatives, can be complex in nature, with intricate structures and strategies. This complexity often results in a lack of transparency, making it difficult for investors to fully understand the risks involved.

Regulatory and Legal Risks: Alternative investments may be subject to less regulatory oversight, leading to increased risk of fraud and malpractice. Additionally, changes in regulations can significantly impact the value of these investments.

High Fees and Costs: Investing in alternatives often incurs higher fees than traditional investments. Management and performance fees for funds, as well as costs associated with buying, storing, and insuring physical assets, can reduce net returns.

Correlation Risks: While alternative investments are often sought for diversification, some may still show correlation to traditional markets, especially during periods of high market stress, potentially undermining their diversification benefits.

Realizing the Potential

Diversification Benefits: Alternative investments can offer diversification benefits, as their returns are often uncorrelated with those of traditional equity and bond markets. This can help in spreading risk and reducing the volatility of an investment portfolio.

Inflation Hedge: Certain alternatives, like real estate and commodities, can act as effective hedges against inflation, preserving the purchasing power of capital in times of rising prices.

High Return Potential: Some alternative assets, such as venture capital, private equity, and cryptocurrencies, have the potential to yield higher returns compared to traditional investments, albeit with higher risk.

Access to Unique Opportunities: Alternative investments provide access to unique market opportunities and sectors not readily available through traditional investments, such as emerging technologies, green energy projects, and niche real estate markets.

Impact and Satisfaction: Investments in art, collectibles, and certain real estate ventures offer not just financial rewards but also personal satisfaction and impact. For instance, investing in sustainable real estate projects or collectibles with historical significance can be gratifying beyond mere financial returns.

In conclusion, while alternative investments can offer attractive opportunities for portfolio diversification and high potential returns, they require a careful assessment of their unique risks. Investors should possess, or seek advice from professionals with, a deep understanding of these asset classes. An informed approach, coupled with a clear alignment of such investments with one's financial goals, risk tolerance, and investment horizon, is essential for successfully incorporating alternative investments into a broader investment strategy.

Understanding the Risks and Potential of Alternative Investments

Alternative investments, encompassing a wide array of assets outside of the traditional realms of stocks, bonds, and cash, offer investors the possibility of high returns and portfolio diversification. However, they also come with a unique set of risks and challenges. Understanding these risks and the potential rewards is crucial for any investor considering an allocation into alternative investments.

Assessing the Risks

Market Volatility and Liquidity Issues: Alternative investments often exhibit higher volatility compared to traditional investments. Additionally, many of these assets face liquidity challenges, meaning they cannot be easily sold or converted into cash without a significant loss in value. This is particularly true for assets like real estate, art, and collectibles.

Complexity and Lack of Transparency: Many alternative investments, such as hedge funds, private equity, and derivatives, can be complex in nature, with intricate structures and strategies. This complexity often results in a lack of transparency, making it difficult for investors to fully understand the risks involved.

Regulatory and Legal Risks: Alternative investments may be subject to less regulatory oversight, leading to increased risk of fraud and malpractice. Additionally, changes in regulations can significantly impact the value of these investments.

High Fees and Costs: Investing in alternatives often incurs higher fees than traditional investments. Management and performance fees for funds, as well as costs associated with buying, storing, and insuring physical assets, can reduce net returns.

Correlation Risks: While alternative investments are often sought for diversification, some may still show correlation to traditional markets, especially during periods of high market stress, potentially undermining their diversification benefits.

Realizing the Potential

Diversification Benefits: Alternative investments can offer diversification benefits, as their returns are often uncorrelated with those of traditional equity and bond markets. This can help in spreading risk and reducing the volatility of an investment portfolio.

Inflation Hedge: Certain alternatives, like real estate and commodities, can act as effective hedges against inflation, preserving the purchasing power of capital in times of rising prices.

High Return Potential: Some alternative assets, such as venture capital, private equity, and cryptocurrencies, have the potential to yield higher returns compared to traditional investments, albeit with higher risk.

Access to Unique Opportunities: Alternative investments provide access to unique market opportunities and sectors not readily available through traditional investments, such as emerging technologies, green energy projects, and niche real estate markets.

Impact and Satisfaction: Investments in art, collectibles, and certain real estate ventures offer not just financial rewards but also personal satisfaction and impact. For instance, investing in sustainable real estate projects or collectibles with historical significance can be gratifying beyond mere financial returns.

In conclusion, while alternative investments can offer attractive opportunities for portfolio diversification and high potential returns, they require a careful assessment of their unique risks. Investors should possess, or seek advice from professionals with, a deep understanding of these asset classes. An informed approach, coupled with a clear alignment of such investments with one's financial goals, risk tolerance, and investment horizon, is essential for successfully incorporating alternative investments into a broader investment strategy.

Incorporating Alternatives into a Diversified Portfolio

Diversification stands as a cornerstone of prudent investment strategy, mitigating risk while potentially enhancing returns. The integration of alternative investments into a portfolio can augment this diversification, provided it is executed with strategic foresight and an understanding of the unique characteristics of these assets. Herein, we shall explore the methodology and considerations for incorporating alternatives into a diversified investment portfolio.

Strategic Allocation

Assessment of Risk Tolerance and Investment Goals: Before incorporating alternative investments, an investor must assess their risk tolerance and long-term investment objectives. Alternatives, with their varied risk-return profiles, should align with the individual's financial goals and capacity to absorb potential losses.

Determining the Appropriate Allocation: The allocation to alternative investments should be based on their correlation with existing assets in the portfolio, potential impact on overall volatility, and contribution to achieving diversification. Common wisdom suggests a modest allocation to alternatives, often recommended between 5% and 20% of the total portfolio, contingent upon the investor's risk appetite and investment horizon.

Selection of Alternative Assets: The choice of specific alternative investments should reflect an investor's knowledge and understanding of the asset class. This includes factors like market trends, liquidity needs, and the time horizon for investment. A diversified mix of alternatives, including real estate, commodities, private equity, hedge funds, and collectibles, can be considered.

Portfolio Construction

Complementary Assets: In selecting alternatives, it is pivotal to identify assets that complement and balance the existing portfolio. For instance, real estate and commodities might provide inflation hedging, while hedge funds may offer unique strategies that are uncorrelated with stock and bond markets.

Diversification Within Alternatives: Just as diversification is essential across a traditional portfolio, it is equally important within the alternative segment. Diversifying across different types of alternative investments can reduce the risk associated with any single asset class.

Rebalancing Regularly: The portfolio should be regularly reviewed and rebalanced to maintain the desired asset allocation. This is especially important for alternatives, which can exhibit significant price volatility and may drift from their intended allocation over time.

Risk Management

Understanding Illiquidity: Many alternative investments are illiquid, meaning they cannot be quickly sold or converted to cash. Investors must manage the liquidity risk by ensuring they have enough liquid assets to meet short-term needs.

Monitoring and Due Diligence: Ongoing monitoring and due diligence are critical, given the complexity and lower transparency of many alternative investments. Staying informed about market changes and the performance of these assets is crucial.

Advisory and Expertise: Given the specialized nature of alternative investments, seeking advice from financial advisors with expertise in these assets can be beneficial. Professional guidance can aid in selecting the right alternatives and managing the associated risks effectively.

In summary, incorporating alternative investments into a diversified portfolio requires a nuanced understanding of these assets, a clear alignment with the investor's overall financial strategy, and a disciplined approach to portfolio construction and risk management. When executed judiciously, alternatives can enhance portfolio diversification, potentially leading to improved risk-adjusted returns. However, investors must navigate this terrain with caution, acknowledging the complexities and unique risks that alternative investments entail.

Tax Considerations in Investing

Investing, while primarily focused on generating returns, is intricately linked with the realm of taxation. Understanding and navigating the tax implications of various investment decisions is crucial for optimizing the overall efficiency of an investment strategy. This discourse aims to elucidate key tax considerations that investors should be aware of, enhancing their ability to make informed decisions that align with their financial objectives while minimizing tax liabilities.

Types of Investment Taxes

Capital Gains Tax: This tax is levied on the profit realized from the sale of a non-inventory asset, such as stocks, bonds, or real estate, when the sale price exceeds the purchase price. Capital gains are classified as either short-term (held for less than a year) or long-term (held for more than a yer), each attracting different tax rates.

Dividend Tax: Dividends, which are distributions of a company's earnings to its shareholders, are subject to taxation. The tax rate on dividends can vary based on whether they are qualified or non-qualified dividends, with qualified dividends generally receiving more favorable tax treatment.

Interest Income Tax: Interest earned from investments like savings accounts, CDs, and bonds is typically subject to income tax. The rate depends on the investor's income tax bracket.

Tax-Efficient Investing Strategies

Holding Periods: Long-term capital gains are usually taxed at a lower rate than short-term gains. Therefore, holding investments for more than a year before selling can lead to significant tax savings.

Tax-Loss Harvesting: This involves selling securities at a loss to offset capital gains tax liability. It's a strategy used to manage taxes while maintaining the desired asset allocation in a portfolio.

Asset Location: Certain investments are more tax-efficient in specific types of accounts. For example, placing high-growth investments in Roth IRAs can be beneficial, as withdrawals are tax-free in retirement.

Retirement Accounts: Contributions to traditional IRAs and 401(k)s may be tax-deductible, and the investments grow tax-deferred until withdrawal. Roth IRAs and Roth 401(k)s offer tax-free growth and withdrawals, although contributions are made with after-tax dollars.

Tax-Advantaged Investments

Municipal Bonds: Often referred to as "munis," these bonds are generally exempt from federal taxes and, in some cases, state and local taxes, particularly if the investor lives in the state where the bond was issued.

Health Savings Accounts (HSAs) and Education Savings Accounts (ESAs): These accounts offer tax-free growth and tax-free withdrawals for qualified medical and educational expenses, respectively.

Navigating Tax Complexity

Professional Advice: Given the complexity of tax laws, consulting with a tax professional or financial advisor can be invaluable. They can provide personalized advice based on an individual's specific financial situation.

Staying Informed: Tax laws can change, and staying informed about these changes is crucial for maintaining a tax-efficient investment strategy.

Record-Keeping: Maintaining accurate records of all investment transactions is essential for calculating capital gains and losses and ensuring compliance with tax laws.

In conclusion, tax considerations play a pivotal role in the realm of investing. A keen understanding of how different investments are taxed, coupled with strategies to minimize tax liabilities, can significantly affect the net return on investment. Investors are encouraged to integrate tax planning into their overall investment strategy, considering the interplay between investment decisions and their tax implications. By doing so, they can enhance the efficiency of their investment portfolio, ensuring that their financial goals are met in a tax-effective manner.

Tax Implications of Different Investment Types

Investing is not only about assessing potential returns but also understanding the tax implications associated with different types of investments. Each investment vehicle carries its unique set of tax rules, affecting the overall profitability and suitability of the investment. This section delves into the tax implications of various investment types, aiming to provide investors with the knowledge necessary to make tax-efficient investment decisions.

1. Stocks

Capital Gains Tax: When stocks are sold for a profit, capital gains tax is applicable. The rate depends on how long the stocks were held. Long-term capital gains (on assets held for over a year) are taxed at lower rates than short-term gains.

Dividend Tax: Dividends paid by stocks can be taxed at either ordinary income rates or at lower qualified dividend rates, depending on various criteria, including the holding period of the stock.

2. Bonds

Interest Income: Interest from bonds is typically taxed as ordinary income in the year it is received. However, some bonds, like municipal bonds, may be exempt from federal and sometimes state and local taxes.

Capital Gains Tax: Similar to stocks, selling bonds at a profit leads to capital gains tax liabilities.

3. Mutual Funds

Distributions: Mutual funds can distribute capital gains and dividends to investors, which are subject to taxes. The tax rate depends on whether these distributions are classified as long-term capital gains or ordinary income.

Tax-Efficiency: Some mutual funds are designed for tax efficiency, minimizing taxable distributions.

4. Real Estate Investments

Rental Income: Income generated from rental properties is taxed as ordinary income. However, investors can deduct expenses such as mortgage interest, property tax, and maintenance costs.

Capital Gains: Selling real estate can result in capital gains tax, although certain exclusions can apply, especially for primary residences.

Depreciation: Investors can depreciate the value of the property over time, providing a tax deduction that can offset rental income.

5. Retirement Accounts (e.g., 401(k), IRA)

Traditional Accounts: Contributions are often tax-deductible, and earnings grow tax-deferred. Taxes are paid upon withdrawal, typically at ordinary income rates.

Roth Accounts: Contributions are made with after-tax dollars, but withdrawals in retirement are tax-free, including the earnings.

6. Exchange-Traded Funds (ETFs)

- **Tax Efficiency:** ETFs are generally more tax-efficient than mutual funds due to their unique structure, which typically allows investors to defer capital gains taxes.
- **Dividends and Interest:** Like stocks and bonds, dividends and interest from ETFs are subject to taxes.

7. Commodities and Precious Metals

- **Physical Holdings:** Sales of physical commodities or precious metals can result in capital gains tax, often at a higher rate for collectibles.
- **ETFs and Mutual Funds:** Investing in commodities through ETFs or mutual funds involves similar tax implications as those funds.

8. Cryptocurrencies

- **Capital Gains:** The sale or exchange of cryptocurrencies can trigger capital gains tax.
- **Income Tax:** Mining or receiving cryptocurrencies as payment is considered taxable income.

9. Options and Futures

- **Complex Tax Rules:** The taxation of options and futures can be complex, involving short-term and long-term capital gains and, in some cases, marked-to-market rules.

Understanding the tax implications of these investment types is crucial for effective portfolio management. It allows investors to anticipate their tax liabilities and make decisions that align with their financial goals and tax situation. In navigating this complex landscape, consulting with a tax professional can be invaluable in optimizing investment strategies for tax efficiency.

Strategies for Tax-Efficient Investing

Tax-efficient investing is a strategic approach to managing your investments in a way that minimizes tax liabilities and maximizes after-tax returns. Given the varying tax treatments of different investment vehicles, it is imperative to understand and employ strategies that align with one's financial goals while being tax-conscious. Herein, we will explore various methods and considerations for achieving greater tax efficiency in your investment portfolio.

1. Utilize Tax-Advantaged Accounts

    Retirement Accounts: Maximize contributions to tax-advantaged accounts like 401(k)s, IRAs (both Traditional and Roth), and other retirement plans. Traditional accounts offer tax-deferred growth, while Roth accounts provide tax-free growth.

    Education Savings: Consider 529 plans or Coverdell Education Savings Accounts for education savings, which offer tax-free growth and withdrawals for qualified education expenses.

2. Hold Investments Long-Term

    Capital Gains Strategy: Aim to hold investments for more than a year to benefit from lower long-term capital gains tax rates, as opposed to higher short-term rates on investments held for less than a year.

3. Asset Location

    Tax-Efficient Placement: Place high-yield investments in tax-advantaged accounts where tax on income can be deferred. Conversely, place more tax-efficient investments, like stocks you intend to hold long-term or tax-exempt municipal bonds, in taxable accounts.

    Consider Roth Conversions: In certain cases, converting Traditional IRA assets to a Roth IRA can be advantageous, particularly if you expect to be in a higher tax bracket in the future.

4. Tax-Loss Harvesting

    Offset Gains with Losses: Sell investments that are at a loss to offset capital gains realized elsewhere in your portfolio. This strategy, known as tax-loss harvesting, can reduce your overall capital gains tax liability.

    Beware of Wash-Sale Rules: Avoid repurchasing the same or substantially similar security within 30 days before or after the sale to ensure the loss remains deductible.

5. Invest in Tax-Efficient Funds

    ETFs and Index Funds: These funds typically have lower turnover rates, resulting in fewer capital gains distributions compared to actively managed funds.

    Municipal Bonds: Interest from municipal bonds is often exempt from federal income tax and sometimes state and local taxes, making them an attractive option for investors in higher tax brackets.

6. Consider the Impact of Dividends

- **Qualified Dividends:** Aim for investments that pay qualified dividends, which are taxed at the lower long-term capital gains rate, as opposed to non-qualified dividends taxed as ordinary income.

7. Gifting and Donations

- **Charitable Contributions:** Donating appreciated securities directly to charity can avoid capital gains taxes and provide a charitable deduction.
- **Gifting to Family Members:** Consider gifting appreciated assets to family members in lower tax brackets, who may be subject to lower capital gains tax rates.

8. Strategic Withdrawals

- **Retirement Withdrawals:** Plan the timing and order of withdrawals from different types of accounts in retirement to minimize taxes. This might include balancing withdrawals from taxable and tax-advantaged accounts.

9. Estate Planning Considerations

- **Step-Up in Basis:** Understand the benefits of the step-up in basis rules for inherited assets, which can minimize capital gains tax for heirs.

10. Continual Review and Adjustment

- **Regular Portfolio Review:** Regularly review and adjust your investment strategy to adapt to changes in tax laws and your personal circumstances.

In conclusion, tax-efficient investing requires a holistic view of your portfolio, taking into consideration the interplay of various investments, tax laws, and personal financial goals. It is often beneficial to collaborate with financial and tax professionals to tailor a strategy that maximizes after-tax returns while adhering to your investment objectives and risk tolerance. Remember, the ultimate goal is not just to maximize returns but to maximize what you keep after taxes.

Understanding Capital Gains and Losses

Capital gains and losses are fundamental concepts in the realm of investing and tax planning. They represent the changes in the value of an investment from the time it is purchased to the time it is sold. Understanding these concepts is crucial for investors as they have significant implications for investment strategies and tax liabilities.

Definition of Capital Gains and Losses

Capital Gain: A capital gain occurs when you sell an asset for more than its purchase price. For example, if you buy a stock for $100 and sell it later for $150, you have a capital gain of $50.

Capital Loss: Conversely, a capital loss happens when you sell an asset for less than its purchase price. Selling the same stock for $80, resulting in a $20 loss, illustrates a capital loss.

Types of Capital Gains

Short-Term Capital Gains: If you hold an asset for one year or less before selling, any profit is considered a short-term capital gain, taxed as ordinary income at your regular income tax rate.

Long-Term Capital Gains: Gains on assets held for more than one year are classified as long-term. These are taxed at a lower rate, which is advantageous for long-term investors.

Calculating Capital Gains and Losses

To calculate your capital gain or loss, subtract the asset's purchase price (basis) from its selling price. If you have incurred additional costs such as brokerage fees, they can be added to the basis, thus reducing the gain or increasing the loss.

Capital Gains Tax Rates

The tax rate on long-term capital gains depends on your taxable income and filing status. Generally, these rates are more favorable than the rates for short-term gains. As of my last update, the long-term capital gains tax rates in the United States were 0%, 15%, or 20%, depending on your income level.

Netting Capital Gains and Losses

Offsetting Gains with Losses: You can use capital losses to offset capital gains. For instance, if you gained $1,000 on one investment but lost $500 on another, you can offset your gains with these losses, resulting in a net gain of $500.

Carryover of Losses: If your capital losses exceed your capital gains, you can use the loss to offset up to $3,000 of other income. If your total net capital loss is more than the limit you can deduct, you can carry over the losses to future years.

Wash Sale Rule

Investors must be aware of the wash sale rule. This IRS rule disallows a tax deduction for a security sold in a loss if you purchase the same or substantially identical security within 30 days before or after the sale.

Capital Gains and Estate Planning

In estate planning, capital gains have unique considerations. Inherited assets typically receive a "step-up" in basis to their market value as of the decedent's date of death, which can significantly reduce capital gains tax if these assets are later sold.

Conclusion

Understanding capital gains and losses is vital for effective investment and tax strategies. These concepts influence decisions on when to buy or sell assets, the types of investments to hold, and how to plan for taxes. Given the complexity of tax laws and their susceptibility to change, investors often benefit from consulting with financial and tax professionals to navigate these waters effectively. This knowledge empowers investors to make informed decisions, potentially reducing their tax burden and optimizing their investment returns.

Building and Managing an Investment Portfolio: A Call to Action

Embarking on the journey of building and managing an investment portfolio is not just a financial decision, but a profound step towards achieving your personal and financial aspirations. This endeavor, while requiring diligence and strategic planning, is a rewarding process that empowers you to take control of your financial future. As we delve into this crucial aspect of wealth creation and preservation, it is imperative to approach it with a clear vision, informed decision-making, and a commitment to ongoing education and adaptation.

Embrace the Role of an Astute Investor

- **Self-Reflection**: Begin by introspecting your financial goals, risk tolerance, and investment horizon. This self-awareness is the cornerstone of a portfolio that truly reflects your unique circumstances and aspirations.
- **Continuous Learning**: The world of investing is dynamic and complex. Commit to educating yourself continuously about different investment vehicles, market trends, and economic factors that influence your portfolio's performance.

Key Strategies for Portfolio Management

Diversification: Learn the art of diversification, not just across asset classes, but also within them. This strategy is fundamental in mitigating risk and enhancing the potential for balanced growth.

Asset Allocation: Understand how to allocate your investments in a way that aligns with your risk tolerance and investment goals. This involves a mix of stocks, bonds, real estate, and possibly alternative investments, each playing a distinct role in your portfolio.

Regular Review and Rebalancing: Your portfolio is not a set-and-forget endeavor. Regular review and rebalancing in response to market changes and life events are essential to maintain alignment with your goals.

Embrace Technological Tools and Professional Advice

Utilize Investment Tools: Leverage technology to track and manage your investments. Numerous apps and platforms can help streamline this process, offering insights and analytics to aid in decision-making.

Seek Professional Guidance: While self-management is possible, consulting with financial advisors can provide deeper insights, especially in complex situations or for sophisticated investment strategies.

Prepare for the Psychological Aspects of Investing

Emotional Discipline: Investing can be an emotional rollercoaster. Prepare to navigate the psychological aspects, including the temptation to react hastily to market volatility. Developing a long-term perspective and emotional resilience is crucial.

A Journey of Financial Empowerment

As you embark on this journey of building and managing your investment portfolio, remember that it is a continuous process of learning, adapting, and growing. Your portfolio is more than just a collection of assets; it is a reflection of your financial savvy, a testament to your discipline, and a tool for building the future you envision.

This section aims not only to educate but to inspire and empower you to take the reins of your financial destiny. Through informed strategies, a balanced approach, and a commitment to your goals, you can build a portfolio that not only grows in value but also brings you closer to realizing your financial dreams. Let us embark on this journey together, with a spirit of optimism, a commitment to excellence, and a vision for a prosperous future.

Strategies for Portfolio Creation and Management: Crafting Your Financial Masterpiece

Creating and managing an investment portfolio is akin to an artist crafting a masterpiece. It requires a blend of knowledge, intuition, and a strategic approach. This section is dedicated to guiding you through the intricacies of portfolio creation and management, ensuring that your investment decisions are not just transactions, but steps towards realizing your financial and personal goals.

1. Setting a Solid Foundation: Goal-Setting and Risk Assessment

- **Clarifying Investment Goals:** Begin by defining clear, achievable goals. Are you saving for retirement, a child's education, or building wealth over the long term? Your goals will dictate your investment strategy.
- **Risk Tolerance Assessment:** Understanding your risk tolerance is crucial. It will determine your asset allocation and help you invest in a manner that aligns with your comfort level and financial objectives.

2. Asset Allocation: The Art of Diversification

- **Balancing Asset Classes:** A well-balanced portfolio typically includes a mix of stocks, bonds, and other asset classes like real estate or alternative investments. The key is to find the right balance that aligns with your goals and risk tolerance.
- **Diversification Within Asset Classes:** Diversification doesn't stop at asset classes. Within each class, such as stocks or bonds, diversify across sectors, geographical regions, and company sizes to mitigate sector-specific or market-wide risks.

3. Strategic Investment Selection

- **Quality Over Quantity:** When selecting individual investments, focus on quality. Research and select stocks, bonds, or funds that have strong fundamentals and align with your investment philosophy.
- **Cost-Conscious Investing:** Be mindful of investment costs, including fund management fees and transaction costs, as they can significantly impact your returns over time.

4. Active Monitoring and Rebalancing

- **Regular Portfolio Reviews:** Regularly review your portfolio to ensure it remains aligned with your goals. Economic conditions, market trends, and personal circumstances can change, necessitating adjustments.
- **Disciplined Rebalancing:** Rebalance your portfolio periodically to maintain your desired asset allocation. This might involve selling some investments and buying others to get back to your target allocation.

5. Risk Management

Hedging Strategies: Consider using hedging strategies to protect your portfolio against market volatility. This could include options, futures contracts, or diversifying into assets inversely correlated with your primary investments.

Emergency Fund: Maintain an emergency fund to avoid liquidating investments in a market downturn, thereby allowing your portfolio to recover and grow over time.

6. Adapting to Life Changes

Responsive Investing: As your life circumstances evolve – such as a career change, marriage, or nearing retirement – your investment strategy should adapt correspondingly. Flexibility and responsiveness to change are key.

7. Leveraging Technology and Expertise

Utilize Financial Tools: Embrace technology for portfolio management, such as investment tracking software, robo-advisors, or analytical tools, to make informed decisions.

Seeking Professional Advice: Consider consulting with financial advisors for tailored advice, especially when dealing with complex scenarios or large investment portfolios.

In Conclusion: Crafting Your Financial Future

Your investment portfolio is more than a collection of assets; it's a reflection of your financial journey and aspirations. By employing these strategies in portfolio creation and management, you are not just investing money; you are crafting a path to financial security and fulfillment. Approach each investment decision with thoughtfulness and strategy, much like an artist with their canvas, and watch as your financial masterpiece comes to life.

Rebalancing and Adjusting Your Portfolio Over Time: The Dynamics of Portfolio Evolution

As an investor, it is imperative to understand that portfolio rebalancing and adjustment is not a mere administrative task, but a fundamental aspect of sound investment management. Over time, the initial asset allocation of your portfolio can drift due to varying performance of the underlying assets. Rebalancing is the process of realigning the weightings of these assets to maintain the desired level of asset allocation and risk.

The Need for Rebalancing: Maintaining Risk Alignment

Drift from Target Allocation: Over time, some investments may outperform others, causing a drift from your intended asset allocation. This drift can alter the risk profile of your portfolio, potentially exposing you to higher risk than desired.

- **Risk Tolerance and Time Horizon:** As personal circumstances and market conditions change, so may your risk tolerance and investment time horizon. Rebalancing allows your portfolio to reflect these changes.

The Rebalancing Process: Steps and Strategies

Review Your Portfolio: Regularly analyze your portfolio to determine how the actual allocation compares with the target allocation. This review should be consistent but need not be overly frequent; many experts suggest a quarterly or semi-annual review.

Decide on a Rebalancing Strategy:

- **Calendar-Based Rebalancing:** Rebalance at regular intervals, such as quarterly, semi-annually, or annually, regardless of market conditions.
- **Threshold-Based Rebalancing:** Rebalance when an asset class's weight deviates by a set percentage from its target allocation, say 5% or 10%.

Executing Rebalancing:

- **Selling Overweighted Assets:** Reduce positions in asset classes that are above their target allocation.
- **Buying Underweighted Assets:** Increase positions in asset classes that are below their target allocation.
- **Tax Considerations:** Be mindful of potential tax implications when selling assets, especially in taxable accounts.

Adjusting Your Portfolio: Adapting to Changing Circumstances

- **Life Events and Financial Goals:** Major life events, like marriage, the birth of a child, or approaching retirement, may necessitate a review and adjustment of your investment strategy.
- **Economic and Market Changes:** Significant changes in the economic landscape or market conditions might require a reassessment of your investment approach.

Automating Rebalancing: The Role of Technology

- **Robo-Advisors:** Many modern investment platforms offer automated rebalancing, ensuring your portfolio remains aligned with your goals without constant manual intervention.
- **Investment Management Services:** For more complex portfolios, professional investment managers can provide personalized rebalancing services, aligning with your specific needs and goals.

Conclusion: Embracing Dynamic Portfolio Management

Rebalancing is not just about buying and selling assets; it is a strategic exercise that keeps your investment journey aligned with your evolving goals and circumstances. It requires a disciplined, proactive approach, ensuring that your portfolio continues to reflect your desired level of risk and investment objectives. By regularly rebalancing and adjusting your portfolio, you are not merely reacting to market movements; you are actively managing your financial future, adapting and evolving as your life and the markets change.

Utilizing Robo-Advisors and Financial Advisors: Navigating the Digital and Human Elements of Investment Management

In the realm of investment management, the modern investor is presented with a choice between two distinct yet complementary resources: robo-advisors and financial advisors. Each offers unique advantages and serves different needs in the journey of portfolio management and financial planning. Understanding how to effectively utilize these tools can significantly enhance your investment strategy and overall financial health.

Robo-Advisors: Harnessing Technology for Efficient Portfolio Management

Definition and Function: Robo-advisors are digital platforms that provide automated, algorithm-driven financial planning services with minimal human supervision. They typically offer services like automatic portfolio rebalancing, tax-loss harvesting, and diversified portfolio construction based on the user's risk tolerance and investment goals.

Advantages of Robo-Advisors:

- **Cost-Effectiveness:** Generally, robo-advisors are less expensive than human advisors, making them an attractive option for new or cost-conscious investors.
- **Accessibility:** They are accessible 24/7, offering convenience and immediacy in portfolio management.
- **Low Account Minimums:** Many robo-advisors have low or no minimum account requirements, opening the door for investors with smaller capital.

Best Suited For: Investors seeking straightforward, passive investment management, especially those who are just beginning their investment journey or have a relatively simple financial situation.

Financial Advisors: The Human Touch in Personalized Financial Guidance

Role and Services: Financial advisors are professionals who help individuals manage their finances by providing personalized advice tailored to the client's individual circumstances. Their services can include investment management, estate planning, retirement planning, and tax planning.

Advantages of Financial Advisors:

- **Personalized Advice:** They offer bespoke advice based on comprehensive understanding of your personal and financial situation.
- **Complex Financial Planning:** Ideal for individuals with complex financial situations, such as business owners or those with significant assets.
- **Emotional Guidance:** They can provide emotional support and rational guidance during volatile market conditions, helping clients avoid emotional decision-making.

Best Suited For: Investors with more complex financial situations or those who prefer a more hands-on approach to their financial planning.

Combining Robo-Advisors with Financial Advisors: A Synergistic Approach

Complementary Benefits: Utilizing both robo-advisors and human advisors can be a powerful strategy. While robo-advisors can efficiently manage and rebalance your investment portfolio, human advisors can provide in-depth, personalized financial planning and advice on more complex matters.

Holistic Financial Strategy: This combination allows for a more holistic approach to your finances, integrating the efficiency and technological prowess of robo-advisors with the personalized, nuanced understanding of a human advisor.

Conclusion: Navigating the Investment Landscape with Technology and Expertise

In conclusion, both robo-advisors and financial advisors offer valuable resources in managing your investments and financial planning. The choice between them, or the decision to use both, should be guided by your individual financial needs, investment goals, and personal preferences. As the investment landscape continues to evolve, the integration of technology and human expertise stands as a testament to the diverse and adaptive nature of modern financial management. By leveraging the strengths of both robo-advisors and financial advisors, investors can create a robust, dynamic strategy for achieving their financial objectives.

Advanced Investment Strategies: Navigating Complex Financial Instruments for Enhanced Portfolio Performance

As we delve into the world of advanced investment strategies, we embark on a journey through the intricate and often complex terrain of sophisticated financial instruments and methodologies. This exploration is not for the faint-hearted investor; it requires a keen understanding of the financial markets, a willingness to embrace higher levels of risk, and an aptitude for navigating the nuanced dynamics of advanced investment options. In this section, we shall dissect and examine these sophisticated strategies, offering insights into how they can be employed to potentially enhance portfolio performance while acknowledging the elevated risks they entail.

Unveiling the Intricacies of Advanced Investment Vehicles

- **Leverage and Margin Trading**: Delve into the realm of using borrowed capital to amplify investment returns, understanding the potential for significant gains alongside the heightened risk of substantial losses.
- **Hedge Funds and Private Equity**: Explore the exclusive world of hedge funds and private equity, where complex strategies and illiquid investments are often employed in pursuit of outsized returns.
- **Derivatives and Options Trading**: Navigate the sophisticated landscape of derivatives and options, instruments that derive their value from underlying assets, offering unique opportunities for hedging and speculating.

Mastering Risk Management in Advanced Investing

- **Balancing High-Reward with High-Risk**: Understand the critical importance of risk management when engaging with advanced investment strategies, recognizing the fine balance between seeking high rewards and mitigating potential losses.
- **Diversification in Advanced Portfolios**: Learn about the role of diversification in an advanced investment portfolio, not just across asset classes, but also across strategies and market conditions.

Ethical Considerations and Regulatory Compliance

- **Navigating the Ethical Landscape**: Address the ethical considerations that come with engaging in complex investment strategies, ensuring that investment decisions align with personal and societal values.

- **Regulatory Frameworks:** Comprehend the importance of adhering to the regulatory frameworks governing advanced financial instruments, a critical aspect for legal compliance and ethical investment practices.

Conclusion: The Art and Science of Advanced Investing

Embarking on advanced investment strategies is akin to navigating a labyrinth; it requires not only a map in the form of financial knowledge and experience but also the wisdom to recognize when to advance and when to retreat. This section is dedicated to equipping the astute investor with the insights and understanding necessary to maneuver through this complex domain, enhancing their ability to make informed decisions that align with their investment goals and risk tolerance. Herein lies the art and science of advanced investing – a field where intellect, strategy, and an appreciation of complexity converge to create opportunities for those prepared to engage with them.

Unveiling the Intricacies of Advanced Investment Vehicles

In the sophisticated realm of investing, advanced investment vehicles stand as formidable tools, offering seasoned investors an array of strategies that transcend the traditional approaches of stocks and bonds. This section delves into the complex world of these vehicles, exploring their mechanics, potential benefits, and inherent risks. We focus on three pivotal areas: leverage and margin trading, hedge funds and private equity, and derivatives and options trading.

Leverage and Margin Trading: Amplifying Gains and Risks

- **Definition and Mechanics:** Leverage involves using borrowed funds to increase an investment's exposure. Margin trading, a form of leverage, allows investors to borrow money from a broker to purchase securities, with the securities themselves serving as collateral.
- **Risk-Return Profile:** While leverage can magnify returns, it also amplifies losses, making it a double-edged sword. The use of margin increases the potential for higher gains but also increases the possibility of significant losses, potentially exceeding the initial investment.
- **Practical Considerations:** Investors must maintain a minimum margin requirement and be prepared for margin calls, where additional funds must be deposited to cover potential losses. This strategy requires constant monitoring and a deep understanding of market dynamics.

Hedge Funds and Private Equity: Exclusive Avenues of Investment

Hedge Funds: Hedge funds are pooled investment funds that employ different strategies to earn active returns for their investors. These funds may use leverage, derivatives, and short selling to achieve their objectives.

- **Strategies:** Common strategies include long-short equity, market neutral, arbitrage, and macro-trends.
- **Investor Profile:** Typically accessible to accredited investors due to their high minimum investment requirements and risk profiles.

Private Equity: Private equity involves investing in private companies or conducting buyouts of public companies, delisting them from stock exchanges.

- **Investment Horizon:** These investments usually have a longer horizon, often requiring several years to mature.
- **Illiquidity and High Potential Returns:** Private equity investments are illiquid but can offer high returns, contingent upon the success and growth of the underlying businesses.

Derivatives and Options Trading: Instruments of Hedging and Speculation

Derivatives: Financial instruments whose value is derived from an underlying asset. They include futures, options, swaps, and forwards.

- **Futures and Forwards:** Commitments to buy or sell an asset at a predetermined future date and price.
- **Swaps:** Contracts to exchange financial instruments or cash flows.

Options Trading: Options provide the right, but not the obligation, to buy or sell an asset at a specific price before a certain date.

- **Call and Put Options:** Calls give the right to buy, while puts give the right to sell.
- **Strategies:** Options can be used for hedging against portfolio losses or for speculative purposes.
- **Complexity and Risk:** Options trading requires an understanding of various strategies and the ability to anticipate market movements and volatility.

Ethical and Regulatory Considerations

Investing in advanced vehicles requires not only a keen financial acumen but also a thorough understanding of the ethical and regulatory landscape. These instruments, often characterized by their opacity and complexity, demand a high level of compliance with financial regulations. Moreover, the ethical implications of such investments, particularly in the context of their impact on broader economic stability and integrity, must be diligently considered.

Conclusion

Advanced investment vehicles offer unique opportunities for high returns, but they are accompanied by a proportionate level of risk and complexity. Navigating these instruments requires a sophisticated understanding of financial markets, a robust risk management framework, and an adherence to ethical standards and regulatory requirements. For the informed and experienced investor, these vehicles can be a powerful addition to a diversified investment portfolio, offering avenues for both wealth creation and hedging against market uncertainties.

Mastering Risk Management in Advanced Investing

In the intricate landscape of advanced investing, risk management is not just a component of the strategy – it is the keystone. As investors journey through the labyrinth of high-stakes investment vehicles, understanding and mastering risk management is paramount. This section provides a comprehensive exploration of the principles and practices that form the backbone of effective risk management in the context of advanced investing.

Understanding Risk in Advanced Investment Contexts

- **Types of Risk:** Recognize the multifaceted nature of risk, which includes market risk, credit risk, liquidity risk, operational risk, and systemic risk. Each type demands specific mitigation strategies.
- **Risk Assessment:** Implementing thorough risk assessments to understand the potential impact of various market scenarios on the investment portfolio.

Developing a Robust Risk Management Framework

- **Diversification:** Beyond the basic tenet of not putting all eggs in one basket, in advanced investing, diversification involves spreading exposure across different asset classes, industries, geographical regions, and investment strategies.
- **Stress Testing and Scenario Analysis:** Using these techniques to simulate the effect of extreme market events on an investment portfolio. This process helps in understanding potential vulnerabilities and planning for unforeseen circumstances.
- **Risk Measurement Tools:** Utilizing tools like Value at Risk (VaR), Conditional Value at Risk (CVaR), and sensitivity analysis to quantify risk exposure and make informed decisions.

Leverage and Margin Management

- **Leverage Ratios:** Maintaining optimal leverage ratios to balance potential returns with the risk of amplified losses.
- **Margin Requirements:** Understanding and adhering to margin requirements to avoid margin calls that can force the liquidation of positions at inopportune times.

Hedging Strategies

Hedging Instruments: Employing derivatives like options, futures, and swaps as hedging instruments to offset potential losses in the primary investments.

Hedging Techniques: Techniques such as delta hedging or using collars for options can protect against adverse price movements while allowing for profit potential.

Risk and Liquidity Management

Liquidity Analysis: Assessing the liquidity profile of investments to ensure that assets can be quickly converted to cash without significant losses.

Liquidity Reserves: Maintaining sufficient liquidity reserves to meet short-term obligations and unforeseen cash flow requirements.

Ethical Considerations and Compliance

Regulatory Compliance: Staying abreast of and complying with relevant financial regulations and standards.

Ethical Investment Practices: Incorporating ethical considerations into investment decisions, recognizing the broader impact of investment activities on the economy and society.

Implementing a Continuous Risk Monitoring System

Real-Time Monitoring: Establishing systems for real-time monitoring of market conditions, portfolio performance, and risk exposure.

Responsive Action Plans: Having pre-established action plans to address significant market shifts or portfolio deviations.

Conclusion

In the realm of advanced investing, risk management is an ongoing, dynamic process. It requires not only the application of sophisticated tools and techniques but also a vigilant, informed approach that adapts to the ever-changing market landscape. By mastering risk management, investors can navigate the complexities of advanced investment vehicles with greater confidence and the ability to capitalize on opportunities while safeguarding their assets against potential pitfalls. This comprehensive approach to risk management is crucial for achieving long-term success and stability in the challenging world of advanced investing.

Ethical and Socially Responsible Investing

As we delve into the realm of Ethical and Socially Responsible Investing (SRI), it is essential to recognize that this approach transcends traditional financial considerations. SRI represents an alignment of investment decisions with personal values, focusing on contributing positively to society and the environment while pursuing financial returns. This is not merely an investment strategy; it's a commitment to principled growth and sustainable development.

Understanding Ethical and Socially Responsible Investing

- **Definition and Evolution:** SRI involves choosing investments based on ethical, social, and environmental criteria alongside financial returns. This evolution in investing reflects a growing awareness of how financial decisions impact the world.
- **Key Concepts:** Central to SRI are Environmental, Social, and Governance (ESG) criteria, guiding investors in selecting companies that align with ethical values.

The Spectrum of Ethical Investing Strategies

- **Negative Screening:** This approach excludes sectors or companies not aligning with certain ethical standards, such as tobacco or fossil fuels.
- **Positive Screening:** In contrast, this strategy focuses on companies contributing positively to societal or environmental causes.
- **Impact Investing:** Going a step further, impact investing aims to create a tangible positive impact alongside financial returns, often in areas like renewable energy or social welfare.

The Business Case for Ethical Investing

- **Risk Mitigation:** Companies with high ESG scores often exhibit lower risk profiles, as they tend to be more conscientious and forward-thinking.
- **Long-Term Performance:** Contrary to some beliefs, ethical investment strategies can be as profitable, if not more, than traditional investment strategies.

Challenges and Considerations in Ethical Investing

- **Defining Ethics:** The subjective nature of 'ethical' can make investment choices challenging, as personal values differ.
- **Performance Misconceptions:** It is a myth that ethical investing automatically leads to lower returns.
- **Greenwashing Risks:** Be aware of companies that may falsely present themselves as environmentally or socially responsible.

The Role of Shareholder Activism

Influencing Corporate Behavior: As a shareholder in responsible companies, you can influence corporate policies towards ethical standards.

Proxy Voting and Resolutions: Utilize your voting rights as a shareholder to drive change in areas like environmental sustainability and corporate governance.

Ethical Investing in Practice

Case Studies: Learn from real-world examples where ethical investment strategies have been successfully implemented.

Tools and Resources: Familiarize yourself with tools for assessing ethical investments, including sustainability indexes and ESG ratings.

Conclusion

Ethical and socially responsible investing is more than a financial strategy; it's a way to make a difference in the world through your investment choices. As this approach continues to gain popularity, it offers a viable path for both individual and institutional investors to align their financial goals with their values, promoting a more sustainable and equitable global economy. This understanding of SRI provides a solid foundation for making informed, responsible investment decisions.

Common Investment Mistakes to Avoid

In the intricate world of investing, navigating the complexities while striving for financial success is a formidable challenge. Even seasoned investors can fall prey to common pitfalls. This section is dedicated to identifying and understanding frequent investment errors, thereby arming you with the knowledge to make more informed decisions and enhance your investment strategy.

Overview of Investment Missteps

Emotional Decision-Making: One of the cardinal sins in investing is letting emotions, like fear and greed, dictate your actions. Rational, well-researched decisions are key.

Failing to Diversify: Over-reliance on a single investment or sector can lead to increased risk. Diversification is a fundamental principle for risk management.

Chasing Performance: Investors often make the mistake of investing in assets or sectors that have recently performed well, ignoring the principle that past performance is not indicative of future results.

Timing the Market: Attempting to predict market highs and lows is notoriously difficult and often counterproductive.

Delving into Specific Errors

- **Neglecting Research:** Inadequate research or due diligence can lead to poor investment choices.
- **Ignoring Fees and Costs:** Overlooking the impact of fees, including fund management fees and transaction costs, can erode returns over time.
- **Misunderstanding Risk Tolerance:** An investor's failure to accurately assess their risk tolerance can lead to unsuitable investment choices.
- **Short-term Focus:** Focusing too narrowly on short-term gains can be detrimental to achieving long-term financial objectives.

Psychological Aspects of Investing

- **Overconfidence:** Confidence is beneficial, but overconfidence can lead to risky behavior and unwise investment decisions.
- **Herd Mentality:** Following the crowd can lead to bubbles and poor investment decisions. Independent, critical thinking is crucial.

Strategies to Mitigate Mistakes

- **Continuous Education:** Staying informed and educated about markets, different investment types, and economic conditions is vital.
- **Setting Realistic Expectations:** Understand that not all investments will yield high returns and that losses are part of the investment journey.
- **Regular Portfolio Reviews:** Periodically assessing your portfolio and adjusting as needed can help avoid long-term mistakes.

Conclusion

Awareness of these common investment mistakes is the first step toward avoiding them. By fostering a disciplined, informed approach to investing, and understanding the psychological aspects that can impact decision-making, you can significantly enhance your prospects for successful and prudent investment. This section will delve deeper into each of these mistakes, offering insights and strategies to help you navigate the investment landscape more effectively and avoid the pitfalls that have ensnared many investors.

Emotional Decision-Making in Investing: Navigating the Emotional Highs and Lows

Picture this: the stock market takes a sudden dip. Your first instinct might be a knee-jerk reaction, perhaps selling off shares to stop potential losses. Or maybe you've watched a particular stock soar and, driven by a fear of missing out, you jump on the bandwagon, buying shares without thorough research. These scenarios are classic examples of emotional decision-making in investing, and they're more common than you might think.

The Impact of Emotions on Investment Decisions

Fear and Greed: These are the two most powerful emotions in the world of investing. Fear can lead to panic selling when markets drop, causing investors to lock in losses. On the flip side, greed can drive investors to make impulsive investments during market highs, often leading to overvalued purchases.

Emotional Roller Coaster: Investing isn't just about numbers and trends; it's also an emotional journey. The market's inevitable ups and downs can evoke strong emotional responses, which, if unchecked, can lead to poor decision-making.

Recognizing Emotional Triggers

Understanding Your Triggers: Self-awareness is key. Recognize what emotional triggers affect your investment decisions. Is it news headlines? Market rumors? The successes or failures of peers?

The Bandwagon Effect: It's easy to get swept up in market trends or the latest 'hot tip.' However, following the herd isn't always the wisest move. What works for others may not align with your investment strategy or risk tolerance.

Strategies to Overcome Emotional Investing

Stick to Your Plan: One of the best antidotes to emotional investing is having a well-thought-out investment plan. When emotions run high, remind yourself of your long-term goals and investment strategy.

Diversification: It's not just a buzzword; diversification can provide a safety net against market volatility, reducing the impact of any one investment's performance on your overall portfolio.

Pause and Reflect: Feeling impulsive? Take a step back. Allow yourself a 'cooling-off' period before making any big decisions, especially during volatile market periods.

Seeking Professional Advice: Sometimes, a third-party perspective can offer clarity. Financial advisors can provide objective advice, helping to take the emotion out of your investment decisions.

Conclusion

Investing is as much about managing emotions as it is about managing money. Recognizing and controlling emotional responses can help prevent costly mistakes and support better financial outcomes. Remember, successful investing is a marathon, not a sprint; it requires patience, discipline, and a level head. So, next time the market takes you on a wild ride, take a deep breath, remember your plan, and keep those emotions in check. After all, in the world of investing, calm and collected often wins the race.

Timing the Market: Risks and Realities

Let's chat about a concept in investing that's as tempting as it is tricky – timing the market. It's like trying to catch the perfect wave; exhilarating if you get it right, but more often than not, you're left treading water or wiping out.

The Lure of Market Timing

- **The Perfect Moment:** The idea behind market timing is seductive. Buy low, sell high – sounds simple, right? Who wouldn't want to jump in just at the right moment when stocks are about to soar or bail right before a major slump?
- **Predicting vs. Reacting:** Many try to predict market highs and lows, but here's the thing – the market is a complex beast, influenced by an intricate web of global events, economic indicators, and investor sentiment. It's more about reacting to market changes than predicting them.

Why Timing the Market is a High-Risk Game

- **Missed Opportunities:** Waiting for the 'perfect' time can often lead to missed opportunities. For instance, after a market dip, many wait to see if it'll dip further. But markets can rebound quickly, leaving you on the sidelines.
- **The Cost of Getting It Wrong:** If your timing is off, and let's be honest, it often is, the costs can be significant. Selling too early or buying too late can mean substantial losses or missed gains.

The Reality of Market Fluctuations

- **Short-term vs. Long-term:** Market fluctuations are normal in the short term. However, over the long term, markets generally trend upwards. This is why many seasoned investors focus on long-term growth rather than short-term gains.
- **Emotional Rollercoaster:** Trying to time the market can be an emotional rollercoaster, leading to stress and potentially impulsive decisions, which aren't great for your financial health.

A More Measured Approach

- **Dollar-Cost Averaging:** Instead of trying to time the market, consider a strategy like dollar-cost averaging. This involves investing a fixed amount of money at regular intervals, regardless of market conditions, which can reduce the impact of volatility.
- **Stay Invested:** History shows that staying invested over the long term tends to yield positive returns. It's not about timing the market, but time in the market that counts.

Conclusion

In the end, timing the market is a bit like gambling; it's not a strategy, it's a guess. And in the world of investing, guesses can be costly. Instead, focus on building a diversified portfolio that aligns with your long-term goals, and let the market do its thing. Remember, even the most seasoned investors rarely get the timing right consistently. So, play the long game – it's usually where the real winners are.

Overlooking Fees and Costs: A Common Oversight

Hey, let's talk about something that might not be the most thrilling part of investing, but it's super important – the fees and costs associated with it. You know, it's kind of like when you're excited about buying a new gadget online, but then you realize the shipping costs are sky-high. A bit of a downer, right? Well, in investing, not paying attention to fees and costs can really eat into your returns over time.

The Sneaky Nature of Fees and Costs

Hidden in Plain Sight: Often, investment fees aren't as obvious as we'd like them to be. They can be buried in the fine print or just not something we think to ask about. But just like small leaks can sink a big ship, small fees can seriously drain your investment earnings.

Types of Fees: You've got transaction fees every time you buy or sell, management fees for having professionals manage your money, and even performance fees if your investments do really well. And let's not forget about the expense ratios in mutual funds – they can vary a lot!

The Real Impact of Fees

Compounding in Reverse: We all love how compound interest works in our favor, right? Well, fees have a compounding effect too, but not in a good way. Over time, they can significantly reduce your investment's growth. Imagine giving up a slice of your pizza every time you take a bite – not cool!

Comparing Costs: It's like shopping around for the best deal. Comparing fees among similar investment options can make a huge difference in your long-term returns.

Keeping an Eye on Costs

Ask and Research: Don't be shy to ask your financial advisor or broker about all the fees involved. Do your homework, read the product disclosures, and know what you're getting into.

Balancing Act: It's not just about going for the lowest fees, though. Balance the cost with the quality of the investment. Sometimes, paying a bit more for better management or performance can be worth it.

Strategies to Minimize Fees

- **Index Funds and ETFs:** Consider low-cost index funds or ETFs. They often have lower expense ratios compared to actively managed funds.
- **Direct Investments:** If you're savvy enough, direct investments in stocks can reduce the need for intermediary fees.
- **Fee-only Advisors:** Look for fee-only financial advisors who charge a flat rate rather than earning commissions on the products they sell. It aligns their interests more closely with yours.

Conclusion

Remember, every dollar you pay in fees is a dollar not invested for your future. By being aware and strategic about fees and costs, you can keep more of your hard-earned money working for you. So, let's not let those sneaky fees nibble away at our investments, okay? Stay informed, stay vigilant, and here's to making every penny count in your investment journey!

Investment Resources and Tools: Navigating the Sea of Information

Alright, let's dive into the world of investment resources and tools. Think of these as your compass and map in the vast ocean of investing. There's a ton of information out there, and having the right tools at your disposal can make all the difference between sailing smoothly towards your financial goals and getting lost at sea.

The Wide Array of Investment Resources

- **Financial News and Publications:** Staying informed is key. Regularly reading financial news and publications gives you a broader understanding of market trends and economic factors that influence investments. Think of sources like The Wall Street Journal, Bloomberg, or The Economist.
- **Online Platforms and Blogs:** The internet is a treasure trove of information. Websites like Investopedia offer educational content, while finance blogs can provide personal insights and strategies.

Tools to Enhance Your Investment Strategy

- **Investment Calculators:** These handy tools help you crunch numbers on potential investment returns, compound interest, retirement savings – you name it. They can be a great starting point to understand the math behind your investment decisions.

Portfolio Management Software: For those looking to get a bit more advanced, portfolio management software can help track your investments, analyze your asset allocation, and even rebalance your portfolio as needed.

Utilizing Apps and Technology

Mobile Investment Apps: Apps like Robinhood, Acorns, or Betterment have revolutionized how we invest, making it more accessible and user-friendly. They're great for keeping tabs on your investments and making trades on the go.

Robo-Advisors: These automated platforms use algorithms to manage your investments based on your risk tolerance and goals. They're a great, low-cost alternative to traditional financial advisors.

Educational Resources for Continuous Learning

Online Courses and Webinars: Platforms like Coursera, Udemy, or even YouTube offer a plethora of courses on investing, ranging from beginner to advanced levels.

Books: Sometimes, nothing beats a good book. Classics like "The Intelligent Investor" by Benjamin Graham or "One Up On Wall Street" by Peter Lynch can provide timeless investment wisdom.

Staying Safe and Avoiding Misinformation

Critical Evaluation: With so much information available, it's crucial to critically evaluate the sources and their credibility. Not all advice is good advice.

Avoiding Scams: Be wary of 'get rich quick' schemes or any resource that promises guaranteed returns. If it sounds too good to be true, it probably is.

Conclusion

In this age of information overload, having the right investment resources and tools is like having a well-equipped ship on your financial voyage. They empower you to make informed decisions, stay on course, and navigate the sometimes choppy waters of the investment world. So, set sail with confidence, continually educate yourself, and remember – the journey to financial success is a marathon, not a sprint. Happy investing!

Conclusion: Building a Secure Financial Future

As we wrap up our journey through the intricacies of financial empowerment, it's essential to pause and reflect on the ground we've covered together. From the foundational principles of investing to the nuanced strategies for wealth creation, our exploration has been both broad and deep, aimed at equipping you with the knowledge to navigate your financial future confidently.

The Essence of Our Financial Expedition

- **Empowerment Through Understanding:** We've demystified complex financial concepts, turning what might once have seemed like a daunting maze into a navigable path. Remember, knowledge is not just power—it's empowerment.
- **The Journey of Personal Growth:** Beyond mere numbers and strategies, we've embarked on a journey of personal growth. Financial planning isn't solely about accruing wealth; it's about setting and achieving life's goals, whether they're retiring comfortably, providing for a family, or leaving a legacy.

Embracing a Future of Financial Confidence

- **Actionable Steps for Real-world Application:** Throughout our discussions, we've emphasized actionable advice—practical steps you can take today to start shaping your tomorrow. Whether it's starting an investment portfolio, creating a budget, or planning for retirement, the path forward is clear.
- **The Power of Personal Stories:** Through shared anecdotes and case studies, we've seen the challenges and triumphs of others. These stories serve as both cautionary tales and beacons of hope, reminding us that while the financial journey is personal, we're not alone in our experiences.

The Continuous Path of Financial Literacy

- **Lifelong Learning:** The landscape of finance is ever-evolving. Embrace the mindset of continuous learning to adapt to new challenges and opportunities. Remember, the most successful investors are also perpetual students.
- **Community and Support:** Leverage the strength of community and the expertise of professionals when needed. Financial journeys are enriched by the perspectives and support of others.

Looking Ahead with Optimism

- **A Future Crafted by You:** Your financial future isn't written in the stars; it's shaped by your actions, decisions, and the wisdom with which you navigate your path.
- **The Role of Resilience and Adaptability:** Embrace resilience and adaptability as your companions. Challenges and uncertainties are part of the journey, but they're also opportunities for growth and learning.

Final Thoughts

As we close this chapter, remember that building a secure financial future is a dynamic and ongoing process. It's about more than just wealth; it's about creating a life rich in fulfillment and peace of mind. With the tools, knowledge, and strategies we've explored, you're well-equipped to take control of your financial destiny.

So, here's to your financial success and the journey ahead. May it be as rewarding as it is prosperous. Keep learning, stay motivated, and never underestimate the power of a well-crafted financial plan. Your future self will thank you.

Chapter 6: Safeguarding Your Financial Journey: Risk Management and Emergency Preparedness

Welcome to a critical chapter on our journey towards financial empowerment: Safeguarding Your Financial Journey through Risk Management and Emergency Preparedness. As we venture deeper into the realms of personal finance, it's essential to recognize that with every opportunity for growth comes potential risks. Understanding these risks and preparing for unforeseen events is not just prudent; it's indispensable for long-term financial stability.

Defining Financial Risk

Imagine you're setting sail across the vast ocean. Just as the sea can be unpredictable, with calm waters one moment and stormy waves the next, so can the financial landscape. Financial risk encompasses the potential for losing some or all of your investment due to various factors, including market volatility, inflation, or unexpected life events. It's the choppy water and the storms we aim to navigate and prepare for.

The Importance of Risk Management in Personal Finance

Risk management in personal finance is like having a well-equipped ship with a seasoned captain at the helm. It's about identifying, assessing, and taking steps to minimize the impact of financial risks on your journey. This doesn't mean avoiding risk altogether—after all, with no risk comes no reward. Instead, it's about making informed decisions that align with your tolerance for risk and your long-term goals.

Assessing Personal Financial Risks

- **Market Risk:** This is the risk of investment losses due to market fluctuations. Whether you're invested in stocks, bonds, or real estate, market conditions can impact your portfolio's value.
- **Liquidity Risk:** Sometimes, you might need to access your funds quickly. Liquidity risk arises when you're unable to do so without incurring significant losses.
- **Interest Rate Risk:** For those invested in bonds or holding debt, changes in interest rates can affect the value of your investments or the cost of your debt.
- **Inflation Risk:** Over time, inflation can erode the purchasing power of your money, affecting your savings and investments' real value.
- **Personal Life Risks:** These include unforeseen events like job loss, illness, or family emergencies that can disrupt your financial plans.

As we embark on this chapter, our goal is to equip you with the knowledge and tools to effectively manage these risks. By doing so, you'll be better prepared to face financial storms, navigate through them, and continue on your path towards a secure and prosperous financial future. So, let's set sail together, with a keen eye on the horizon and a solid plan to safeguard our journey.

Identifying Potential Risks in Personal Finances

Embarking on the journey of personal finance management is akin to navigating a vast and sometimes unpredictable ocean. Just as a seasoned sailor must be aware of potential storms, hidden reefs, and changing winds, you too must identify the potential risks that could impact your financial well-being. Understanding these risks is the first step in crafting a resilient financial plan that can withstand the storms of life.

Types of Personal Financial Risks

Income Risk: This involves the potential for a sudden loss of income due to job loss, business failure, or health issues. It's like sailing into a fog bank where you can't see what's ahead, impacting your ability to navigate forward financially.

Expense Risk: Unexpected expenses, such as emergency repairs, medical bills, or legal issues, can suddenly emerge like a rogue wave, threatening to capsize your financial stability.

Debt Risk: High levels of debt, especially with high interest rates, can anchor you down, making it difficult to move forward or respond to financial opportunities and challenges.

Investment Risk: The volatility of the stock market, real estate market fluctuations, or investments in start-ups can be as unpredictable as the sea. These investments can offer high rewards but also come with the risk of substantial losses.

Inflation Risk: Over time, inflation can erode the purchasing power of your money, like a slow leak in a boat that gradually lowers it into the water.

Health Risk: Unexpected health issues or accidents can not only lead to significant medical expenses but also reduce your ability to earn an income, affecting your financial journey.

Longevity Risk: Living longer than expected can be a double-edged sword, posing the risk of outliving your savings and investments.

Strategies for Identifying Risks

Financial Health Check-Up: Regularly review your financial statements, budget, debts, and investments to identify areas of vulnerability.

Risk Assessment Tools: Utilize online calculators and tools to assess your risk exposure, especially when it comes to investments and retirement planning.

Professional Advice: Consider consulting with a financial advisor to get an expert perspective on potential risks and how to mitigate them.

Education: Stay informed about financial trends, market conditions, and new investment opportunities. Knowledge is power when it comes to identifying and managing risks.

Conclusion

Identifying potential risks in your personal finances is like charting a course before setting sail. It involves understanding where the dangers lie, anticipating changes in the financial climate, and preparing accordingly. By recognizing these risks early, you can steer your financial ship with confidence, knowing you're prepared to face whatever challenges come your way. Remember, the goal isn't to avoid all risks but to navigate them wisely, ensuring your financial journey is both rewarding and secure.

Conducting a Personal Risk Assessment

Navigating the waters of personal finance requires a keen understanding of the potential risks that might disrupt your journey toward financial stability and growth. Conducting a personal risk assessment is akin to charting your course before embarking on a sea voyage, ensuring you're prepared for whatever lies ahead. Let's explore how to conduct this assessment effectively, ensuring that you can sail smoothly towards your financial goals.

Step 1: Inventory of Current Financial Situation

- **Assess Your Assets and Liabilities:** Begin by compiling a comprehensive list of your assets (savings, investments, property, etc.) and liabilities (debts, loans, mortgages). This financial inventory provides a clear starting point for understanding your net worth.
- **Evaluate Income Streams:** Consider the stability and sustainability of your current income sources. Are they dependent on a single employer, client, or investment?

Step 2: Identify Potential Risks

- **Income Risks:** Assess the risk of losing your primary income source. How likely is job loss, business downturn, or other income interruptions?
- **Expense Risks:** Identify potential unforeseen expenses. Could health issues, home repairs, or family needs arise unexpectedly?

Investment Risks: Review your investment portfolio for potential volatility. Are your investments diversified enough to withstand market fluctuations?

Life Changes: Consider life events that could impact your financial situation, such as marriage, having children, or planning for retirement.

Step 3: Assess Risk Tolerance

Emotional Tolerance: How much financial uncertainty can you comfortably handle without stress?

Financial Tolerance: Financially, how much risk can you afford to take? Consider your current savings, debts, and financial commitments.

Step 4: Develop Risk Mitigation Strategies

Emergency Fund: Building an emergency fund can provide a financial buffer against unexpected expenses or income loss.

Insurance: Evaluate your need for insurance policies (health, life, disability, property) to mitigate significant financial risks.

Diversification: Diversify your investment portfolio to spread risk across different assets.

Debt Management: Develop a plan to manage or reduce high-interest debt, decreasing financial vulnerability.

Step 5: Implement and Monitor the Plan

Action Plan: Create a detailed action plan based on your risk assessment. Set clear, achievable goals for risk mitigation.

Regular Reviews: Financial situations and risks can change. Regularly review and adjust your plan as necessary to stay on course.

Conclusion

Conducting a personal risk assessment is a critical step in securing your financial future. It allows you to identify potential hazards on your financial journey and prepare adequately to navigate them. Remember, the goal of this assessment is not to eliminate all risks but to understand them thoroughly and develop strategies to manage them effectively. With a well-charted course and a keen eye on the horizon, you're well-equipped to sail toward financial success, regardless of the storms you may encounter along the way.

The Role of Insurance in Risk Management

In the vast and unpredictable ocean of personal finance, insurance serves as one of the most effective lifeboats, designed to protect you and your loved ones from the financial storms that life can unexpectedly bring. Understanding the role of insurance in risk management is akin to knowing how to navigate through rough waters, ensuring that you remain afloat even when facing the most daunting waves. Let's delve into how insurance can be a pivotal component in safeguarding your financial journey.

The Essence of Insurance in Personal Finance

- **Financial Shield:** Insurance acts as a financial shield, absorbing the shock of unforeseen losses such as illness, accidents, property damage, or loss of life. Without it, these events can have a devastating impact on your financial stability and long-term plans.
- **Risk Transfer Mechanism:** At its core, insurance is a risk transfer mechanism. By paying a relatively small premium, you transfer the potential financial burden of a significant loss to the insurance company. This transfer allows you to manage financial risks that would be otherwise unbearable.

Key Types of Insurance for Comprehensive Protection

- **Health Insurance:** Covers medical expenses arising from illnesses and injuries, protecting you from high healthcare costs that can deplete savings.
- **Life Insurance:** Provides financial support to your dependents in the event of your untimely death, ensuring their financial security.
- **Disability Insurance:** Offers income replacement if you're unable to work due to a disability, safeguarding your ability to meet your financial obligations.
- **Property and Casualty Insurance:** Protects your property (home, car, etc.) against losses from accidents, theft, or natural disasters.
- **Liability Insurance:** Shields you from financial losses if you're found legally responsible for causing harm to another person or their property.

Integrating Insurance into Your Financial Plan

- **Assessing Needs:** Start by evaluating your specific financial situation and the potential risks you and your family face. Consider factors like health, dependents, assets, and career.
- **Choosing the Right Coverage:** Not all insurance policies are created equal. Select coverage that aligns with your risk assessment, ensuring that it's neither inadequate nor excessively burdensome in terms of premiums.
- **Regular Reviews and Adjustments:** Life changes, and so do your insurance needs. Regularly review your policies to ensure they remain aligned with your current circumstances and financial goals.

The Strategic Use of Insurance in Wealth Preservation

Estate Planning: Life insurance can play a crucial role in estate planning, providing tax-advantaged wealth transfer to your heirs.

Asset Protection: Certain types of insurance, like umbrella policies, can protect your assets from being depleted by lawsuits or liability claims.

Conclusion

In the journey of financial management and planning, insurance is not just an optional accessory but a fundamental component of a comprehensive risk management strategy. It provides a safety net, ensuring that unexpected events do not derail your financial goals or jeopardize your family's security. By thoughtfully integrating insurance into your financial plan, you're not merely preparing for potential risks; you're actively securing your path towards a stable and prosperous financial future. Remember, in the realm of personal finance, being well-insured is synonymous with being well-prepared.

Let's dive a little deeper into the sea of insurance, shall we? Picture this: you're sitting down for coffee with a friend who's about to unravel the mysteries of insurance for you. No jargon, no complex terms—just a straightforward chat about how insurance is pretty much your financial safety net.

Health Insurance: The First Line of Defense

"Think of health insurance as your personal health guardian," your friend begins. "It's there to catch you if you fall—literally. Whether it's a minor injury or something more serious, health insurance helps cover those medical bills so you're not left with a financial headache on top of everything else."

Life Insurance: Protecting Your Greatest Asset

"Next up, we have life insurance," they continue. "It's something a lot of people don't like to think about, but it's really about protecting your loved ones. If something were to happen to you, life insurance ensures that your family is taken care of financially. It's like leaving them a financial safety net, so they can keep moving forward without you."

Property Insurance: Shielding Your Castle

"Property insurance is like the shield for your castle. Whether you own a home, rent an apartment, or drive a car, this insurance helps protect your possessions from damage, theft, or other disasters. It's about making sure that if something happens to your stuff, you can get it fixed or replaced without it draining your savings."

Disability Insurance: Ensuring Your Paycheck

"Imagine if you couldn't work for a while due to an injury or illness. Disability insurance is like having a backup plan that ensures you still get a 'paycheck' even when you're unable to earn your usual one. It's about keeping the bills paid and your financial life intact, even when life throws you a curveball."

Liability Insurance: Your Financial Guard

"Lastly, there's liability insurance. This one's a bit like having a legal guardian ready to defend you. If you accidentally cause damage or injury to someone else, liability insurance can help cover the costs or legal fees. It's about protecting your wallet from unexpected 'oops' moments that could otherwise cost you big time."

Wrapping Up

Your friend leans back, smiling. "So, that's the basics of insurance—your financial safety nets, designed to catch you and protect you from life's unexpected drops. Each type has its role, safeguarding different parts of your life so you can focus on living it to the fullest, without worrying about the 'what-ifs.'"

As you finish your coffee, you realize that insurance isn't just about policies and premiums; it's about peace of mind and financial security. And with this chat, the world of insurance suddenly seems a lot less daunting and a lot more like a friend you can count on.

Health Insurance: Your Health's Bodyguard

First up, we've got health insurance, standing tall like a trustworthy bodyguard for your health. It's there to cover your medical bills, from routine check-ups to unexpected hospital stays. Think of it as your financial ally against the high costs of healthcare, ensuring that a doctor's visit or a prescription doesn't throw your budget overboard.

Life Insurance: The Financial Protector of Your Loved Ones

As we move along, you'll notice life insurance, a solemn but significant presence. It's not so much about you as it is about the people you love. Should the unexpected happen, life insurance ensures your family can maintain their lifestyle, cover funeral expenses, or even support long-term goals like college tuition. It's your way of saying, "I've got you covered," even when you're not around.

Property Insurance: Guardian of Your Treasures

Next, let's chat about property insurance, which covers your home, car, and personal belongings. It's like a shield guarding your castle and chariot against storms, fires, theft, and other mishaps. Whether you own or rent, it helps repair or replace what's damaged, so a disaster doesn't have to mean starting from scratch.

Disability Insurance: Ensuring Your Income Streams

Disability insurance might not catch your eye immediately, but it's a crucial stall in our market. If you're unable to work due to illness or injury, this insurance acts as a stand-in for your paycheck, covering a portion of your lost income. It's like having a safety net that catches you, ensuring your financial goals don't fall by the wayside during tough times.

Liability Insurance: Your Financial Defender

As we weave through the crowd, we'll find liability insurance. This one's all about protecting you if you're ever held responsible for injuring someone or damaging their property. It's your legal defense and settlement coverage, keeping your savings intact if accidents happen.

Wrapping Up Our Market Stroll

And there you have it—a quick tour through the vibrant market of insurance options. Each type serves a unique purpose, protecting different aspects of your life and giving you peace of mind. Like picking the right ingredients for a meal, choosing the right insurance mix is about making sure you and your loved ones are well-protected, come what may. So, as we end our stroll, think about which stalls caught your eye and how they might fit into your life's blueprint.

Navigating the maze of insurance options can feel like trying to find the perfect recipe for a dish you've never cooked before. You know you need the right ingredients in the right amounts, but where do you start? Let's break it down into simpler steps, just like deciding whether you're baking a cake or grilling a steak. Here's how you can determine the right insurance coverage for your individual needs, keeping the conversation as light and straightforward as a chat over coffee.

Step 1: Assess Your Life's Recipe

First things first, take stock of what's on your plate. Are you single, supporting a family, running a business, or maybe nearing retirement? Your life stage is like choosing the dish you want to prepare; it sets the foundation for what ingredients (or coverage) you'll need.

- **Single and Independent:** You might focus on health, disability, and renters' insurance.
- **Family Life:** Life insurance, health insurance, and homeowners' or renters' insurance become crucial.
- **Business Owners:** Liability, property, and possibly health insurance for employees are key.
- **Retirement Planning:** Health (including long-term care) and life insurance adjustments are in focus.

Step 2: Inventory Your Ingredients

Look at what assets, liabilities, and responsibilities you have. This step is like checking your pantry before you start cooking. What's valuable and needs protection? Your home, car, health, ability to earn an income, and even your pets might need coverage.

- **Assets:** Homes, vehicles, and personal property.
- **Liabilities:** Any potential legal responsibilities, like if someone gets injured on your property.
- **Income:** Your biggest asset. Disability insurance can protect this.

Step 3: Consider Your Dietary Restrictions (Risk Tolerance)

Just as some folks avoid gluten or dairy, your financial situation might have its own sensitivities. How much risk can you stomach? If the thought of unexpected medical bills or property damage gives you indigestion, you'll want more comprehensive coverage.

- **High Risk Tolerance:** You might opt for higher deductibles to lower premiums, assuming you can handle potential out-of-pocket costs.
- **Low Risk Tolerance:** You'll likely prefer broader coverage and lower deductibles, even if it means paying higher premiums.

Step 4: Taste Test (Shop Around)

Just as you might sample a bit of sauce before adding more salt, it's smart to shop around and compare policies. Look for the best combination of coverage, company reputation, and cost. Online comparison tools can be a great way to do a quick taste test across different providers.

Step 5: Adjust the Seasoning (Customize Your Policy)

Most dishes need a little adjustment to get them just right. Similarly, customize your insurance policies through riders or endorsements to make sure they fit your specific needs. Maybe you need extra coverage for that heirloom jewelry or want to ensure your home business equipment is covered.

Step 6: Set a Timer (Review Regularly)

Just as some dishes need to be checked periodically to avoid overcooking, your insurance coverage needs regular review. Life changes—marriage, children, new homes, and new jobs—can all affect your insurance needs. Make it a habit to review your coverage annually or after major life events.

Wrapping Up

Determining the right insurance coverage is about mixing the right ingredients to suit your life's recipe. It might require a bit of prep work and some taste testing, but the peace of mind it brings is like enjoying a perfect meal you've made yourself—satisfying and essential. So, take your time, do your homework, and don't be afraid to ask for advice from a financial advisor or insurance agent. After all, even the best chefs had to learn from someone.

Understanding Insurance Policies and Terms: A Guide to Decoding the Menu

Imagine you're at a new restaurant, and the menu is filled with terms you've never seen before. Without a little help, you might end up ordering something that's not quite what you expected. The world of insurance can feel similar, with its own language full of terms and conditions that can seem daunting at first glance. But fear not! Let's break down the essentials, turning that confusing menu into a guide you can navigate with confidence.

The Menu (Policy Document)

Think of your insurance policy as the menu for your coverage. It lists everything you need to know: what's included (coverage), what's not (exclusions), how much you'll pay (premiums), and what you need to do if you need to make a claim (claims process).

Appetizers (The Basics)

Premium: This is the price you pay for insurance, typically charged monthly or annually. It's like the cover charge at a club—paying it lets you in, ensuring you're covered.

Deductible: The amount you pay out of pocket before your insurance kicks in. If your deductible is $500 and the repair costs $1,500, you pay the first $500, and your insurance covers the rest. It's like a minimum spend before the insurance company picks up the tab.

Coverage Limits: The maximum amount your insurance will pay out for a claim. It's the cap on what the insurance company will cover, much like a spending limit on a prepaid card.

Main Course (Types of Coverage)

Comprehensive: This is broad coverage that includes protection against a wide range of risks, except those specifically excluded. It's the full-course meal of insurance, covering more than just the basics.

Liability: Covers costs if you're responsible for causing harm or damage to someone else. It's like having insurance for accidentally spilling wine on a stranger's expensive suit.

Collision: For car insurance, this covers damage to your vehicle from a collision, whether it's with another vehicle or an object. It's like having coverage for when you accidentally bump your car into a post.

Side Dishes (Add-Ons and Riders)

- **Riders:** Additional coverage options you can add to your policy, for an extra cost. Think of them as side dishes that complement the main meal, offering specialized coverage for valuables, specific disasters, or additional liability beyond your basic policy.

Desserts (Benefits)

Claim: A request for payment from your insurance company to cover a loss. It's like asking for a refund for a meal that didn't meet the promised standard.

Adjuster: An insurance professional who assesses the damage and determines the payout. They're the sommelier of the insurance world, assessing the situation to recommend the appropriate "wine" (payout).

The Bill (Policy Exclusions)

- **Exclusions:** These are the conditions or situations not covered by your policy. Just as some dishes might not be available for dietary reasons, certain claims won't be covered by your insurance.

Tips for a Satisfying Meal (Tips for Policyholders)

Read Your Policy Carefully: Understanding your policy is key. Take the time to read it as you would a menu before ordering, ensuring you know what you're getting.

Ask Questions: If something isn't clear, don't hesitate to ask your insurance agent for clarification, just as you'd inquire about a dish's ingredients.

Review Regularly: Your insurance needs can change, just like your taste in food. Regularly review your policy to ensure it still meets your needs.

Understanding your insurance policy and its terms doesn't have to be daunting. With a little effort, you can become fluent in the language of insurance, making informed decisions that protect you and your loved ones. Just like mastering the art of ordering at a gourmet restaurant, navigating your insurance policy can be satisfying and empowering, ensuring you enjoy the peace of mind that comes with being well-protected.

Building and Maintaining an Emergency Fund: A Financial Chef's Secret Ingredient

Imagine you're a chef in the kitchen of life, whipping up your financial future with skill and care. Every chef knows the importance of having a few secret ingredients up their sleeve, and in the realm of personal finance, one of the most crucial is the emergency fund. Let's break down how to build and maintain this fund, making it as straightforward as following a simple recipe.

Step 1: Understanding the Importance

An emergency fund is like your kitchen's pantry, stocked for unexpected guests or a sudden storm that keeps you indoors. It's a stash of money set aside to cover unforeseen expenses—be it a car repair, job loss, or medical emergency. Having this fund means you won't have to raid your savings or resort to credit cards, keeping your financial goals on track.

Step 2: Determining How Much You Need

The size of your emergency fund can vary based on your life recipe. A good starting point is to aim for three to six months' worth of living expenses. Consider your ingredients: Are you single or feeding a family? Is your income steady, or does it fluctuate like the seasons? Adjust your fund size accordingly, just as you would modify a recipe based on who's coming to dinner.

Step 3: Finding the Right Ingredients

Start Small: Begin by setting aside a small portion of your income, even if it's just $50 from each paycheck. Think of it as seasoning your dish—a little at a time until it's just right.

Increase Gradually: As you get more comfortable, increase the amount gradually. Maybe you get a raise or pay off a debt; redirect some of that newfound cash into your emergency fund.

Use a High-Yield Savings Account: Store your fund in a high-yield savings account. It's like putting your ingredients in the right environment to keep them fresh—accessible but also growing a bit with interest.

Step 4: Cooking the Meal (Building Your Fund)

Automate Your Savings: Set up automatic transfers to your emergency fund. It's like having a slow cooker; you set it up, forget it, and let it do its work.

Cut Back on Non-Essentials: Find areas where you can cut back—dining out, subscriptions you don't use—and reroute that money to your fund. It's akin to opting for home-cooked meals over expensive takeout to save money.

Use Windfalls Wisely: Got a tax refund or a bonus? Resist the urge to splurge and put a portion into your emergency fund instead.

Step 5: Maintenance and Adjustments

Review Regularly: Just as a good chef tastes their dish throughout cooking, review your emergency fund regularly. Your financial situation can change, and so should your fund.

Avoid Unnecessary Dips: Withdraw from your emergency fund only for actual emergencies. If you do need to use it, make a plan to replenish it.

Increase as Necessary: As your living expenses increase, so should your emergency fund. Keep it proportional to your needs, ensuring it always covers several months of expenses.

Conclusion: Savoring the Security

An emergency fund is more than just money in the bank; it's peace of mind. It's knowing that when life throws a surprise your way, you have a financial cushion to land on. By building and maintaining an emergency fund, you ensure that unexpected expenses don't derail your financial plans. Just like a well-stocked pantry ensures you're ready for any culinary challenge, an emergency fund ensures you're prepared for life's financial surprises. Start small, build gradually, and enjoy the security and peace of mind that comes with having your very own financial safety net.

The Essential Ingredient: The Importance of an Emergency Fund

Imagine navigating the journey of life as if you were piloting a ship across the vast oceans. Just as a seasoned captain prepares for unforeseen storms, having an emergency fund is akin to keeping a lifeboat on board—it's essential for weathering financial squalls that might otherwise capsize your budget.

A Safety Net for the Unexpected

Life, much like the sea, is unpredictable. Emergency funds serve as a financial safety net, ready to catch you when unexpected expenses fall into your lap. Whether it's a sudden job loss, an urgent car repair, or a medical emergency, having this fund means you can cover these costs without derailing your long-term financial plans.

Keeping Debt at Bay

Without an emergency fund, you might be tempted to turn to credit cards or loans, leading to high interest and a debt cycle that's hard to escape. An emergency fund keeps you afloat, providing a buffer that can prevent the need for borrowing and the stress that comes with debt.

Peace of Mind

Beyond the practical benefits, an emergency fund contributes significantly to your mental and emotional well-being. Knowing you have a financial cushion can reduce stress and anxiety associated with unexpected expenses, allowing you to focus on solving the problem at hand without worrying about financial fallout.

Financial Independence and Freedom

An emergency fund is a cornerstone of financial independence. It gives you the freedom to make decisions based on what's best for you and your family, rather than being cornered by financial desperation. Whether it's leaving a job that's not the right fit, handling a household emergency, or navigating a global pandemic, your emergency fund gives you options and control over your life choices.

How Much is Enough?

The size of your emergency fund can vary based on your lifestyle, expenses, and income stability. A common guideline is to aim for three to six months' worth of living expenses, though some may need more for added security. Assessing your situation and adjusting your fund accordingly is key.

In Conclusion

The importance of an emergency fund cannot be overstated. It's the lifeboat of your financial ship, designed to keep you safe when the waters get rough. Building and maintaining it should be a priority in your financial planning, ensuring that when storms hit, you're ready to weather them with confidence. Like any essential ingredient in a well-prepared dish, an emergency fund can make the difference between a financial crisis and a manageable inconvenience. Start small, build steadily, and watch as this fund transforms from a simple financial tool into a pillar of your personal financial security.

Crafting Your Financial Safety Net: Guidelines for Your Emergency Fund

When it comes to saving for an emergency fund, envision yourself as an architect designing a safety net. It must be strong enough to catch you, yet flexible enough to fit your unique life structure. The question of 'How much?' is pivotal, akin to deciding the dimensions of your net. Here's a guide to help you determine the right size for your emergency fund, ensuring it's both robust and responsive to your needs.

Start with a Foundation

The conventional wisdom suggests starting with a fund that can cover three to six months' worth of living expenses. This range isn't arbitrary; it's designed to provide a buffer for life's most common financial disruptions, like job loss or unexpected medical bills.

- **Three Months:** Considered the minimum, suitable for those with a stable income and fewer dependents.
- **Six Months or More:** Recommended for individuals with fluctuating incomes, single-income households, or those with dependents.

Tailor to Your Architectural Design (Life Circumstances)

Just as no two buildings are alike, your emergency fund should reflect your personal financial landscape.

- **Fixed vs. Freelance Income:** If your income is variable, consider leaning towards the higher end of the savings spectrum to account for dry spells.

Family Structure: Single earners with dependents should aim for a larger fund, as more lives depend on a single income source.

Health Considerations: If you or a family member has ongoing health issues, a more substantial emergency fund can mitigate unexpected medical costs.

Calculate Your Living Expenses

Begin by defining "living expenses." These are your non-negotiable costs: housing, food, utilities, insurance premiums, and transportation. Exclude luxuries to ensure your calculation reflects true needs, not wants.

Incremental Steps to the Summit

Building your emergency fund is a marathon, not a sprint. Start with achievable milestones:

$1,000 Mini-Fund: A preliminary target to cover small emergencies.

One Month of Expenses: Once you hit the first goal, aim to cover a month's worth of living expenses.

Three to Six Months: Gradually work your way up to this more substantial safety net.

Location, Location, Location: Where to Keep Your Fund

Your emergency fund should be easily accessible but not so accessible that you're tempted to dip into it for everyday expenses. High-yield savings accounts are ideal, offering better interest rates than regular savings accounts without compromising on accessibility.

Regular Maintenance

Review your emergency fund annually or after significant life events (e.g., a new job, marriage, or a new family member). Adjust your contributions to reflect changes in your income and living expenses, ensuring your safety net remains adequate.

In Summary

Building an emergency fund is a personalized process, akin to constructing a safety net tailored to your life's architecture. By assessing your specific needs, setting clear milestones, and choosing the right storage location, you can ensure that your emergency fund provides the financial security you need. Remember, this fund isn't just about the money—it's about peace of mind, stability, and having the freedom to navigate life's challenges with confidence.

Best Practices for Building and Maintaining an Emergency Fund

Creating a robust emergency fund is akin to constructing a lighthouse—it serves as a beacon of safety, guiding you through the tumultuous seas of financial uncertainty. Here are best practices to ensure your emergency fund is as steadfast and reliable as a lighthouse on a stormy night.

1. Start with a Clear Goal

- **Define Your Target:** Begin by determining how much you need in your emergency fund, typically three to six months' worth of living expenses. Tailor this amount to your personal circumstances, such as job stability, health, and family obligations.

2. Establish a Separate Account

- **Accessibility vs. Temptation:** Place your emergency fund in a separate high-yield savings account. This makes the money easily accessible while keeping it distinct from your daily spending accounts to avoid temptation.

3. Automate Your Savings

- **Set and Forget:** Automate transfers to your emergency fund from your checking account. By treating these contributions like any other recurring bill, you ensure consistent growth without having to remember to make transfers manually.

4. Gradually Increase Contributions

- **Scale with Success:** As you pay off debts or if your income increases, redirect a portion of those funds to your emergency savings. Even small increments can significantly accelerate the growth of your fund.

5. Monitor and Adjust Your Fund

- **Annual Review:** Life changes—so should your emergency fund. Regularly review your fund to ensure it matches your current living expenses and adjust your contributions as necessary.

6. Resist the Urge to Dip In

- **True Emergencies Only:** Reserve your emergency fund for true emergencies, such as unexpected medical bills, essential home repairs, or in case of job loss. Avoid dipping into it for non-essentials.

7. Replenish Any Withdrawals

Restore Balance: If you need to use your emergency fund, prioritize replenishing it. Treat the replenishment as you would any other financial obligation until the fund is restored to its full amount.

8. Increase Your Financial Literacy

Knowledge as Power: Enhance your understanding of personal finance. The more you know, the better equipped you are to make informed decisions about saving, spending, and investing, all of which can contribute to a more substantial emergency fund.

9. Seek Additional Income Streams

Diversify Your Income: Look for opportunities to increase your income through side hustles, freelance work, or passive income streams. Additional income can be directed towards your emergency fund or other financial goals.

10. Stay Motivated

Visualize Your Safety Net: Keep the purpose of your emergency fund in mind. Visualizing the security and peace of mind it provides can be a powerful motivator to keep building and maintaining your fund.

In Summary

Building and maintaining an emergency fund is a foundational aspect of financial well-being. Like a lighthouse guiding ships to safety, your emergency fund offers guidance and protection through life's unexpected financial storms. By adhering to these best practices, you can ensure that your emergency fund remains a reliable source of financial security, ready to illuminate your path through even the darkest of times.

Navigating the Seas of Investment: Risks and Mitigation Strategies

Investing is akin to setting sail on the vast ocean of financial opportunity. While the potential rewards can be great, so too can the risks. Understanding these risks and how to mitigate them is essential for any investor seeking to navigate these waters safely. Here's a guide to the common investment risks and strategies to mitigate them, ensuring a more secure journey towards your financial goals.

Market Risk (Systematic Risk)

Nature of the Risk: Market risk refers to the potential loss due to factors that affect the entire market or asset class. Economic downturns, political instability, or significant events like pandemics can lead to market-wide drops.

Mitigation Strategy: Diversification is key. Spread your investments across different asset classes (stocks, bonds, real estate, etc.) and geographies. This way, a downturn in one market or sector won't capsize your entire investment portfolio.

Credit Risk (Default Risk)

Nature of the Risk: This risk arises when a borrower fails to make payments on debt securities, such as bonds. It can lead to lost interest payments or, in worst cases, losing the principal investment.

Mitigation Strategy: Research and invest in high-quality bonds issued by reputable entities with strong credit ratings. Diversifying your bond investments across different issuers and sectors can also reduce credit risk.

Interest Rate Risk

Nature of the Risk: Interest rate changes can affect the value of bonds inversely; as rates rise, bond prices typically fall, and vice versa.

Mitigation Strategy: Ladder your bond investments by purchasing bonds with varying maturities. This approach can help manage the effects of interest rate fluctuations. Considering bonds with different durations can also help balance this risk.

Liquidity Risk

Nature of the Risk: Liquidity risk involves being unable to sell an investment at or near its value due to a lack of buyers. This can be a significant issue with more obscure or complex investments.

Mitigation Strategy: Focus on investments with higher liquidity, such as stocks of large companies traded on major stock exchanges. Keep a portion of your portfolio in highly liquid assets for emergencies.

Concentration Risk

Nature of the Risk: This risk occurs when an investor's portfolio is heavily weighted towards a single investment, asset class, or market sector. Significant losses can occur if that specific area underperforms.

Mitigation Strategy: Ensure your investments are well-diversified across different sectors, industries, and asset classes. Regularly review and adjust your portfolio to avoid over-concentration.

Inflation Risk

Nature of the Risk: Inflation can erode the purchasing power of your investments, particularly fixed-income securities like bonds, which may not yield enough to outpace inflation.

Mitigation Strategy: Consider investments that tend to fare well during inflationary periods, such as stocks, real estate, or Treasury Inflation-Protected Securities (TIPS).

Emotional Risk

Nature of the Risk: Emotional decision-making can lead to buying high out of greed and selling low out of fear, resulting in significant losses.

Mitigation Strategy: Develop a disciplined investment strategy and stick to it, avoiding impulsive decisions based on market volatility. Consider working with a financial advisor to maintain an objective perspective.

Currency Risk

Nature of the Risk: For investments in foreign markets, currency risk arises from fluctuations in the exchange rate that could reduce the investment's value when converted back to your home currency.

Mitigation Strategy: Diversify globally with a mindful approach to how currency fluctuations could impact your portfolio. Currency-hedged funds can also mitigate this risk.

Conclusion

Just as a skilled sailor uses charts, compasses, and the stars to navigate, so too must investors use diversification, research, and a disciplined approach to mitigate the risks of the investment seas. By understanding these risks and employing effective strategies to mitigate them, you can set a course towards achieving your financial objectives with confidence. Remember, the goal isn't to eliminate risk but to manage it wisely, ensuring it aligns with your investment horizon, goals, and tolerance for volatility.

Chatting About Identifying Risks in Investment Portfolios

Hey there! Let's have a little heart-to-heart about something super important but often overlooked—identifying risks in your investment portfolio. Think of it as checking the weather before you head out for a sail. You wouldn't want to get caught in a storm without the proper gear, right? So, let's dive into how you can spot those stormy clouds in your investments.

The Sneaky Risks Lurking Around

First off, it's all about knowing what could go bump in the night (or in your portfolio). Risks in investing aren't just about one thing going wrong; they're about everything from market swings to the chance that the company you've invested in decides to take an unexpected "sabbatical" (aka goes belly-up).

Market Mood Swings

Market risk, my friend, is like the weather—it changes. One day it's sunny, and stocks are up; the next, it's raining because of an economic downturn, and so are your investments. It's the whole market feeling a bit moody, not just a few stocks.

That One Friend Who Never Pays Back

Then there's credit risk, especially if you're into bonds. It's like lending money to a friend who sometimes forgets to pay you back. Some companies or governments are more likely to give you your money back with interest. Others, not so much.

The Interest Rate Dance

Interest rates and bonds have this dance they do. When rates go up, bond prices usually take a dive, and vice versa. It's all about timing and not stepping on each other's toes.

The Party No One Shows Up To

Imagine throwing a party (selling an investment) where no one shows up (no buyers). That's liquidity risk for you. You're stuck with leftovers that nobody wants, at least not at a price you'd like.

Too Many Eggs in One Basket

Concentration risk is when you're a little too enthusiastic about one type of investment. It's like only having pizza every day. Sure, pizza is great, but what if suddenly there's a tomato sauce shortage? Diversify your "diet" to stay healthy.

The Sneaky Thief: Inflation

Inflation is that sneaky thief that comes in and lowers the value of your money over time. Imagine buying a candy bar for $1 today, but next year, due to inflation, that same bar costs $1.10. If your investments aren't keeping up with or beating inflation, you're losing purchasing power.

Keeping a Weather Eye on the Horizon

So, how do you keep your portfolio shipshape amidst all these risks? It's all about being the captain of your ship.

- **Stay Vigilant:** Regularly check your investment weather forecast. A little review now and then helps you see if there are any storm clouds on the horizon.
- **Diversify:** Don't put all your treasures in one chest. Spread them out across different types of investments (stocks, bonds, real estate, etc.). It's like having a well-balanced diet.
- **Understand What You Own:** Know your investments like the back of your hand. If you wouldn't be comfortable explaining it to a friend, maybe it's time to reconsider that investment.

Wrapping It Up

Identifying risks in your investment portfolio doesn't have to be a chore or something to dread. Think of it as preparing for an adventure, making sure you have all the right gear, and knowing the terrain. By staying informed, diversified, and proactive, you're not just avoiding risks; you're setting sail towards your financial goals with confidence. So, keep a keen eye, adapt as needed, and remember, every great navigator knows how to navigate through both calm and stormy seas. Let's make your investment journey one for the history books!

Diving into Diversification and Other Risk Mitigation Strategies in Investing

Alright, let's break this down like we're trying to explain Netflix's algorithm to our grandparents—simply, with patience, and maybe a little humor. We're tackling how to keep your investments as chill as a cucumber in a spa, despite the rollercoaster ride that is the stock market. So, grab your financial floaties; we're wading into the deep end of diversification and other savvy strategies to keep your portfolio buoyant.

The Magic of Diversification

Imagine you're at a potluck dinner. Instead of filling your plate with just lasagna (because let's face it, lasagna is awesome), you sample a little bit of everything. That way, if the lasagna is a bit too crispy (burnt), your entire meal isn't ruined. Diversification in investing works the same way. By spreading your investments across various asset classes (stocks, bonds, real estate, gold, the latest and greatest tech startups), sectors, and geographical locations, you're not putting all your financial hopes in one basket. If one investment tanks, you've got others to keep your portfolio from hitting rock bottom.

The Bond Balancing Act

Stocks are the life of the party, but bonds are the designated drivers—less exciting, but they get you home safely. Having a mix of both can balance out the risk. When the stock market's doing its best impression of a yo-yo, bonds often remain more stable, providing a comforting predictability to your investment journey.

The Global Gala

Why limit yourself to home turf? Investing in international markets can be like adding a dash of exotic spices to a dish—it can enhance the flavor (returns) but also comes with its own set of risks (currency fluctuations, geopolitical tensions, etc.). The key is to not go overboard. A sprinkle here and there can diversify your portfolio and potentially tap into growth opportunities abroad.

Alternative Assets Alley

Ever thought about investing in a vineyard, artwork, or even cryptocurrencies? These are called alternative investments, and they march to the beat of their own drum, often not following the ups and downs of traditional stock and bond markets. Including a smidgen of these in your portfolio might add that je ne sais quoi, potentially boosting returns or reducing overall risk. Just remember, these can be the wild cards—exciting but unpredictable.

Timing is Everything... Or Is It?

Here's the thing about trying to time the market—it's like trying to catch a greased pig. It's slippery, stressful, and you're likely to end up face-first in the mud. Instead of trying to buy low and sell high based on predictions (which are as reliable as a weather forecast), consider a strategy like dollar-cost averaging. This means investing a fixed amount regularly, regardless of the market's mood swings. It takes the guesswork out and can smooth out the volatility.

Knowledge as Armor

Staying informed is your best defense. Understanding the basics of economic cycles, how different asset classes behave, and keeping abreast of financial news can help you make more informed decisions. Knowledge is power, and in the world of investing, it can be the difference between making a strategic move and a costly mistake.

The Financial Safety Net: Emergency Funds

Before you even think about investing, ensure you've got a rainy day fund tucked away. This isn't just good advice; it's your financial safety net. Having 3-6 months' worth of living expenses saved up means you won't have to liquidate investments (potentially at a loss) if life throws you a curveball.

Wrapping It Up

So there you have it—a beginner's guide to navigating the choppy waters of investing with diversification and other risk mitigation strategies. Think of your investment portfolio as a ship setting sail. With the right balance, a keen eye on the horizon, and a diverse cargo, you're set for an adventurous but secure voyage toward your financial goals. Remember, every investor's journey is unique, so tailor these strategies to fit your personal financial landscape and risk tolerance. Happy investing!

Navigating the Tightrope: Balancing Risk and Return in Long-Term Investments

Hey there! Let's chat about something that might seem as complex as deciding between hitting snooze or getting up for that early morning run—balancing risk and return in long-term investments. It's all about finding that sweet spot, where you're not lying awake at night worrying about your investments, but you're also not letting your money snooze when it could be out there working for you. Ready to dive in? Let's do this!

Understanding the Basics: Risk vs. Return

First off, imagine you're at an amusement park. You've got the merry-go-round (low risk, low return) and the giant roller coaster (high risk, high return). Your choice depends on what kind of thrill you're after—or can handle without losing your lunch. Investments work similarly. Generally, the higher the risk, the higher the potential return. The key for long-term investors is to not just go for the biggest thrill but to choose rides (investments) that provide the right balance of excitement and safety for their comfort level.

The Long-Term Perspective: A Marathon, Not a Sprint

Investing with a long-term perspective is like training for a marathon. It's about endurance, pacing yourself, and not getting overly worked up about the ups and downs along the way. Over time, markets tend to go up, but there will be plenty of bumps (and maybe a few bruises) along the route. By staying focused on the finish line, you can afford to take some risks early on, knowing you have time to recover from any missteps.

Diversification: The Art of Spreading Your Bets

Here's a secret weapon for balancing risk and return: diversification. Think of it as not putting all your eggs in one basket. Instead, you're spreading your eggs across several baskets—stocks, bonds, real estate, maybe even some commodities or crypto if you're feeling adventurous. This way, if one basket takes a tumble, you're not scrambling to make an omelet with what's left. Diversification can help smooth out the ride and potentially increase your overall returns while managing risk.

Risk Tolerance: Know Thyself

Balancing risk and return is also about knowing your own risk tolerance. This is deeply personal and can change with life stages. Maybe you're a daredevil in your 20s, but by your 40s, you've become more of a cautious navigator. Adjust your investment strategy accordingly. There are no right or wrong answers here, just what feels right for you and your financial goals.

The Role of Asset Allocation

Asset allocation is your game plan. It's deciding what portion of your investment portfolio goes into stocks, bonds, and other assets. Younger investors often lean heavier on stocks for growth, while those closer to retirement may shift towards bonds for stability. Revisiting and adjusting your asset allocation over time ensures your investment strategy stays aligned with your evolving risk tolerance and financial goals.

Staying the Course: The Discipline of Long-Term Investing

Here's where the rubber meets the road: sticking to your plan. Markets will test your resolve with volatility that can make a roller coaster seem tame. It's tempting to react to short-term market movements, but remember, you're in this for the long haul. Staying disciplined, keeping an eye on your asset allocation, and resisting the urge to make impulsive decisions are key to navigating the path to long-term financial success.

Regular Check-Ins: Adjusting as You Go

Just like you might adjust your marathon training based on how you're feeling, regular check-ins on your investment portfolio are crucial. Life changes—marriages, babies, new careers—and your investment strategy should evolve too. These check-ins are opportunities to rebalance your portfolio, reassess your risk tolerance, and ensure you're still on track to meet your financial goals.

Wrapping It Up

Balancing risk and return in long-term investments doesn't have to feel like walking a tightrope without a net. With a clear understanding of your risk tolerance, a well-diversified portfolio, and a disciplined approach to asset allocation and rebalancing, you can stride confidently towards your financial goals. Remember, investing is a journey, not a race. By keeping a steady pace and adjusting as needed, you're setting yourself up for a successful and rewarding investment experience. Happy investing!

Legal and Tax Risks: Navigating the Regulatory Maze of Investing

Welcome to the less talked about, but equally thrilling side of investing—navigating the intricate world of legal and tax risks. Think of this as the hidden level in a video game, where the rewards can be substantial, but so can the pitfalls if you're not careful. Let's embark on a journey through the regulatory maze, armed with knowledge and a flashlight, to uncover how you can safeguard your investments from potential legal and tax headaches.

The Legal Landscape: More Than Just Fine Print

When you dive into investing, you're entering a world brimming with regulations, compliance requirements, and legal obligations. It's like playing a game where the rules change depending on where you're standing. From the securities you choose to invest in, to the way you report your earnings, the legal landscape can significantly impact your investment strategy and outcomes.

Regulatory Compliance: Just as traffic laws keep roads safe, investment regulations protect investors and maintain market integrity. Non-compliance, whether intentional or not, can lead to penalties, fines, or worse. It's crucial to stay informed about the regulations that apply to your investments, especially if you're venturing into areas like cryptocurrencies or international markets, where the rules can be markedly different.

Legal Structures and Implications: Different investment vehicles and strategies come with their own set of legal considerations. For example, investing through a corporation, partnership, or solo can have varied implications for liability and legal protection. Understanding the nuances of each structure can help you make informed decisions that align with your risk tolerance and investment goals.

Tax Risks: The Certainty of Uncertainty

Benjamin Franklin famously said, "In this world, nothing is certain except death and taxes." The realm of investing is no exception. Tax implications can significantly affect your returns and, therefore, must be navigated with care.

Capital Gains and Losses: The joy of selling an investment for a profit comes with the obligation to pay taxes on those gains. Conversely, understanding how to legally use capital losses to offset gains can be a strategic advantage. The key is to know the rules, including how long you've held an investment, as it can affect the tax rate applied to your gains.

Tax-Efficient Investing: Certain accounts and investments offer tax advantages. Roth IRAs, 401(k)s, and 529 plans in the U.S., for instance, can provide tax-free growth or deductions. Similarly, choosing investments like municipal bonds for tax-exempt income can be a smart move. Familiarizing yourself with these options can help you build a more tax-efficient portfolio.

Reporting and Compliance: Proper reporting of investments and income to tax authorities is non-negotiable. Mistakes or omissions can lead to audits, penalties, or interest on unpaid taxes. Utilizing professional advice or reliable tax software can ensure you stay on the right side of the law.

Staying Ahead of Legal and Tax Risks

Education is Your Best Defense: Keeping abreast of legal and tax changes is vital. Tax laws, in particular, can evolve, impacting your investment strategy. Regularly consulting with a financial advisor or tax professional can keep you informed and compliant.

Professional Guidance: For complex investment portfolios or strategies, the cost of professional legal and tax advice is often outweighed by the benefits of compliance and optimized tax strategies. Consider it an investment in your peace of mind.

Record-Keeping: Maintain meticulous records of all your investments, transactions, and related documents. Good record-keeping not only simplifies tax reporting but can also protect you in the event of a dispute or audit.

Wrapping Up

Legal and tax risks in investing might seem daunting, but they don't have to be barriers to your success. With a proactive approach, a willingness to learn, and perhaps a bit of professional help, you can navigate these complexities confidently. Remember, the goal is not just to maximize returns but to do so in a way that is both legally sound and tax-efficient. By staying informed and compliant, you can focus on growing your investments while keeping legal and tax risks in check. Happy investing, and here's to a journey that's both profitable and compliant!

Unraveling Legal Risks in Personal Finance: Liabilities, Estate Planning, and Beyond

When we talk about personal finance, it's like entering a vast sea aboard your financial vessel. Navigating through the waters of wealth accumulation, you must also be vigilant about the undercurrents of legal risks that could potentially capsize your journey. Today, let's chart the course through the choppy waters of legal risks in personal finance, focusing on liabilities, estate issues, and other lurking legal icebergs.

The Anchors of Liability: More Than Just a Weight

Liabilities in personal finance aren't just about the debts you owe; they extend to any legal responsibilities that can impact your financial health. Imagine you're the captain of a ship. Just as you're responsible for any damages your ship might cause, in life, various forms of liability can tie you down.

Personal Liability: This can arise from everyday activities, such as being involved in an accident. If found liable, your assets could be at risk to cover damages. It's like having a hole in your boat; if you're not prepared, you could sink fast.

Property Ownership: Owning property comes with its set of risks. For instance, if someone is injured on your property, you could be held liable. It's akin to having passengers on your ship; you need to ensure their safety to avoid trouble.

Professional Liability: For those navigating the waters of self-employment or business ownership, professional liability can arise from the services you provide. It's important to have the right measures in place, like liability insurance, to protect against claims that could financially drown you.

Estate Planning: Charting the Course Beyond the Horizon

Estate planning is about ensuring your assets are distributed according to your wishes after you've sailed into the sunset. Without a proper map (will or estate plan), your assets could end up marooned in probate court, costing time and money, and leading to potential family disputes.

- **Wills and Trusts:** These are the compasses that guide the distribution of your assets. A will provides directions on who gets what, while a trust can offer more control over how and when your assets are distributed.
- **Power of Attorney:** This legal document is like appointing a first mate. It gives someone you trust the authority to make decisions on your behalf if you're unable to do so, ensuring your financial ship stays on course.
- **Healthcare Directives:** These ensure your wishes regarding medical treatment are followed if you're incapacitated. It's like setting the rules for how to navigate in case of a storm.

Navigating Through Legal Icebergs

- **Marital and Family Law:** Changes in your family structure, such as marriage, divorce, or the birth of a child, can have significant legal and financial implications. It's crucial to adjust your financial plan accordingly, ensuring your assets are protected and your estate plan reflects your current wishes.
- **Debt and Bankruptcy:** Understanding your rights and responsibilities when it comes to debt and the potential of bankruptcy is crucial. It's about knowing when to bail water out of your boat versus when it might be time to signal for help.
- **Tax Obligations:** Taxes are the perpetual winds affecting your financial journey. Failing to navigate these waters correctly can lead to legal troubles with tax authorities. Ensure you're aware of your obligations and take advantage of legal ways to minimize your tax burden.

Keeping Your Financial Ship Afloat

- **Legal Shield:** Consider legal insurance or retaining a lawyer to help navigate complex legal situations. It's like having an experienced navigator aboard.
- **Insurance:** Beyond just liability insurance, various types of insurance can protect you from unforeseen legal risks. It's the lifeline that can save you from financial distress.
- **Education:** Stay informed about the legal aspects of personal finance. The more you know, the better you can steer clear of legal pitfalls.

In Closing

Understanding and managing legal risks in personal finance are crucial to safeguarding your wealth and ensuring your financial journey is smooth sailing. By taking preemptive measures, such as proper estate planning, liability management, and continuous education, you can protect your financial ship from unexpected legal storms. Remember, in the vast ocean of personal finance, a little legal foresight can go a long way in ensuring a prosperous voyage.

Navigating Tax Risks and Compliance: A Roadmap to Financial Serenity

In the realm of personal finance, the topic of taxes often evokes a spectrum of emotions, ranging from mild apprehension to downright trepidation. It's a labyrinthine world of legislation, dotted with pitfalls for the unwary and opportunities for the informed. Let's embark on a journey together, navigating the complexities of tax risks and compliance, with the aim of transforming potential anxieties into a state of financial serenity.

Understanding the Landscape

Tax laws are notoriously fluid, evolving with each legislative session. This constant state of flux can seem daunting, but it's also replete with opportunities for optimization. Consider this: each change in the tax code opens a door to new strategies for minimizing liabilities and maximizing returns. The key lies in staying informed and adaptable, qualities that empower you to navigate this terrain with confidence.

Personal Anecdotes: Lessons from the Front Lines

I recall a year when, like many, I was blindsided by a significant, unexpected tax liability. The oversight stemmed from a lack of understanding of how freelance income, side hustles, and investment returns intersected with my tax bracket. This experience was a crucible, forging a more disciplined approach to tax planning in me. It underscored the importance of proactive engagement with my finances, transforming what was a reactive stance into a strategic, forward-looking mindset.

Actionable Advice: Fortifying Your Financial Defenses

To mitigate tax risks, consider these actionable steps:

- **Quarterly Reviews**: Regularly assess your income streams and tax liabilities. This approach, akin to a gardener tending to their plants, ensures that there are no unpleasant surprises come tax season.
- **Maximize Contributions to Tax-Advantaged Accounts**: Whether it's a 401(k), IRA, or HSA, these vehicles offer a dual benefit—reducing taxable income and fostering wealth growth.
- **Seek Professional Guidance**: A tax professional can be a navigator in the choppy waters of tax legislation, offering personalized advice tailored to your unique financial situation.

Philosophical Insights: Embracing the Journey

The journey towards financial independence is as much about mindset as it is about tactics. Consider the philosophy of stoicism, which teaches the value of focusing on what we can control while accepting what we cannot. In the context of tax planning, this means embracing the inevitability of taxes while assertively seeking ways to minimize their impact through lawful and ethical means.

Engaging Narratives: Historical Perspectives

History is replete with tales of financial ingenuity in the face of tax adversity. For instance, consider the story of John D. Rockefeller, who, faced with the introduction of the federal income tax, diversified his wealth into philanthropic foundations, thereby mitigating his tax liabilities while contributing to societal welfare. These narratives not only illustrate strategic financial planning but also serve as a reminder of the dynamic interplay between personal wealth and societal obligations.

Conclusion: Charting Your Course with Confidence

Navigating tax risks and compliance is an integral part of securing financial well-being. It requires a blend of knowledge, vigilance, and strategic action. By embracing this journey with a mindset of growth and empowerment, you can transform the daunting into the doable. Remember, the goal is not merely to survive the tax season but to thrive within it, crafting a narrative of financial success that is uniquely yours.

In closing, let us approach the topic of taxes not as a burden but as a challenge to be mastered. With the right strategies, a proactive mindset, and a touch of historical wisdom, we can all become adept navigators of the financial seas, charting a course towards a future of prosperity and peace of mind.

Seeking professional advice for complex legal and tax matters.
Seeking professional advice for complex legal and tax matters is not merely a prudent step; it is a strategic necessity in today's intricate financial and legal landscapes. The intricacies of law and taxation can be as labyrinthine as they are dynamic, presenting both challenges and opportunities. In this discourse, we shall explore the imperative of engaging with professionals in these fields, underscoring the multifaceted benefits such collaborations can yield.

The Imperative of Expert Guidance

Navigating Complexity

The complexity of legal and tax environments cannot be overstated. Laws and regulations are in a state of perpetual evolution, shaped by legislative changes, judicial interpretations, and administrative guidelines. This fluidity, while reflective of societal progress, necessitates expert navigation. Professionals in legal and tax advisories are not just repositories of knowledge; they are interpreters of complexity, adept at translating abstract regulations into actionable strategies.

Customized Solutions

Every individual and business entity has a unique financial fingerprint, characterized by specific needs, goals, and challenges. Professional advisors excel in crafting customized solutions that align with these unique profiles. This personalized approach ensures that strategies are not just effective in a general sense but are optimized for the individual or entity in question.

Risk Mitigation

Engaging with legal and tax professionals is akin to fortifying one's financial and legal defenses. These experts not only identify potential risks but also devise strategies to mitigate them. From tax planning to compliance audits, and from legal risk assessment to dispute resolution, professional advisors serve as both shield and strategist, protecting against and navigating through potential legal and financial pitfalls.

The Value of Professional Advice

Strategic Planning

Professional advisors contribute to strategic planning by identifying opportunities for tax optimization, legal protection, and financial growth. Their expertise can uncover avenues for savings and efficiency that lay hidden within the complex interplay of regulations and statutes.

Compliance Assurance

Compliance with legal and tax regulations is not merely about avoiding penalties; it is about ensuring operational integrity and reputation. Professional advisors ensure that compliance is integrated seamlessly into strategic planning and operational execution, thereby safeguarding against both financial penalties and reputational damage.

Informed Decision-Making

Decisions informed by professional expertise are invariably more robust than those based on cursory understanding. Legal and tax advisors provide the depth of knowledge necessary for informed decision-making, empowering individuals and businesses to make choices with confidence.

Selecting the Right Professional

Choosing the right advisor is critical. This decision should be informed by the advisor's expertise, experience, and alignment with one's specific needs. It is advisable to seek professionals who not only have a deep understanding of the law and taxation but also possess a keen insight into the industry and personal circumstances involved.

Questions to Consider

- What is the professional's expertise and experience in areas relevant to your needs?
- How does the professional communicate complex information? Is it accessible and understandable?
- Can the professional provide references or case studies that demonstrate their impact?
- Does the professional's approach align with your values and objectives?

Conclusion: A Partnership for Prosperity

The pursuit of professional advice in complex legal and tax matters is more than a mere tactical move; it is a cornerstone of strategic financial management. This partnership between individuals/businesses and their advisors fosters a proactive approach to financial health, legal compliance, and strategic growth. In essence, it is a collaboration that not only navigates the present with confidence but also charts a course toward a prosperous and secure future.

Emergency Preparedness Beyond Finances

Emergency preparedness transcends the realm of financial readiness, encompassing a comprehensive strategy to safeguard personal well-being, secure assets, and ensure resilience in the face of unforeseen circumstances. This discourse aims to illuminate the multifaceted aspects of emergency preparedness, advocating for a holistic approach that integrates physical safety, mental preparedness, and community engagement alongside financial security.

Physical Preparedness: The Foundation of Resilience

The cornerstone of emergency preparedness is the physical safeguarding of oneself and one's dependents. This encompasses a spectrum of measures:

Emergency Kits: Assembling emergency kits for both home and vehicles is fundamental. These kits should include essentials such as water, non-perishable food, first aid supplies, flashlights, batteries, and personal hygiene items. Tailoring these kits to accommodate specific medical needs or dietary restrictions of family members is crucial.

Evacuation Plans: Developing and practicing evacuation plans for various scenarios (natural disasters, fires, etc.) ensures that all family members are aware of how to safely exit the home and where to reconvene.

Home Safety Checks: Regular safety audits of the home to identify and mitigate potential hazards (e.g., securing heavy furniture, checking smoke detectors) can significantly reduce the risk of injury during an emergency.

Mental Preparedness: Cultivating Resilience

Equally important to physical readiness is mental preparedness. The ability to remain calm and make informed decisions under pressure is invaluable during emergencies.

Education and Training: Participating in emergency preparedness workshops and first aid training can empower individuals with the knowledge and skills to respond effectively to crises.

Stress Management Techniques: Developing stress management skills, such as deep breathing exercises or mindfulness, can enhance one's ability to maintain composure and clarity of thought during stressful situations.

Financial Security: An Integral Component

While this discourse extends beyond financial preparedness, acknowledging its importance remains essential. A solid financial plan for emergencies includes:

Emergency Fund: Maintaining an emergency fund with sufficient resources to cover at least three to six months of living expenses provides a financial buffer against unexpected setbacks.

Insurance Coverage: Regularly reviewing and adjusting insurance policies (health, property, life) to ensure adequate coverage is fundamental in mitigating financial risks associated with emergencies.

Community Engagement: Strengthening Collective Resilience

The fabric of community plays a pivotal role in emergency preparedness. Engaging with local community emergency response teams, neighborhood associations, and support networks fosters a collective resilience.

Community Resources: Familiarizing oneself with community emergency plans, shelters, and resources can enhance individual preparedness efforts.

Volunteering: Participating in local emergency response teams or community support initiatives not only contributes to community resilience but also provides individuals with additional training and preparedness skills.

Conclusion: A Holistic Approach to Preparedness

Emergency preparedness, in its most effective form, is a holistic endeavor that interweaves physical safety, mental readiness, financial security, and community engagement. It demands a proactive and comprehensive approach, one that prepares individuals not just to survive, but to thrive in the aftermath of unforeseen events. This integrative strategy ensures that when faced with emergencies, individuals and communities are not merely reacting, but are equipped, resilient, and poised for recovery. Embracing this multifaceted approach to preparedness can transform the unpredictability of emergencies into manageable challenges, thereby safeguarding not only personal well-being but also the collective strength of the community.

Creating a comprehensive emergency plan.

Creating a comprehensive emergency plan is a pivotal task that requires meticulous attention to detail, foresight, and a strategic approach to ensure the safety, security, and resilience of individuals and their families. This plan should be designed to address a wide range of potential emergencies, including natural disasters, medical emergencies, and unforeseen personal crises. The following steps outline a structured methodology for developing an effective emergency plan:

Step 1: Risk Assessment

- **Identify Potential Emergencies**: Begin by assessing the types of emergencies most likely to occur in your geographical area and personal life. This could range from natural disasters (earthquakes, hurricanes, floods) to health emergencies and financial crises.
- **Evaluate Vulnerabilities**: Consider the specific needs of your household, including pets, individuals with disabilities, elderly family members, and children, to identify any unique vulnerabilities.

Step 2: Establish Communication Strategies

- **Emergency Contacts**: Compile a list of emergency contacts, including family members, friends, healthcare providers, and local emergency services. Ensure everyone in the household has access to this list.
- **Communication Plan**: Develop a plan for staying in touch with family members during an emergency, especially if you are separated. This should include backup communication methods, such as text messaging or social media, in case phone lines are overwhelmed.

Step 3: Evacuation and Shelter Plans

- **Evacuation Routes**: Identify safe evacuation routes from your home and local area. Familiarize yourself with alternate routes in case the primary paths are blocked.
- **Shelter Locations**: Know the location of nearby shelters and understand under what circumstances you would need to evacuate versus when it is safer to shelter in place.

Step 4: Emergency Kits

Home Emergency Kit: Assemble a comprehensive emergency kit for your home, including water, non-perishable food, first-aid supplies, flashlights, batteries, and necessary medications. Tailor the kit to the specific needs of your household.

Go Bags: Prepare portable "go bags" for each family member, including basic supplies and personal items, in case you need to evacuate quickly.

Step 5: Financial Preparedness

Emergency Fund: Build an emergency fund that can cover several months of living expenses.

Important Documents: Keep important documents (birth certificates, insurance policies, medical records) in a secure, easily accessible location, and consider having digital backups.

Step 6: Plan Maintenance and Practice

Review and Update: Regularly review and update your emergency plan to reflect any changes in your family situation, residence, or potential risks.

Drills and Practice: Conduct drills to practice evacuation routes, communication plans, and the use of emergency supplies. Familiarity with these procedures can reduce panic and confusion during an actual emergency.

Step 7: Community Integration

Community Resources: Engage with your local community to understand available resources and how you can contribute to or benefit from community emergency response efforts.

Neighborhood Plans: Coordinate with neighbors to share plans and resources. A community that works together is more resilient in emergencies.

Conclusion: Empowering Through Preparedness

A comprehensive emergency plan is an empowering tool that prepares individuals and families to face unforeseen events with confidence. By systematically assessing risks, establishing clear communication strategies, preparing for evacuation and shelter, assembling emergency kits, ensuring financial readiness, regularly updating and practicing the plan, and integrating with community resources, you can build a robust framework for emergency preparedness. This proactive approach not only enhances safety and security but also fosters a sense of community and mutual support, which are invaluable in times of crisis.

Essential documents and information management in emergencies.
In the context of emergency preparedness, the management of essential documents and information is a critical component that ensures individuals can access vital records and communicate effectively during and after an emergency situation. Proper organization, protection, and accessibility of these documents can significantly mitigate the administrative and logistical challenges often encountered in the wake of unforeseen events. Herein, we will delineate a systematic approach to managing essential documents and information for emergencies.

Identification of Essential Documents

Firstly, it is imperative to identify which documents are considered essential in emergency situations. These typically include:

- **Personal Identification**: Passports, driver's licenses, and birth certificates.
- **Legal and Financial Records**: Wills, powers of attorney, insurance policies, bank account information, and investment records.
- **Medical Information**: Health insurance cards, medical records, prescriptions, and contact information for healthcare providers.
- **Property Documents**: Deeds, leases, vehicle titles, and mortgage information.
- **Emergency Contacts**: Comprehensive list of personal contacts, local emergency numbers, and contacts for financial and medical institutions.

Protection and Storage Strategies

Once identified, the next step involves the protection and storage of these documents to ensure they are secure yet accessible when needed.

- **Physical Copies**: Keep original documents in a waterproof, fireproof safe or lockbox in your home. This safe should be easily accessible in the event of an evacuation.
- **Digital Copies**: Scan or photograph documents and store them digitally using secure cloud storage services. This ensures access to documents even if physical copies are lost or destroyed.
- **Encryption and Security**: For digital storage, use encryption and strong passwords to protect sensitive information against unauthorized access.

Accessibility and Portability

In emergencies, quick access to these documents can be crucial. Implementing strategies for accessibility and portability is essential.

- **Emergency Kits**: Include copies of essential documents in your "go bag" or emergency kit. This ensures you have necessary information if you need to evacuate quickly.

Cloud Access: Ensure you know how to access digital copies of your documents from any device. Familiarity with login credentials and navigation of cloud storage platforms is vital.

Trusted Contacts: Consider sharing copies or access to certain essential documents with trusted family members or friends. This can be particularly useful if you are unable to access them yourself.

Regular Updates and Reviews

The utility of these documents in an emergency can be compromised if the information is outdated. Regularly review and update your documents to reflect any changes in personal circumstances, financial situations, or medical conditions.

Annual Reviews: Establish a routine, such as an annual review, to update documents and information. This can coincide with other annual tasks, such as tax filing, to ensure it becomes a regular part of your administrative activities.

Changes in Circumstances: Update your documents and information promptly following significant life events, such as marriage, divorce, birth of a child, changes in financial status, or medical diagnoses.

Communication Plan

Incorporate the management of essential documents into your broader emergency communication plan. Ensure that all family members understand where documents are stored, how to access them, and whom to contact in case of an emergency.

Education and Training: Educate family members about the importance of these documents and train them on accessing both physical and digital copies.

Emergency Contacts: Include instructions within your emergency plan on who to contact for help in accessing or using these documents.

Conclusion: A Foundation for Resilience

Effective management of essential documents and information forms a foundational pillar of comprehensive emergency preparedness. By ensuring that vital records are identified, protected, accessible, and regularly updated, individuals can significantly enhance their resilience in the face of emergencies. This strategic approach not only facilitates a more effective response during crises but also aids in the recovery process, allowing for a quicker return to normalcy. Implementing these measures diligently prepares one to navigate the complexities and challenges of emergency situations with confidence and assurance.

Community resources and support systems.

In the tapestry of emergency preparedness and response, community resources and support systems represent vital threads that strengthen the overall fabric of resilience and recovery. These entities not only provide immediate aid and assistance during crises but also play a crucial role in the long-term recovery and rebuilding efforts. A comprehensive understanding of community resources and the mechanisms for leveraging these support systems is essential for individuals and families to navigate the aftermath of emergencies effectively. Here, we explore the spectrum of community resources available and strategies for engaging with and benefiting from these support systems.

Types of Community Resources

Community resources in the context of emergency preparedness and response can be broadly categorized into several key areas:

- **Government Agencies**: Entities such as FEMA (Federal Emergency Management Agency) in the United States, and similar organizations worldwide, provide emergency assistance, disaster relief, and information on recovery programs.
- **Local Emergency Services**: Fire departments, police, and emergency medical services (EMS) are frontline responders providing critical assistance during emergencies.
- **Non-Governmental Organizations (NGOs)**: Organizations like the Red Cross, Salvation Army, and community food banks offer various forms of support, including shelters, food, clothing, and medical aid.
- **Community Centers and Religious Institutions**: Local community centers and places of worship often serve as hubs for distributing aid and organizing volunteer efforts in the wake of disasters.
- **Neighborhood Associations and Social Networks**: Grassroots organizations and social networks can facilitate localized support, information sharing, and resource distribution.

Engaging with Community Resources

Maximizing the benefits from community resources requires proactive engagement and a strategy that encompasses preparation, collaboration, and participation:

Preparation

- **Research**: Familiarize yourself with the community resources available in your area. Identify contact information, services offered, and the process for accessing these services.
- **Documentation**: Keep a list of essential community resources, including addresses, phone numbers, and websites. Include this list in your emergency plan and share it with family members.

Collaboration

Network Building: Establish connections with community resource providers before emergencies occur. This can include attending community meetings, participating in local emergency preparedness events, and volunteering.

Partnerships: For businesses and local leaders, forming partnerships with NGOs and government agencies can facilitate coordinated response efforts and resource sharing during emergencies.

Participation

Community Drills and Training: Participate in community emergency response drills and training sessions. Programs such as the Community Emergency Response Team (CERT) in the United States offer training in basic disaster response skills.

Volunteering: Offer your time and skills to local emergency response and recovery efforts. Volunteering not only contributes to the community but also enhances your understanding of local resources and networks.

Leveraging Support Systems

In the aftermath of an emergency, effectively leveraging support systems involves several key actions:

Immediate Assistance: Reach out to emergency services and local NGOs for immediate needs such as shelter, food, and medical care.

Information Gathering: Use community centers, online platforms, and social networks to stay informed about available resources, recovery programs, and volunteer opportunities.

Long-Term Recovery: Engage with government agencies and NGOs involved in long-term recovery efforts to access services such as counseling, financial assistance, and housing.

Conclusion: A Community-Centric Approach to Resilience

Community resources and support systems play an indispensable role in enhancing the resilience of individuals and communities to emergencies. By understanding the spectrum of available resources, engaging proactively with these entities, and leveraging the support offered, communities can not only respond more effectively to crises but also foster a culture of preparedness and mutual aid. This community-centric approach underscores the importance of solidarity, collaboration, and active participation in building a resilient and supportive community network, ready to face and overcome the challenges posed by emergencies.

Risk Management in Real Estate and Large Investments

Risk management in real estate and large investments is a sophisticated discipline that necessitates a comprehensive understanding of the various risks involved and the implementation of strategies to mitigate these risks. The objective is to safeguard assets, ensure sustainability, and maximize returns while minimizing potential losses. This discussion elucidates the principles and practices central to effective risk management in these sectors, highlighting the multifaceted nature of risks and the strategic approaches for their mitigation.

Understanding the Spectrum of Risks

Risk management begins with a thorough assessment of the potential risks that can impact real estate and large investments. These risks can be categorized into several key areas:

- **Market Risks**: Fluctuations in the market that affect property values, rental income, and investment returns. Factors include economic downturns, changes in interest rates, and shifts in supply and demand dynamics.
- **Credit Risks**: The risk of loss arising from a borrower's failure to repay a loan or meet contractual obligations. For real estate, this could involve tenants defaulting on lease payments or borrowers failing on mortgage commitments.
- **Operational Risks**: Risks associated with the day-to-day operations of managing real estate or investments, including management inefficiencies, property maintenance issues, and technology failures.
- **Legal and Regulatory Risks**: The potential for legal disputes, changes in property law, zoning regulations, and compliance with environmental standards.
- **Environmental Risks**: Risks related to natural disasters (floods, earthquakes, hurricanes) and environmental contamination that can affect the value and usability of property.
- **Geopolitical Risks**: The impact of political instability, policy changes, and international conflicts on investment security and returns.

Strategies for Risk Mitigation

Effective risk management in real estate and large investments involves the implementation of strategies designed to mitigate these risks:

Diversification

- **Portfolio Diversification**: Spreading investments across different geographical locations, property types (residential, commercial, industrial), and investment vehicles (REITs, direct ownership, real estate funds) to reduce exposure to market volatility.

Due Diligence

- **Comprehensive Research**: Conducting thorough due diligence before acquiring a property or making a large investment, including market analysis, property inspection, and legal checks.
- **Financial Analysis**: Evaluating the financial stability and creditworthiness of tenants and borrowers to minimize credit risk.

Insurance

Risk Transfer: Utilizing insurance policies to transfer financial risks associated with property damage, liability claims, and loss of income due to unforeseen events.

Legal and Regulatory Compliance

Legal Advisory: Engaging legal counsel to navigate zoning laws, regulatory compliance, and contractual obligations to mitigate legal and regulatory risks.

Environmental Assessments: Conducting environmental assessments to identify and address potential contamination issues, thereby minimizing environmental risks.

Operational Efficiency

Property Management: Implementing effective property management practices to ensure proper maintenance, enhance tenant satisfaction, and optimize operational performance.

Technology Integration: Leveraging technology for property management, market analysis, and financial tracking to improve efficiency and decision-making.

Financial Management

Leverage Management: Carefully managing debt levels to maintain financial flexibility and reduce the risk of over-leverage.

Cash Flow Management: Ensuring adequate liquidity to cover operational expenses, debt service, and unexpected costs.

Conclusion: A Proactive Approach to Risk Management

In conclusion, risk management in real estate and large investments demands a proactive and strategic approach. By understanding the diverse array of risks, investors can implement comprehensive mitigation strategies to protect their assets and optimize returns. Diversification, due diligence, insurance, legal compliance, operational efficiency, and financial management are fundamental components of a robust risk management framework. Through diligent application of these principles, investors can navigate the complexities of the real estate and investment landscapes with confidence, ensuring long-term sustainability and success in their ventures.

Addressing risks in real estate investments.
Addressing risks in real estate investments involves a multifaceted approach that requires investors to identify, assess, and mitigate potential hazards that could affect the profitability and viability of their investments. The real estate market is influenced by a variety of factors, including economic trends, market dynamics, regulatory changes, and environmental considerations.

Effective risk management strategies are essential for preserving capital, maximizing returns, and ensuring the long-term success of real estate ventures. Below, we outline key strategies and practices for addressing risks in real estate investments.

1. Market Risk Assessment

- **Market Analysis**: Conduct thorough market research to understand current trends, including supply and demand dynamics, rental yields, and property appreciation rates in the target area.
- **Economic Indicators**: Monitor economic indicators such as GDP growth, employment rates, and interest rate trends that can impact real estate markets.
- **Flexibility**: Maintain flexibility in investment strategies to adapt to changing market conditions. This may involve reevaluating investment timelines or property types based on market forecasts.

2. Financial Risk Management

- **Diversification**: Diversify the investment portfolio across different types of real estate (residential, commercial, industrial) and geographical locations to spread risk.
- **Financial Analysis**: Perform detailed financial analysis including cash flow projections, expense estimates, and sensitivity analysis to understand potential financial outcomes under various scenarios.
- **Debt Management**: Manage leverage carefully, ensuring that debt levels are sustainable and aligned with investment cash flows. Opt for fixed-rate financing when possible to hedge against interest rate fluctuations.

3. Operational Risk Reduction

- **Professional Property Management**: Engage professional property managers to ensure efficient operation, maintenance, and tenant relations, which can mitigate operational risks and enhance property value.
- **Technology Utilization**: Leverage technology for property management, including automated systems for rent collection, maintenance requests, and tenant communication to reduce operational inefficiencies.

4. Legal and Regulatory Compliance

- **Legal Due Diligence**: Prior to investment, conduct legal due diligence to uncover any potential legal issues, zoning restrictions, or title discrepancies that could impact the property.
- **Regulatory Awareness**: Stay informed about local, state, and federal regulations affecting real estate, including tenant rights, building codes, and environmental laws, to ensure compliance and avoid legal pitfalls.

5. Environmental and Physical Risk Considerations

Environmental Assessments: Conduct environmental assessments to identify potential risks such as soil contamination or flood risk, which could affect property value and usability.

Insurance Coverage: Obtain comprehensive insurance coverage, including property damage, liability, and in certain areas, specific policies for natural disasters (flood, earthquake, hurricane) to protect against physical and environmental risks.

6. Tenant and Credit Risk Strategies

Tenant Screening: Implement rigorous tenant screening processes to assess creditworthiness and reduce the risk of rental defaults.

Lease Agreements: Craft clear, comprehensive lease agreements that outline tenant responsibilities and conditions for lease termination to protect the investment and ensure steady rental income.

7. Strategic Exit Planning

Exit Strategy Development: Develop clear exit strategies for each investment, considering the best timing and methods for sale or repositioning to maximize returns.

Market Timing: Continuously assess market conditions to identify optimal exit points, taking into account capital gains tax implications and market liquidity.

Conclusion

Addressing risks in real estate investments requires a proactive and strategic approach, encompassing market research, financial diligence, operational efficiency, legal compliance, environmental awareness, tenant management, and strategic exit planning. By implementing these strategies, investors can not only mitigate risks but also capitalize on opportunities, ensuring the growth and sustainability of their real estate portfolios. Effective risk management is integral to navigating the complexities of the real estate market and achieving long-term investment success.

Protecting large investments and assets from unforeseen circumstances.

Protecting large investments and assets from unforeseen circumstances requires a robust and comprehensive approach to risk management. This encompasses a variety of strategies aimed at identifying potential risks, implementing preventative measures, and preparing for the mitigation of adverse effects should those risks materialize. The goal is to safeguard the value of investments and ensure their sustainability over the long term. Below are key strategies for protecting large investments and assets against unforeseen circumstances.

Diversification

Principle: Don't put all your eggs in one basket.

- **Asset Diversification**: Spread investments across different asset classes (e.g., real estate, stocks, bonds, precious metals) to reduce exposure to a single market's volatility.
- **Geographical Diversification**: Invest in different geographic locations to mitigate the impact of regional economic downturns, political instability, or natural disasters.

Insurance

Principle: Transfer risk to a third party.

- **Comprehensive Coverage**: Obtain insurance policies tailored to the specific risks associated with each asset. This may include property insurance, liability insurance, business interruption insurance, and specialized policies for natural disasters or political risks.
- **Regular Policy Review**: Ensure insurance coverage is regularly reviewed and updated to reflect changes in asset values and risk exposure.

Legal Protection

Principle: Shield assets through legal structures and compliance.

- **Asset Protection Structures**: Utilize trusts, limited liability companies (LLCs), and other legal entities to provide a layer of protection against lawsuits and creditors.
- **Regulatory Compliance**: Adhere strictly to legal and regulatory requirements to avoid fines, penalties, and reputational damage that can adversely affect asset value.

Financial Resilience

Principle: Maintain liquidity and financial flexibility.

- **Emergency Fund**: Establish an emergency fund to cover unforeseen expenses without the need to liquidate investments prematurely under unfavorable conditions.
- **Debt Management**: Manage leverage and debt obligations carefully to avoid overextension and ensure financial stability during economic downturns.

Strategic Planning and Review

Principle: Anticipate and prepare for the unexpected.

- **Scenario Planning**: Conduct scenario analysis to understand potential impacts of various unforeseen events on your investments and develop contingency plans.

Regular Asset Review: Perform regular reviews of investment performance and risk exposure, adjusting strategies as necessary to address changing circumstances.

Technological Safeguards

Principle: Use technology to monitor and protect assets.

Security Systems: Implement advanced security systems for physical assets, including surveillance, alarms, and access controls.

Cybersecurity Measures: For digital assets, ensure robust cybersecurity measures are in place, including firewalls, encryption, and multi-factor authentication.

Community and Network Support

Principle: Leverage collective knowledge and resources.

Professional Advice: Engage with financial advisors, legal experts, and insurance professionals who can provide specialized knowledge and guidance on protecting your assets.

Networking: Participate in networks and forums with other investors to share strategies, insights, and alerts on emerging risks.

Conclusion

Protecting large investments and assets from unforeseen circumstances is a dynamic and ongoing process. It requires a blend of diversification, insurance, legal protections, financial resilience, strategic planning, technological safeguards, and community support. By adopting a holistic approach to risk management, investors can not only shield their assets from potential threats but also position themselves to navigate uncertainties with greater confidence and agility. This proactive stance is crucial for preserving and growing asset value in the face of an ever-changing risk landscape.

Debt Management and Risk

Debt management and its associated risks play a crucial role in both personal and corporate finance, directly impacting financial stability and growth potential. Effective management of debt is essential for maintaining a healthy financial status, avoiding excessive liabilities, and mitigating associated risks. Below, we explore strategies for managing debt and minimizing the risks it poses.

Understanding Debt and Its Risks

Debt can be a valuable tool for financing growth, investments, and personal needs. However, it carries risks such as high interest costs, potential for default, and negative impacts on credit scores. Risks vary depending on the type of debt—secured vs. unsecured, fixed-rate vs. variable-rate, short-term vs. long-term—and the borrower's financial health.

Strategies for Effective Debt Management

1. Assessing and Prioritizing Debt

- **Inventory of Debts**: Compile a comprehensive list of debts, including amounts, interest rates, and terms. This inventory will provide a clear picture of your debt obligations.
- **Prioritize Repayments**: Focus on paying off high-interest and non-tax-deductible debts first, as they cost the most over time. Strategies such as the debt snowball or avalanche method can be effective.

2. Refinancing and Consolidation

- **Refinancing**: Securing a new loan with lower interest rates to pay off existing debts can reduce interest costs and monthly payments.
- **Consolidation**: Combining multiple debts into a single loan with a lower interest rate simplifies payments and can reduce costs.

3. Budgeting and Expense Management

- **Creating a Budget**: Implement a budget that accounts for debt repayments, ensuring that spending aligns with income while prioritizing debt reduction.
- **Cutting Expenses**: Identify and reduce non-essential spending to free up more funds for debt repayment.

4. Establishing an Emergency Fund

- **Financial Buffer**: An emergency fund provides a financial safety net, reducing the need to take on additional debt during unexpected financial difficulties.

5. Negotiating with Creditors

- **Payment Terms**: In cases of financial hardship, communicating with creditors to negotiate more favorable payment terms or temporary relief can prevent default.

6. Monitoring and Adjusting Strategies

- **Regular Reviews**: Continuously monitor your debt management plan, adjusting as necessary to accommodate changes in financial circumstances or to take advantage of better terms.

Risks of Poor Debt Management

Credit Score Impact: Late payments and high debt levels can significantly damage credit scores, affecting the ability to borrow in the future.

Financial Stress: High debt burdens can lead to financial stress, impacting mental and physical health.

Legal Consequences: Defaulting on debt obligations can lead to legal actions, including foreclosure or bankruptcy.

Mitigating Debt-Related Risks

Risk Management Plan: Incorporate debt management into a broader financial risk management plan, considering insurance products, investment diversification, and legal structures to protect assets.

Professional Advice: Consult with financial advisors for personalized strategies to manage and mitigate debt risks effectively.

Conclusion

Effective debt management is pivotal for financial health and risk mitigation. By understanding the structure and implications of their debt, individuals and businesses can implement strategies to manage and reduce their debt efficiently. This proactive approach not only safeguards against the adverse effects of excessive debt but also positions them for sustainable financial growth and stability.

The relationship between debt and financial risk.
The relationship between debt and financial risk is both intricate and profound, impacting individuals, businesses, and economies on multiple levels. Debt, when managed judially, can be a powerful tool for leveraging opportunities, facilitating growth, and achieving financial objectives. However, it also introduces significant financial risks that can undermine fiscal stability and sustainability if not carefully managed. This relationship is characterized by several key dynamics, which include leverage, liquidity, solvency, and the cost of capital.

Leverage Effect

Debt amplifies the leverage effect in financial operations, meaning it can significantly increase the return on investment (ROI) when the returns generated from debt-financed projects exceed the cost of debt. Conversely, leverage also magnifies losses when returns fall short of the cost of debt, thereby increasing financial risk. The higher the degree of leverage, the greater the risk of volatility in earnings and return on equity.

Liquidity Risks

Liquidity refers to the ability to meet short-term obligations without incurring substantial losses. High levels of debt may compromise liquidity, as significant portions of cash flow are diverted to service debt, leaving less available for operations, investment, and unexpected expenses. This can make it challenging to respond to market opportunities or financial emergencies, increasing the risk of default.

Solvency Concerns

Solvency is the ability of an entity to meet its long-term financial commitments. Excessive borrowing can jeopardize solvency, especially if the debt is not used for income-generating investments or if the investments do not yield the expected returns. High debt levels relative to equity (high debt-to-equity ratio) can signal potential solvency issues, raising concerns among investors and creditors about the borrower's financial health and stability.

Cost of Capital

Debt influences an entity's cost of capital, which is the cost of obtaining funds through borrowing, equity, or other financial instruments. While debt can initially be a cheaper source of finance due to tax deductions on interest payments, excessive borrowing can lead to higher interest rates as lenders demand more significant premiums for increased risk. This elevates the cost of capital, potentially diminishing investment returns and eroding shareholder value.

Credit Ratings and Access to Finance

Credit ratings, which assess the creditworthiness of borrowers, are directly influenced by debt levels and financial risk management practices. Higher debt levels can lead to downgrades in credit ratings, making it more difficult and expensive to access finance in the future. This can create a vicious cycle where the cost of servicing existing debt rises, further straining financial resources.

Strategic Flexibility

Financial risk associated with debt also affects strategic flexibility. Companies or individuals with high debt burdens may find themselves constrained in their ability to pursue new opportunities or pivot in response to market changes. The obligation to prioritize debt repayments can limit investment in research and development, expansion, or other strategic initiatives.

Conclusion

The relationship between debt and financial risk underscores the importance of strategic debt management. By carefully balancing the benefits of debt against its inherent risks, entities can harness debt as a tool for growth while safeguarding against its potential to exacerbate financial vulnerability. This equilibrium requires diligent planning, ongoing risk assessment, and adaptive management strategies to align debt levels with financial capacity, investment returns, and market conditions. Understanding and navigating the nuances of this relationship is fundamental to achieving long-term financial stability and success.

Strategies for managing and reducing debt risk.

Managing and reducing debt risk is essential for maintaining financial stability and achieving long-term financial goals. Effective strategies for debt risk management involve a combination of prudent financial planning, disciplined budgeting, and informed decision-making. Below are several strategies designed to help individuals and businesses manage and reduce their debt risk.

1. Comprehensive Debt Assessment

Inventory Debts: Start by compiling a complete list of all debts, including amounts owed, interest rates, and repayment terms. This overview provides a clear picture of the total debt burden and priorities for repayment.

2. Prioritize High-Cost Debt

Debt Avalanche Method: Focus on paying off debts with the highest interest rates first while maintaining minimum payments on other debts. This approach reduces the amount of interest paid over time.

3. Debt Consolidation

Consolidate Loans: Combining multiple debts into a single loan with a lower interest rate can simplify repayments and reduce interest costs. However, it's crucial to carefully consider the terms of consolidation to ensure they are favorable.

4. Refinancing

Refinance High-Interest Loans: If possible, refinance high-interest loans to secure lower interest rates. This is particularly relevant for mortgages, car loans, and student loans.

5. Budgeting and Expense Management

Create a Budget: Develop a realistic budget that prioritizes debt repayment. Identify areas where expenses can be reduced to allocate more funds toward paying off debt.

Emergency Fund: Aim to build an emergency fund to cover unexpected expenses. This reduces the need to incur new debt in case of unforeseen financial needs.

6. Increase Income

- **Supplemental Income**: Seek opportunities to increase income through side gigs, overtime, or selling unused items. Direct additional income towards debt repayment.

7. Negotiate with Creditors

- **Improved Terms**: Contact creditors to negotiate more favorable repayment terms, including lower interest rates or extended repayment periods. Many creditors are willing to work with borrowers to avoid default.

8. Use Windfalls Wisely

- **Apply Windfalls to Debt**: Use any unexpected windfalls, such as tax refunds, bonuses, or inheritance, to pay down debt. Even small amounts can significantly impact over time.

9. Avoid Accumulating New Debt

- **Spend Wisely**: Resist the temptation to take on new debt. Adopt a cash-only spending policy if necessary to prevent accruing additional liabilities.

10. Financial Education

- **Stay Informed**: Enhance financial literacy by learning about debt management, personal finance, and investment strategies. Knowledge is a powerful tool in making informed financial decisions.

11. Professional Advice

- **Seek Professional Help**: Consider consulting with a financial advisor or credit counselor. Professional guidance can provide personalized strategies and solutions for managing and reducing debt.

12. Leverage Technology

- **Use Financial Apps**: Numerous apps and online tools can help track spending, budget more effectively, and strategize debt repayment. These tools can provide reminders, insights, and encouragement to stay on track.

Conclusion

Managing and reducing debt risk requires a proactive and disciplined approach. By assessing debts comprehensively, prioritizing high-cost debts, utilizing consolidation and refinancing, managing expenses, increasing income, and seeking professional advice, individuals and businesses can effectively mitigate the risks associated with debt. Implementing these strategies not only enhances financial stability but also paves the way for achieving financial freedom and long-term economic well-being.

Psychological Aspect of Financial Risks

The psychological aspect of financial risks plays a crucial role in how individuals perceive, react to, and manage financial uncertainties. These psychological factors can significantly influence financial decision-making processes, often leading to behaviors that diverge from what traditional economic models predict. Understanding these psychological dimensions is essential for managing financial risks more effectively and making informed decisions. Below, we explore key psychological concepts related to financial risks and strategies to address them.

1. Risk Tolerance and Perception

Definition: Risk tolerance is the degree to which an individual is willing to endure financial uncertainty and volatility. It varies greatly among individuals, influenced by psychological factors, life experiences, and financial goals.

Impact: An individual's perception of risk can significantly affect their investment choices and financial decisions. For example, those with low risk tolerance may avoid high-return investments due to fear of loss, potentially missing out on growth opportunities.

2. Overconfidence and Optimism Bias

Overconfidence: Many investors overestimate their knowledge, skills, and ability to predict market movements, leading to riskier financial decisions than warranted.

Optimism Bias: This bias leads individuals to believe they are less likely to experience negative outcomes compared to others, underestimating the risks involved in their financial decisions.

3. Loss Aversion

Definition: Loss aversion refers to the tendency to prefer avoiding losses rather than acquiring equivalent gains. The pain of losing is psychologically about twice as powerful as the pleasure of gaining.

Impact: This can lead to holding onto losing investments too long, hoping to break even, or avoiding investments with short-term volatility despite their long-term benefits.

4. Herd Behavior

- **Definition**: Herd behavior is the tendency to follow and mimic what a majority of others are doing. In finance, it manifests as investors buying or selling assets because others are doing so, often without considering their own financial situation or the asset's fundamentals.
- **Impact**: This can lead to asset bubbles or crashes, as decisions are driven more by emotion and social influence than by rational analysis.

Strategies for Addressing Psychological Aspects of Financial Risks

Enhance Financial Literacy

- **Education**: Improving one's understanding of financial markets, investment principles, and risk management can help mitigate the effects of psychological biases.

Diversify Investments

- **Balanced Portfolio**: Diversification can reduce the impact of volatility on investment portfolios, addressing loss aversion by spreading risk across different asset classes.

Set Clear Financial Goals

- **Goal-Setting**: Establishing clear, achievable financial goals can help individuals maintain focus and make decisions aligned with their long-term objectives, reducing the influence of herd behavior and overconfidence.

Develop a Financial Plan

- **Planning**: A well-structured financial plan that includes risk assessment and management strategies can provide a roadmap, helping to navigate financial decisions with a rational framework.

Seek Professional Advice

- **Professional Guidance**: Financial advisors can offer objective advice and insights, helping individuals understand their risk tolerance, counteract emotional biases, and make informed decisions.

Practice Mindfulness and Emotional Regulation

Mindfulness: Being aware of one's emotional state and cognitive biases can help individuals recognize when their decisions might be unduly influenced by psychological factors.

Conclusion

The psychological aspect of financial risks underscores the complexity of human behavior in financial decision-making. By recognizing and addressing these psychological factors, individuals can better navigate the uncertainties of financial markets, make decisions that align with their goals and risk tolerance, and ultimately achieve greater financial stability and success.

Understanding the emotional impact of financial risks.
The emotional impact of financial risks significantly influences individuals' well-being, decision-making processes, and overall quality of life. Financial risks, encompassing the potential for loss or adverse outcomes associated with financial decisions and market fluctuations, can elicit a wide range of emotional responses. These responses are rooted in the deeply personal nature of financial security and aspirations. Below, we explore the emotional dimensions of financial risks and offer insights into managing these emotional impacts constructively.

Emotional Responses to Financial Risks

Anxiety and Stress: Uncertainty and the potential for financial loss can lead to heightened anxiety and stress. These emotions stem from concerns over the ability to meet financial obligations, maintain lifestyle standards, or achieve long-term financial goals.

Fear and Panic: In times of significant financial downturns or personal financial crises, individuals may experience fear and panic. These intense reactions can precipitate rash decision-making, such as panic selling or abrupt changes in financial strategies without thorough analysis.

Frustration and Regret: Decision regret, especially after taking financial risks that do not pan out as expected, can lead to frustration. This often involves ruminating over 'what could have been' if different choices had been made.

Hope and Optimism: On the flip side, taking calculated financial risks can lead to feelings of hope and optimism, especially if those risks start to show potential for positive returns. These emotions can motivate further engagement with financial planning and investments.

Disappointment and Despondency: When financial outcomes fail to meet expectations, individuals may experience disappointment and despondency. This can affect motivation and confidence in making future financial decisions.

Managing the Emotional Impact of Financial Risks

Developing Emotional Resilience

- **Awareness and Acceptance**: Recognize and accept that emotional responses to financial risks are natural. Acknowledging these feelings without judgment can be the first step in managing them effectively.
- **Mindfulness Practices**: Incorporate mindfulness and stress-reduction techniques, such as meditation, deep breathing, or yoga, to mitigate anxiety and maintain emotional equilibrium.

Enhancing Financial Literacy

- **Education**: Increasing one's understanding of financial principles, market dynamics, and risk management can build confidence in decision-making processes, reducing fear and stress associated with financial risks.

Strategic Financial Planning

- **Diversification**: Diversify investments to spread risk and potentially reduce the volatility of returns, which can alleviate the emotional rollercoaster associated with financial investments.
- **Long-term Perspective**: Maintain a long-term perspective on investments and financial goals. This approach can help smooth out short-term market fluctuations and reduce reactionary emotional responses.

Seeking Professional Support

- **Financial Advisors**: Engage with financial advisors for personalized advice tailored to your financial situation and goals. Professional guidance can provide reassurance and clarity, helping to mitigate emotional distress.
- **Counseling**: In cases where financial stress significantly impacts mental health, seeking counseling or therapy can be beneficial. Professionals specializing in financial therapy can offer strategies to cope with financial stress and anxiety.

Building a Support Network

- **Community and Peer Support**: Sharing experiences and strategies with a supportive community or peers facing similar financial challenges can provide emotional comfort and practical insights.

Conclusion

The emotional impact of financial risks is a complex interplay of psychological responses to the uncertainties inherent in financial decisions and market behaviors. By understanding and acknowledging these emotional dimensions, individuals can employ strategies to manage their emotional responses constructively. Developing emotional resilience, enhancing financial literacy, engaging in strategic financial planning, seeking professional support, and building a supportive community are pivotal in navigating the emotional landscape of financial risks. These approaches not only foster healthier emotional responses but also contribute to more informed, deliberate, and strategic financial decision-making.

Coping strategies for financial stress and anxiety.
Financial stress and anxiety can significantly impact one's mental health and overall quality of life, arising from concerns about debt, savings, investments, and the uncertainty of financial futures. Effective coping strategies can help mitigate these effects, enabling individuals to manage financial stress more constructively and make informed decisions. Here, we outline several key strategies designed to address financial stress and anxiety.

1. Financial Planning and Budgeting

Create a Budget: Develop a detailed budget that tracks income, expenses, and savings. This can provide a sense of control over financial matters and help identify areas for cost reduction.

Set Realistic Goals: Establish achievable financial goals, both short-term and long-term. Breaking these down into manageable steps can reduce the overwhelm and create a sense of progress.

2. Building Financial Literacy

Educate Yourself: Enhance your understanding of financial management, investment options, and risk mitigation strategies. Knowledge can empower you to make more confident decisions.

Seek Professional Advice: Consulting with financial advisors can provide personalized insights and strategies to navigate financial challenges and plan for the future.

3. Establishing an Emergency Fund

Start Small: Aim to save a small portion of your income regularly, gradually building an emergency fund. This can reduce anxiety associated with unexpected expenses or financial setbacks.

4. Practicing Mindfulness and Stress Reduction Techniques

Mindfulness Meditation: Engage in mindfulness practices to cultivate a present-focused mindset, reducing rumination and worry about financial matters.

- **Physical Exercise**: Regular exercise can significantly reduce stress and anxiety levels, improving overall mental health and resilience.

5. Prioritizing Debt Management

- **Debt Repayment Plan**: Organize your debts and develop a structured repayment plan, prioritizing high-interest or high-stress debts.
- **Negotiate Terms**: Contact creditors to discuss repayment options, such as reduced interest rates or extended payment terms, which can alleviate financial pressure.

6. Enhancing Communication

- **Family Discussions**: Openly discuss financial concerns with family members to share responsibilities, set collective goals, and support each other through challenges.
- **Peer Support**: Engage with friends or support groups who understand financial stress. Sharing experiences and strategies can provide relief and practical advice.

7. Adjusting Lifestyle and Spending Habits

- **Review Spending**: Regularly assess spending habits and identify areas where you can cut back without significantly impacting your quality of life.
- **Value-based Spending**: Focus on spending that aligns with your core values and brings genuine satisfaction, rather than succumbing to impulse buys or societal pressure.

8. Seeking Professional Mental Health Support

- **Counseling Services**: If financial stress is overwhelming, consider seeking support from mental health professionals who can offer coping mechanisms and therapeutic strategies.
- **Financial Therapy**: Some therapists specialize in financial issues, offering targeted support to address the emotional and psychological aspects of financial stress.

Conclusion

Coping with financial stress and anxiety requires a multi-faceted approach, combining practical financial management strategies with psychological and emotional support mechanisms. By implementing these strategies, individuals can gain greater control over their financial situation, reduce stress and anxiety levels, and lay the groundwork for a more secure and fulfilling financial future. Remember, it's crucial to approach financial wellness as a component of overall well-being, requiring attention, care, and proactive management.

Maintaining a healthy perspective on risk and uncertainty.

Maintaining a healthy perspective on risk and uncertainty is essential for both financial well-being and general mental health. In the realm of personal finance, investments, and life decisions, risk and uncertainty are inevitable. However, the manner in which one perceives and manages these factors can significantly influence outcomes and overall satisfaction. Below are strategies to cultivate a balanced and healthy perspective towards risk and uncertainty.

1. Understand the Nature of Risk and Uncertainty

Educate Yourself: Enhance your knowledge about financial markets, investment principles, and the nature of economic cycles. Understanding that markets fluctuate and that risk is a natural part of investing can help temper emotional responses.

Differentiate Between Risk and Uncertainty: Risk involves known probabilities, while uncertainty involves unknowns. Recognizing this difference can aid in developing appropriate strategies for each.

2. Develop a Long-Term Perspective

Focus on Long-Term Goals: Short-term volatility can lead to anxiety and reactionary decisions. Focusing on long-term financial goals helps to contextualize and mitigate the impact of temporary uncertainties.

Historical Context: Remember that markets have recovered from downturns historically. Keeping a long-term view can provide comfort during periods of market stress.

3. Embrace a Mindset of Flexibility and Adaptability

Stay Flexible: Be prepared to adjust your plans as circumstances change. Flexibility can reduce the stress associated with trying to predict and control the future.

Adaptability: Cultivate the ability to adapt to changing conditions. This resilience can transform challenges into opportunities for growth and learning.

4. Practice Risk Management

Diversification: Spread investments across different asset classes to mitigate the impact of any single adverse event.

Emergency Fund: Maintain an emergency fund to cover unexpected expenses, providing a financial buffer that reduces the need to make hasty decisions under pressure.

5. Cultivate Emotional Resilience

- **Mindfulness and Stress Reduction**: Engage in practices such as meditation, yoga, or deep breathing exercises to manage stress and anxiety levels.
- **Positive Reframing**: Train yourself to reframe challenges as opportunities for learning and growth, rather than threats.

6. Seek Professional Guidance

- **Financial Advisors**: Consulting with a financial advisor can provide personalized advice tailored to your risk tolerance and financial goals.
- **Therapy and Counseling**: For those who find their anxiety or stress levels are significantly impacted by financial concerns, professional mental health support can be invaluable.

7. Foster Open Communication

- **Discuss Concerns**: Share your concerns and perspectives with trusted friends, family, or financial advisors. Open communication can provide new insights and emotional support.

8. Engage in Continuous Learning

- **Stay Informed**: Keep abreast of financial news and trends, but be wary of sensationalism. Seek out reputable sources of information that provide balanced viewpoints.
- **Lifelong Learning**: View your financial journey as a continuous learning experience. This mindset encourages curiosity and openness, reducing fear of the unknown.

Conclusion

Maintaining a healthy perspective on risk and uncertainty involves a combination of knowledge, emotional resilience, strategic planning, and open communication. By adopting these strategies, individuals can navigate financial and life decisions with greater confidence and equanimity, turning potential stressors into opportunities for growth and achievement. Remember, risk and uncertainty are not just challenges to be managed but are also inherent to the pursuit of any worthwhile goal.

Future-Proofing Your Finances

Future-proofing your finances is a strategic approach to ensure that your financial health remains robust across various economic conditions and life stages. This proactive stance involves planning, preparation, and adaptation strategies designed to safeguard against unforeseen challenges while capitalizing on opportunities for growth. Below, we explore comprehensive steps to future-proof your finances, ensuring long-term security and prosperity.

1. Establish a Solid Emergency Fund

Objective: Aim to save at least 3-6 months' worth of living expenses in a readily accessible savings account. This fund acts as a financial buffer against unexpected job loss, medical emergencies, or urgent home repairs.

2. Diversify Your Income Streams

Multiple Sources of Income: Explore opportunities for additional income beyond your primary job, such as freelance work, investments, or a side business. This can reduce dependency on a single income source, spreading risk.

3. Invest Wisely with a Long-Term Perspective

Long-Term Investments: Focus on building a diversified investment portfolio that aligns with your risk tolerance and financial goals. Consider retirement accounts, stocks, bonds, real estate, and other assets that offer growth potential over time.

Continuous Learning: Stay informed about market trends and investment strategies. Knowledge is a powerful tool for making informed decisions.

4. Stay Insured

Comprehensive Coverage: Ensure you have adequate insurance coverage, including health, life, disability, and property insurance. Review and adjust your coverage regularly to match changing life circumstances.

5. Manage Debt Strategically

Debt Reduction: Prioritize paying off high-interest and non-productive debts. Consider debt consolidation or refinancing options for more favorable terms.

Avoid Unnecessary Debt: Practice cautious borrowing, focusing on debt that contributes to financial growth, such as mortgages or education loans.

6. Plan for Retirement

Retirement Savings: Contribute regularly to retirement accounts like 401(k)s, IRAs, or other pension plans. Take advantage of employer match programs, if available.

Retirement Planning: Work with a financial planner to develop a retirement strategy that considers your desired lifestyle, expected expenses, and income sources in retirement.

7. Maintain Good Credit

- **Credit Health**: Regularly monitor your credit score and report. Good credit can be crucial for securing loans with favorable terms, renting properties, and even job opportunities in some industries.

8. Estate Planning

- **Wills and Trusts**: Create or update your will and consider setting up trusts to ensure your assets are distributed according to your wishes.
- **Advance Directives**: Include healthcare directives and a durable power of attorney to manage your affairs if you become unable to do so.

9. Continuous Education and Adaptability

- **Lifelong Learning**: Commit to ongoing financial education to adapt to changing economic landscapes and opportunities.
- **Flexibility**: Be prepared to adjust your financial plans as your personal circumstances, economic conditions, and goals evolve.

10. Seek Professional Advice

- **Financial Advisors**: Consult with financial professionals for personalized advice tailored to your unique situation, helping you make informed decisions and adjust strategies as needed.

Conclusion

Future-proofing your finances is an ongoing process that requires vigilance, discipline, and a proactive approach to financial management. By building a strong financial foundation, diversifying income and investments, managing risks through insurance and debt strategies, planning for retirement, and staying adaptable to change, you can navigate the uncertainties of the future with confidence. Remember, the goal is not just to survive potential financial challenges but to thrive, achieving financial independence and security.

Planning for long-term financial security.
Planning for long-term financial security is a comprehensive process that requires foresight, discipline, and strategic action. It involves setting clear financial goals, understanding your financial situation, and implementing a plan that will grow your wealth, protect your assets, and ensure that you can maintain your desired lifestyle in the future. Below, we outline key steps and strategies to help you plan for long-term financial security.

1. Define Your Financial Goals

Set Clear Objectives: Identify your long-term financial goals, such as retirement, homeownership, education funding, or wealth transfer. Be specific about what you want to achieve and by when.

Prioritize Goals: Recognize that not all goals can be pursued simultaneously. Prioritize them based on importance and timeline.

2. Assess Your Current Financial Situation

Net Worth Analysis: Calculate your net worth by subtracting liabilities from assets. This provides a clear picture of your current financial health and helps track progress over time.

Cash Flow Analysis: Understand your income and expenses to identify opportunities for savings and areas where spending can be reduced.

3. Create a Comprehensive Financial Plan

Budgeting: Develop a budget that allocates funds towards savings, investments, and debt repayment while covering essential living expenses.

Emergency Fund: Build an emergency fund covering at least 3-6 months of living expenses to safeguard against unexpected financial shocks.

4. Invest for Growth

Diversification: Spread investments across various asset classes (stocks, bonds, real estate) to mitigate risk and capitalize on different growth opportunities.

Retirement Accounts: Maximize contributions to retirement accounts like 401(k)s, IRAs, or equivalent vehicles, taking advantage of tax benefits and compound interest.

5. Implement Risk Management Strategies

Insurance: Ensure adequate coverage (health, life, disability, property) to protect against significant financial losses.

Debt Management: Strategically manage debt, focusing on paying down high-interest or non-deductible debt first.

6. Plan for Taxes

Tax Planning: Consider the tax implications of investment decisions, income sources, and retirement withdrawals. Utilize tax-advantaged accounts and strategies to minimize tax liabilities.

7. Prepare for Retirement

- **Retirement Strategy**: Estimate your retirement needs based on your desired lifestyle, expected lifespan, and inflation. Adjust your savings and investment strategies accordingly.
- **Healthcare Considerations**: Plan for healthcare costs in retirement, including Medicare and long-term care insurance.

8. Estate Planning

- **Wills and Trusts**: Ensure your assets are distributed according to your wishes by creating a will and considering trusts for more complex situations.
- **Advance Directives**: Establish powers of attorney and healthcare directives to manage your affairs in case of incapacity.

9. Continuous Review and Adaptation

- **Regular Reviews**: Periodically review and adjust your financial plan to reflect changes in your personal circumstances, financial goals, and the economic landscape.
- **Professional Advice**: Seek ongoing advice from financial advisors, tax professionals, and estate planners to navigate complex issues and optimize your financial strategy.

10. Focus on Financial Education

- **Lifelong Learning**: Stay informed about financial markets, investment strategies, and economic trends. Continuous education empowers you to make knowledgeable decisions.

Conclusion

Planning for long-term financial security is an iterative and dynamic process that adapts to your changing life circumstances and goals. By taking a structured and proactive approach to financial planning, you can build a solid foundation that supports your aspirations, protects against unforeseen challenges, and ensures a secure and fulfilling financial future.

Adapting to changing economic and personal circumstances.

Adapting to changing economic and personal circumstances is crucial for maintaining financial stability and achieving long-term security. The economic landscape and personal life situations are inherently dynamic, often changing in unpredictable ways. Whether it's a shift in the global economy, a change in employment status, or a personal milestone, the ability to adapt financially can significantly influence one's resilience and success. Below, we explore strategies to effectively navigate and adapt to these changes.

1. Maintain Financial Flexibility

Emergency Fund: An essential buffer against financial uncertainty, an emergency fund should cover 3-6 months of living expenses, providing protection against sudden job loss, medical emergencies, or unexpected repairs.

Liquid Assets: Keeping a portion of your assets in liquid form ensures that you can access funds quickly without incurring significant losses.

2. Continuous Financial Planning and Review

Regular Assessments: Conduct periodic reviews of your financial plan to adjust for changes in income, expenses, and financial goals. This includes revisiting your budget, investment portfolio, and savings strategies.

Adaptation: Be prepared to make adjustments to your financial plan in response to significant life events, such as marriage, childbirth, or retirement, ensuring that your financial strategies align with your current needs and goals.

3. Diversify Income Sources

Multiple Streams: Cultivate multiple streams of income to reduce dependence on a single source. This could include freelance work, rental income, investments, or starting a side business.

Skill Development: Invest in education and skill development to enhance your employability and open up new income opportunities.

4. Stay Informed

Economic Awareness: Keep abreast of global and local economic trends that could impact your finances, such as inflation rates, interest rate changes, and market fluctuations.

Professional Advice: Seek guidance from financial advisors for insights into how economic changes may affect your financial plan and strategies to mitigate potential risks.

5. Invest Wisely

Risk Management: Ensure your investment portfolio is diversified across different asset classes, sectors, and geographies to mitigate risk.

Long-Term Perspective: Focus on long-term investment strategies that can weather short-term market volatility.

6. Embrace Technology

Financial Tools: Utilize financial management software and apps to track spending, budget, and monitor investments, enabling more informed and timely decisions.

- **Online Learning**: Take advantage of online courses and resources to stay current on financial planning, investment strategies, and economic trends.

7. Develop Resilience and Adaptability

- **Mindset**: Cultivate a mindset of resilience and adaptability, viewing challenges as opportunities for growth and learning.
- **Stress Management**: Practice stress-reduction techniques such as mindfulness, exercise, or hobbies to maintain mental and emotional well-being during times of change.

8. Plan for Retirement and Future Needs

- **Future Projections**: Regularly update your retirement planning to account for changes in your life expectancy, desired lifestyle, and potential healthcare needs.
- **Savings Adjustments**: Adjust your savings rate to stay on track with your retirement goals, especially after major life or economic changes.

9. Protect Your Assets and Identity

- **Insurance Coverage**: Review and adjust your insurance coverage (health, life, property) to ensure it meets your current needs and provides adequate protection.
- **Identity Protection**: Stay vigilant against identity theft and fraud, especially during times of economic turmoil, by monitoring your financial accounts and credit report.

Conclusion

Adapting to changing economic and personal circumstances requires a proactive, informed approach to financial planning. By maintaining flexibility, diversifying income sources, investing wisely, and staying informed, you can navigate life's uncertainties with confidence. Cultivating resilience, seeking professional advice, and regularly reviewing your financial plan will equip you to make adjustments that align with both your immediate needs and long-term goals.

Continuous education and staying informed about financial risks.
Continuous education and staying informed about financial risks are indispensable strategies for navigating the complex and ever-evolving financial landscape. In an era marked by rapid economic changes, technological advancements, and global interconnectedness, understanding financial risks and how to manage them effectively is crucial for personal financial stability and growth. Below are strategies and resources to facilitate continuous education and awareness regarding financial risks.

1. Leverage Educational Resources

Online Courses and Webinars: Numerous platforms offer courses on finance, economics, and risk management. These range from introductory courses for beginners to advanced programs for seasoned investors.

Books and Journals: Reading books by financial experts and academic journals can provide deep insights into financial risk management theories and practices.

Financial News and Publications: Regularly reading reputable financial news outlets, magazines, and online publications helps keep you updated on market trends, economic indicators, and emerging risks.

2. Participate in Financial Workshops and Seminars

Community Programs: Look for workshops and seminars offered by community centers, libraries, or financial institutions. These events can provide valuable information and networking opportunities.

Professional Associations: Joining professional associations related to finance or your specific industry can offer access to exclusive resources, conferences, and seminars.

3. Engage with Online Communities and Forums

Financial Forums: Platforms like Reddit, Quora, and specific finance-related forums host vibrant communities where individuals share experiences, advice, and strategies related to financial risk management.

Social Media: Follow financial analysts, economists, and professionals on social media platforms for insights and commentary on current financial risks and opportunities.

4. Utilize Financial Planning and Analysis Tools

Software and Apps: There are numerous financial planning and analysis tools available that can help you assess and manage financial risks. These tools often include features for budgeting, investment analysis, and scenario planning.

Risk Assessment Tools: Specific tools designed to evaluate investment risks, such as Monte Carlo simulations, can be invaluable for understanding potential outcomes and making informed decisions.

5. Consult with Financial Advisors

- **Professional Guidance**: Regular consultations with financial advisors can provide personalized advice tailored to your financial situation, goals, and risk tolerance. They can offer insights into managing risks associated with investments, retirement planning, and tax strategies.

6. Continuous Learning in Professional Settings

- **Professional Development**: Take advantage of professional development opportunities offered by employers, including workshops, courses, and conferences related to finance and risk management.
- **Certifications**: Pursuing certifications in financial planning, investment management, or risk analysis can deepen your expertise and enhance your ability to manage financial risks effectively.

7. Stay Informed About Global Economic Trends

- **Global Awareness**: Understanding global economic trends and geopolitical events is crucial, as they can have significant impacts on financial markets and investment risks. Follow international news sources and analyses to gain a broader perspective.

8. Practice Critical Thinking and Analysis

- **Skepticism and Analysis**: Approach financial information and advice with a critical mind. Analyze sources for bias, credibility, and relevance to your personal financial context.

Conclusion

Continuous education and staying informed are vital for effectively managing financial risks. By leveraging educational resources, engaging with professional communities, utilizing analysis tools, and seeking professional advice, individuals can enhance their financial literacy and resilience. This proactive approach empowers you to make informed decisions, adapt to changing economic conditions, and achieve long-term financial security.

Conclusion: Embracing Resilience in Your Financial Journey

Embracing resilience in your financial journey is not merely a strategy but a mindset that underscores the importance of preparation, adaptability, and continuous learning in navigating the complexities of personal finance. Financial resilience involves developing the capacity to withstand economic shocks, recover from setbacks, and adapt to changing circumstances, all while maintaining a focus on long-term goals and well-being.

Cultivating a Resilient Financial Mindset

Proactive Planning: Resilience begins with foresight and the willingness to prepare for the unexpected. This means establishing robust emergency funds, insuring adequately against risks, and diversifying income sources and investments to mitigate potential impacts of market volatility.

Adaptability: The ability to adapt to changing financial landscapes—whether due to personal life changes, shifts in the global economy, or emerging investment opportunities—is crucial. This requires staying informed, being open to adjusting financial plans, and making decisions based on current realities rather than past assumptions.

Learning from Experiences: Every financial challenge presents an opportunity for learning. Reflecting on past decisions, understanding what worked or didn't, and applying these lessons moving forward can enhance your financial resilience.

Strategies for Building Financial Resilience

Continuous Education: Engage in lifelong learning about financial management, investment strategies, and economic trends. Knowledge empowers you to make informed decisions and recognize potential risks and opportunities.

Professional Guidance: Leveraging the expertise of financial advisors can provide personalized insights and strategies tailored to your unique situation, enhancing your ability to navigate uncertainties.

Emotional Intelligence: Managing the emotional aspects of financial decision-making, such as stress, anxiety, and impulse control, is as important as managing the finances themselves. Practices such as mindfulness can help maintain emotional equilibrium, ensuring that decisions are driven by logic rather than fear or euphoria.

The Role of Community and Support Networks

Peer Support: Sharing experiences and strategies with others, whether through online communities, local workshops, or informal networks, can provide moral support and practical advice, reminding you that you're not alone in facing financial challenges.

Mentorship: Seeking mentors who have navigated their financial journeys successfully can offer valuable perspectives and guidance, helping you avoid common pitfalls and make more strategic decisions.

Embracing Technology

Financial Tools and Apps: Utilizing technology to track spending, investments, and financial progress can streamline management processes and provide real-time insights into your financial health.

Online Resources: The wealth of financial education resources available online, from blogs and podcasts to webinars and courses, offers endless opportunities for enhancing your understanding and skills.

Conclusion

Embracing resilience in your financial journey is about more than just surviving economic downturns or personal financial setbacks; it's about thriving despite them. By cultivating a resilient mindset, adopting strategic practices, leveraging community and professional resources, and utilizing technology, you can build a financial foundation that not only withstands challenges but also capitalizes on opportunities for growth and fulfillment. Remember, resilience is a journey, not a destination, and each step taken strengthens your capacity to achieve long-term financial security and success.

www.ingramcontent.com/pod-product-compliance
Lightning Source LLC
La Vergne TN
LVHW030311070526
838199LV00008B/374